NATIONAL POLITICAL SCIENCE REVIEW

EDITOR
Lucius J. Barker
Washington University

ASSOCIATE EDITOR
Michael Preston
University of Southern California

BOOK REVIEW EDITOR
Paula D. McClain
School for Public Affairs
Arizona State University

EDITORIAL BOARD

Marguerite R. Barnett
University of Missouri,
St. Louis

Michael Combs
University of
Nebraska

William Crotty
Northwestern
University

William Daniels
Union College

Richard Fenno
University of
Rochester

Charles Hamilton
Columbia University

Mathew Holden, Jr.
University of
Virginia

Mack Jones
Prairie View A&M
University

Dennis Judd
University of Missouri,
St. Louis

E. Walter Miles
San Diego State
University

William Nelson
Ohio State
University

Dianne Pinderhughes
University of
Illinois

Jewel Prestage
Iowa University

Mitchell Rice
Louisiana State
University

Robert Salisbury
Washington
University

Elsie Scott
National Organization of
Black Law Executives

Ron Walters
Howard
University

Hanes Walton
Savannah State
College

Susan Welch
University of
Nebraska

Linda Williams
Joint Center for
Political Studies

Ernest Wilson
University of
Michigan

NEW PERSPECTIVES
IN AMERICAN POLITICS

National Political Science Review

Volume 1

NEW PERSPECTIVES
IN AMERICAN POLITICS

National Political Science Review

Volume 1

Lucius J. Barker, Editor

Transaction Publishers
New Brunswick (U.S.A.) and Oxford (U.K.)

Copyright © 1989 by Transaction Publishers.
New Brunswick, New Jersey 08903

All rights reserved under International and Pan-American Copyright Con,en-
tions. No part of this book may be reproduced or transmitted in any form or
by any means, electronic or mechanical, including photocopy, recording, or
any information storage and retrieval system, without prior permission in
writing from the publisher. All inquiries should be addressed to Transaction
Publishers, Rutgers—The State University, New Brunswick, New Jersey
08903.

ISSN: 0896-629-X
ISBN: 0-88738-744-6 (cloth)
ISBN: 0-88738-280-0 (paper)
Printed in the United States of America

CONTENTS

BOOK FORUM

Review Essays: Jesse Jackson and Presidential Politics

Bibliographic Essays

Book Reviews

Editor's Note

This first volume of the *National Political Science Review (NPSR)* represents the culmination of many years of ideas, discussions, and planning. It also represents an important step in the growth and development of the National Conference Of Black Political Scientists (NCOBPS) as a professional scholarly organization. For, at bottom, the central purpose of the NCOBPS, no less than of similar organizations, is to facilitate scholarly research and communication and further the environment in which this can be most effectively done.

Since our founding in 1971, the NCOBPS annual meetings have provided the principal method through which our organization could promote such scholarly information and exchange. And though over the years our individual members have contributed research to other professional reviews and journals, the *NPSR* represents our goal to expand the traditional research agenda by promoting the communication and dissemination of varied research interests, methodologies, and ideas. This first volume—*New Perspectives in American Politics*—reflects this objective. Our ultimate hope, of course, is that this venture will lead to new information, insights, and findings that add both to our basic knowledge as well as prove helpful in understanding and dealing with important ongoing problems in our politics and society.

The contributions in the first volume suggest a bright future for the *NPSR*. Articles include topics that focus on the first term of the Rehnquist court, political movements in American politics, political party efforts to *get out* the black vote, liberalism and black political thought, and second generation discrimination. The issue also includes two symposia that focus on the Iran–Contra affair and bicentennial assessments on black Americans and the Constitution. Although articles on the Rehnquist court and political movements were especially solicited for this first issue, they, too, were subject to peer review screening before publication. A similar procedure was followed with respect to contributions for the two symposia.

Starting a venture of this kind has not been easy, and there are many persons to whom we owe many thanks. Clearly, the general membership of the NCOBPS must be credited with providing the *NPSR* with the vision, courage, and the support needed to launch a project that stands to benefit not only NCOBPS members but the political science profession and the scholarly community generally. Similarly, we appreciate the interest and supportive environment provided by the Department of Political Science and the Faculty of Arts and Sciences at Washington University—St. Louis. This environment maximized the chances for the *NPSR* to get started on a fast track.

In addition, our editorial staff and assistants have been indispensable in this effort. Through her ingenuity and stamina, Paula D. McClain has pulled together one of the most thorough and innovative book review sections that can be found in any scholarly journal. And Michael Preston, as associate editor, has provided me with steady counsel and willing assistance in undertaking any task at hand, and there were many. My two graduate assistants, Kevin Lyles and Robert Pultz, provided organizational and systematic help that greatly facilitated the work of the NPSR. And in Molly Bunton, we were fortunate to have a secretary who kept everything in tow, seeing that manuscripts were processed and deadlines met.

At bottom, however, our greatest appreciation goes to the authors whose contributions appear in this volume as well as those whose submissions enlarged our range of choices from which selections could be made. We also owe a great debt to the many reviewers who invariably heeded our request to give rather detailed comments on the various contributions and who somehow managed to do so within reasonable time frames.

The book forum section merits special comment. In addition to traditional book reviews, the section includes two review essays that allow authors to place in perspective three recent publications on Jesse Jackson and presidential politics. The section also includes four bibliographic essays that offer commentaries in the areas of black politics, women in politics, Chicano politics, and politics of American Indians.

As we celebrate this first volume, our readers should know that the *NPSR* hopes to become a major forum for the publication of scholarly research and sincerely welcomes all contributions and suggestions.

Lucius J. Barker
Editor

Liberalism and Black Political Thought: The Afro-American Dilemma

Stuart Alan Clarke

Yale University

The work of Jennifer Hochschild is used to locate an Afro-American dilemma that exists within the gap that separates the formal guarantees made to individuals by a liberal democratic society and the social and ideological conditions that allow particular groups to sustain, concretize, and transmit group values. Defined as the relationship between black Americans and American liberalism, this 'gap' is understood to have analytical, political, and ideological components. This essay considers the task of contextualizing investigations of Afro-American political thought in order to more clearly define (and perhaps redefine) the ideological component of the relationship between black Americans and American liberalism.

In her book, *The New American Dilemma: Liberal Democracy and School Desegregation* (Hochschild, 1984), Jennifer Hochschild analyzes Gunnar Myrdal's conception of the "American Dilemma." Hochschild's analysis adequately addresses the problem that presents itself to (white) liberal policy makers, a problem that she labels the new American dilemma. Although she also locates what might be termed a second-order dilemma within this new American dilemma, this second dilemma does not occupy much of her analytical attention.

This second-order dilemma involves a dynamic tension that sets important tasks for students and practitioners of black American political thought. Between the formal political guarantees made to individuals by a liberal democratic society and the social and ideological conditions that allow particular groups to sustain, concretize, and transmit group values lies a forest of practical and theoretical problems. Ultimately black thinkers will have to clear their own paths through this forest. In this chapter I would like to suggest one direction that these path-clearing efforts might take.

I begin by discusssing Professor Hochschild's work for two reasons. First, she helps us to focus on the practical significance of this second-order dilemma. Second, her work demonstrates how easily even well-intentioned observers can elide issues that are of fundamental importance for black Americans.

American Dilemmas

Hochschild is primarily concerned with public policy, especially educational policy. She wants to show how school desegregation can, in her words, "foster excellence rather than exacerbating shoddiness." It is within this context that she considers Myrdal's "American Dilemma." She concludes that Myrdal was wrong to characterize the coexistence of racism and liberal democracy as anomalous. She believes that this characterization must give way to explanations that assert the existence of a symbiotic relationship between racism and liberal democracy.

Hochschild understands Myrdal to have insisted that the American dilemma was simply the failure of liberal democratic practices to coincide with liberal democratic theory. For Hochschild, there are two claims implicit in this argument. The first claim is that the standard practices and procedures of American policymaking are adequate to the task of abolishing racism. The second claim is that the (white) American people do, in fact, wish to abolish racism. For Myrdal then, the American dilemma was only skin deep.

In contrast to the anomaly thesis, Hochschild poses a symbiosis thesis that suggests that:

> liberal democracy and racism in the United States are historically, even inherently reinforcing; American society as we know it exists only because of its foundation in racially based slavery, and it thrives only because racial discrimination continues (Hochschild, 1984:5).

Hochschild abstracts this thesis from commentary ranging from Edmund Morgan's argument for the positive relationship between slavery and the development of a republican ideology of freedom, to contemporary Marxist accounts of the functional utility of racism within a capitalist economy.

Hochschild then sets out to test the validity of Myrdal's thesis. She operationalizes standard practices and procedures as incremental policymaking, (Hochschild, 1984:35-6) and hypothesizes that the existence of effective measures of popular control insure the integrity of public policy relative to the desires of the American people. She then:

> examines these two arguments by asking whether the United States wishes to, and can, end racism without severe dislocations. If so, then the anomaly thesis gains support . . . If not, then the symbiosis thesis gains support, and we face a dilemma much less tractable than the one (Myrdal) so eloquently described (Hochschild 1984:8-9).

For reasons that are not entirely clear she establishes school desegregation as the mechanism that might eradicate racism in the United States. This leads to the proposition that if the American public school system can be effectively desegregated in a manner that is both incremental and subject to popular control, then Myrdal's position is upheld.

After considering the theory and historical practice of school desegregation in the United States, Hochschild concludes that incrementalism,

> works poorly in two ways to desegregate schools. It does less than full scale, rapid, extensive . . . change to improve race relations, achievement, and community acceptance and to minimize white flight . . . Both minorities and Anglos can end up worse off in a halfhearted, restricted, timid . . . "reform" than if nothing had been done . . . Half a loaf in this case, may be worse than nothing at all (Hochschild 1984:91).

These findings force Hochschild to the conclusion that severe dislocation is unavoidable if school desegregation is to be effectively pursued, and therefore Myrdal's anomaly thesis must be rejected. She maintains that rather than being understood as the tension between liberal democratic theory and liberal democratic practice, the American dilemma must be understood as the more fundamental and intractable problem of reconciling liberalism with democracy. Eschewing (or at least postponing) this reconciliation, Hochschild suggests that the practical solution to the dilemma may be to shift the balance of liberalism and democracy: "If most citizens choose not to grant the rest of the citizens their full rights, then perhaps democracy must give way to liberalism" (Hochschild 1984:145). By this, she seems to mean that some of our concern for popular control may simply have to be subordinated to an active respect for the rights of minorities.

What is of interest from my perspective is that Hochschild recognizes that the new American dilemma is not really quite this simple. She first hints at its complexity in a footnote in the early part of her book. "Some communities," she observes, "for religious, ethnic, or other reasons reject transportation of students for any purpose into or out of their geographic bounds . . . Such claims are hard for liberal policy makers to deal with" (Hochschild 1984:61fn). It is not, however, until the final eight pages of her 200-page text that the rest of this camel of cultural integrity bursts unceremoniously into the liberal tent. As late as page 169, she is asserting that "after all, liberal democracy can take the form of people creating and controlling their own institutions and rules within the bounds set by basic rights; it need not entail majorities creating and controlling a single community in which all must live." But then, she is ultimately moved to admit that "diversity breeds inequality. People not only separate into in-groups and out groups; they add a vertical dimension that creates topdogs and underdogs." Her analysis of the racial significance of this vertical stratification is important enough to quote at length:

> Thus whites see blacks as not merely different but inferior; Princetonians are not merely different but superior. Even these psychological hierarchies would not matter much to policy makers if they remained merely sentiments, but they have profound political and economic consequences. blacks or Hispanics are not hired or encouraged to move next door, or elected president . . . thus diversity turns into inequality which inhibits freedom of movement . . . by freedom of movement I mean the classic liberal promise of individual opportunity, the right to pursue

happiness wherever and however one desires . . . Thus racial and cultural diversity illegitimately inhibits freedom of movement. If we value the former more heavily than the latter we will endorse neighborhood schools, black control of the ghetto schools, and Hispanic control of barrio schools . . . If we could figure out how to make diversity mean simply difference, not inequality, we would not have to choose (Hochschild 1984:198-9).

Here we can spy what might be considered the Afro-American dilemma nestled within Hochschild's new American dilemma. This Afro-American dilemma issues in the problem of reconciling the (ostensibly) illiberal project of racial and cultural autonomy with the liberal requirement of freedom of movement. Hochschild acknowledges that claims to the autonomy that is necessary for racial diversity are "hard for liberal policy makers to deal with" and so, in good liberal policy maker fashion, she chooses to ignore them. She does, however, precisely locate the analytical problem:

(B)y redefining diversity, freedom of movement, liberalism, or democracy we may be able to wriggle out of the contradictions that I have posited. But no one has done so yet in a way that commands universal assent (Hochschild 1984:200).

The Black Intellectual and the Terms of Exchange

The issue that is raised by Hochschild's two American dilemmas is that of the *costs* of liberal freedom. That is, the need to interrogate the terms upon which Americanness has historically been offered to black men and women. That these terms could be problematic, that the game could, at some point be unworthy of the candle, was confirmed for W. E. B. DuBois in 1934 when he left the NAACP. He had, of course, located the existential root of the problem three decades earlier:

It is a peculiar sensation, this double consciousness, this sense of always looking at one's self through the eyes of others, of measuring one's soul by the tape of a world that looks on in amused contempt and pity. One ever feels his twoness, an American, a Negro; two souls, two thoughts, two unreconciled strivings; two warring ideals in one dark body, whose dogged strength alone keeps it from being torn asunder (DuBois 1965:214-215).

Sixty years later when Harold Cruse compared the aspirations of newly freed colonial subjects with those of American racial integrationists, he, too, was attempting an interrogation of the terms of the "deed of gift". "They are seeking their identity," he stormed, "while we are endeavoring to lose ours in exchange for a brand of freedom in a never never land of racial differences" (Cruse 1969:63).

Finally, it is a measure of continuity as well as change that Martin Kilson can, some twenty years after Cruse, locate the paradox of blackness in the fact that in white hands, "blackness can be converted into sizable commercial (and even intellectual) value" and yet blacks still search in vain for political and economic parity (Kilson 1986:70-78).

Although artifacts of the black American life would have been abstracted and integrated into the American consumer culture, flesh and blood black Americans remain (with important and problematic exceptions) on the periphery of American society. Kilson's call for black intellectuals to "invent a response to white competition for the cultural and market values of blackness" is a prosaic, but no less profound insistence that we interrogate the terms under which black "freedom" has been and is being achieved.

Interrogating the terms upon which freedom has been offered to black Americans is a large task. As my consideration of Hochschild's work ought to suggest, it includes (but is certainly not limited to) investigating the ideological and cultural forces that have conditioned both the "offer(s)" and the response(s) that it (they) has (have) provoked. Whatever else this task involves, it must include an examination of the terms of American liberalism.

Unfortunately, the relationship between the black American experience and the terms and forms of American liberalism has never been drawn very precisely. This is as true of discursive practices as it is of analytical forms and historical practice. Although works by Bernard Boxhill and Edwin Dorn have attempted to locate black American concerns within the context of contemporary analytical political philosophy, there remains much to be done in this area. (Boxhill, 1984; Dorn, 1984) In particular, 'communitarian' critics who question the capacity of liberal political philosophy to provide adequate accounts of community and the public good, offer possibilities for the construction of a framework within which we can ask whether liberalism offers freedom only at the cost of identity (Hirsch, 1986).

There has, by and large, been a greater effort to "integrate Afro American history into American history" (Huggins, 1986) than is the case with analytical political theory. There are, for example, important studies that attempt to explain the civil rights movement with reference to the evolution of the thought and practice of American liberalism. (Reed, 1987) This is to a lesser extent true of black politics during the New Deal as well. (Kirby, 1980) Nevertheless, much of our understanding of black American political history remains cast in terms like self help and protest, terms that bear an uncertain relationship to the historical reality of American liberal political practice.

It is in the relationship between black American political discourse and the discourse of American liberalism that the task of the black intellectual, alluded to earlier, crystallizes. It is in this relationship that we should be able to most clearly locate and assess an interrogation of the terms upon which freedom has been offered to black Americans. Unfortunately, there has been, probably, less attention paid to articulating this relationship than to either of the others.

A Life on the Horns of the White Man's Dilemma

There has been a distinct disjuncture between the historiography of Anglo-American political thought and the historiography of black American political thought. Dominant characterizations of Anglo-American political thought have moved from Hartz's 'Lockean consensus' of the 1950s (Hartz 1955) through a 'republican revolt' of the 1960s and early 1970s (Shallhope, 1972) to what might be termed a contemporary liberal restoration (Diggins, 1984, 1985; Greenstone, 1986). Throughout, the structuring principle for interpretations has been the relationship between Anglo-American political thought and European philosophical traditions. This principle has issued in a focus on the role that concepts like interest, virtue, individual, and community have played in the history of Anglo-American political thought.

Broad characterizations of black American political thought have been drawn quite differently. In the prevailing tendency to ignore the intellectual and discursive contexts within which black American political thinking has taken place, writers on the subject have appeared to assimilate Gunnar Myrdal's pronouncement on the 'defensive' nature of black thought.

> Negro thinking is almost completely determined by white opinions . . . it develops as an answer to the popular theories prevalent among whites by which they rationalize their upholding of caste. In this sense it is a derivative, or secondary thinking (Myrdal, 1942:784).

Whatever the reason, critics have based their characterizations on the strategic positions that various thinkers have taken. More often than not, this has resulted in the construction of a left-center-right continuum, with nationalism, integrationism, and 'accomodationism' as the respective reference points. (Meier, Rudwick, and Broderick, 1971; Walton, 1970)

Recently, a group of black social critics have individually and perhaps unintentionally, contributed to the strength of this assumption of derivativeness. Within the work of Alex Willingham, Lucius Outlaw, and Cornel West, there can be found a pronounced insistence on the need to forge new, race-specific, theoretical tools for social and political criticism. (Outlaw, 1983: West 1982, 1983, 1987; Willingham, 1986). This insistence is grounded in an assertion of the sterility of most existing black political discourse, and it issues in grand visions for the construction of a black American theoretical edifice. Willingham would have us think "in terms of a critical social theory which . . . dialectically relates political, cultural, and economic matters into a theoretical form" (Willingham, 1986:20). Outlaw seeks the "elaboration of a global, critical, socio-political-economic-cultural theory. (Outlaw, 1983:72). West, drawing on the work of Derrida, Foucault, and Said among others, wants to clear the ground for a "genealogical materialist analysis of Afro American oppression" (West, 1987 passim).

Although I do not want to suggest that these critics necessarily agree among themselves on the particular direction that this theory building must take, they do seem, in at least one important respect, to begin from the same place. In Willingham's words, "criticism in the black community suffers from the inability to transcend the categories of liberal ideology" (Willingham, 1986:21). Concerning this 'liberal confinement,' Outlaw notes that

> Throughout the history of the presence of African people in this country, the dominant theoretical framework out of which we have struggled has been that provided by the Declaration of Independence, the Constitution and the Bill of Rights (Outlaw, 1983:72).

This is seen by Outlaw to have spelled the impoverishment of black American political discourse and created the need for radically new theoretical formulations.

A resigned acceptance may ultimately be the appropriate response to Myrdal's dictum. Nevertheless, there is force in the objection raised by Ralph Ellison.

> But can a people (its faith in an idealized American Creed notwithstanding) live and develop for over three hundred years simply by reacting? Are American Negroes simply the creation of white men, or have they at least helped to create themselves out of what they found around them? Men have made a way of life in caves and upon cliffs, why cannot Negroes have made a life upon the horns of the white man's dilemma? (Ellison, 1972:315-316).

Accepting a degree of social determination in the thought of black Americans leaves open the question of the amount of latitude that is still possible. It is in recognition of the fact that black thinkers respond not simply to white thought but to the conditions in which they find themselves as well that led Hanes Walton to argue that black political thought, having developed from many different situations, has been as different as those different black experiences (Walton 1970). If we grant, as I think we must, that the thinking of black Americans is conditioned both by their particular (individual and group) situations in America and by pervasive discursive environments, it is still the case that important questions remain unanswered. We should still wish to understand how much distinctiveness is possible under these circumstances of determination and how much distinctiveness has in fact been achieved.

This brings us back to the need to examine the relationship between black American discourse and the discourses of American liberalism. I do not think that we can avoid this task by shifting to new theoretical frameworks, as important as such a shift may ultimately prove to be. In fact, I think that it is crucially important that any attempt to "transcend the categories of liberal ideology" be informed by a text-specific understanding of both the severity and the consequences of the liberal grip on the black American imagination. Encouragement to leave our liberal intellectual baggage behind (on our trip to the critical theoretical promised land) should include the how and why of our liberal confinement. In other words, it is idle for us to expect political commentary to transcend the categories of liberal ideology unless and until the precise hold of these categories on the black American imagination has been accurately illustrated.

Such illustrations would constitute some of the substance of a strong critical tradition in the interpretation of black American political thought. This type of tradition would produce and encourage 'rich' and 'integrated' interpretations of black American political texts.

'Rich' interpretations uncover the philosophical and normative commitments that drive a text; commitments of which the author may or may not have been aware. "Integrated" interpretations reveal the relationships between the text at hand and other intellectual discourses (Hollinger, 1985). Through articulating and developing these relationships, integrated interpretations can confront broad questions about politics and society that, once again, the text at hand may not have been specifically intended to address.

This type of "strong criticism" would require, at a minimum, an investigation of the relationship between black political discourse and its discursive context. This means at least two things. First, it means arguing about (rather than simply asserting) the liberal confinement of black American political discourse within the context of historiographical debates about the general character of Anglo-American political thought. Second, the imperatives of strong criticism suggest the need to locate and describe black political discourses within the context of the historical development of Anglo-American political thought.

I have argued that, in her consideration of liberal democracy and school desegregation, Jennifer Hochschild (almost in spite of herself) precisely locates a dilemma that exists in the gap between the formal guarantees made to individuals by a liberal democratic society and the social and ideological conditions that allow particular groups to sustain, concretize, and transmit group values. This dilemma has particular salience when issues of personal identity are understood to be inextricably tied to the life and values of the group, that is, when one is a black American.

This salience was understood by W. E. B. DuBois when he suggested that the history of the black American can best be understood as the struggle to "merge his double self into a better and truer self" without losing either one of the older selves. Martin Kilson also seems to understand it when he recognizes the ability of liberal democratic capitalism to valorize the commodification of blackness at the same time that it degrades and marginalizes those who cannot "de-black" as easily as unbraiding their hair or cutting off their Walkman.

I have suggested that Hochschild's dilemma presents itself as the need for black people (especially black intellectuals) to interrogate the terms upon which American freedom has been offered to them and the terms upon which they have responded. This interrogation involves, among other things, an investigation of the ideological and cultural conditions within which the offer and the response have occurred. This investigation must consider the relationship between the black American experience and American liberalism.

This relationship takes analytical, historical and discursive forms. I have focused on the discursive forms because I find them to be both interesting and neglected. In addition to setting the historical record straight with richer and more integrated interpretations of black American political discourse, attention to the different discursive forms that the relationship has taken may be repaid in analytical dividends. That is, considering the real ways in which real black people have confronted the terms of liberal freedom may help to concretize what might otherwise be arid and abstract "redefinitons of diversity, freedom of movement, liberalism, or democracy."

I can imagine two objections to the line of inquiry that I propose. The first objection holds that it is essentially a waste of time because consideration of the manner in which black intellectuals have interrogated the terms of liberal freedom will only yield a dismal record of failure. This is the contention that black American political discourse is best characterized by an inability to transcend the categories of liberal ideology. If redefinitions are necessary, they are best pursued directly, without reference to past mistakes.

It is always difficult to argue people out of positions that they have not argued themselves into; it is tempting to oppose assertions with counterassertions. I doubt if imputations of liberal confinement are absolutely and categorically true of black American discourse. If they are, however, that is worthy of demonstration. I think that demonstration must be made along something like the lines that I have set out.

The second objection is a bit more difficult. This position holds (as I take Willingham, Outlaw, and West to hold) that the point is not to redefine the terms of liberalism but to replace liberalism with something else. I find myself sympathetic to this position. Nevertheless, it is important to note that all three theoreticians want their new theoretical forms to be firmly grounded in norms that can be drawn from the history, cultural heritage, and political struggles of black folks in America. Although it may be that, to paraphrase Henry Louis Gates, the terms of our political self-representation have been provided by the master, this is, in important respects, also true of the cultural self-representations that West and Outlaw seem to privilege. Indeed, Outlaw recognizes that

> Oppressed people come to embody in their very being the negations imposed upon them and thus, in the reproduction of their lives, perpetuate their own enslavement (Outlaw 1983:71).

Therefore, even attempts to construct new race-specific theoretical formulations on the foundation of black American life worlds ought not slight the explicitly political self-representations that help to constitute those life worlds.

Once projects along the lines that I have outlined have been carried out, it may in fact turn out to be the case that most extant expressions of black social and political thought are derivative and disposable. But it seems to me that a proper burial is no more than common decency requires.

References

Boxhill, Bernard. 1984. *Blacks and Social Justice*. Totowa, N.J.: Rowman & Allanheld.

Cruse, Harold. 1969. *Rebellion or Revolution?* New York, N.Y.: William Morrow & Co.

Diggins, John P. 1984. *The Lost Soul of American Politics*. Chicago, Ill.: U. of Chicago Press.

_____. 1985. "Comrades and Citizens: New Mythologies in American Historiography." *American Historical Review* 90: 614–638.

Dorn, Edwin. 1984. *Rules and Racial Equality*. New Haven, Ct.: Yale University Press.

DuBois, W. E. B. 1965. *The Souls of Black Folk*. In John Hope Franklin, ed., *Three Negro Classics* New York, N.Y.: Avon Books.

Ellison, Ralph. 1972. *Shadow and Act*. New York, N.Y.: Vintage Press.

Greenstone, J. David. 1986. "Political Culture and American Political Development: Liberty, Union and the Liberal Bipolarity." *Studies in American Political Development* 1: 1–49.

Hartz, Louis. 1955. *The Liberal Tradition in America*. New York, N.Y.: Harcourt Brace Jovanovich.

Hirsch, H. N. 1986. "The Threnody of Liberalism." *Political Theory* vol. 14, no. 3 (August).

Hochschild, Jennifer. 1984. *The New American Dilemma*. New Haven, Ct.: Yale University Press.

Hollinger, David. 1985. *In The American Province*. Bloomington, Ind.: Indiana University Press.

Huggins, Nathan. 1986. "Integrating Afro American History into American History." In Darlene Clark Hine. ed., *The State of Afro American History*. Baton Rouge, LA.: L. S. U. Press.

Kilson, Martin. 1986. "Paradoxes of Blackness: Notes on the Crisis of Black Intellectuals." *Dissent* (Winter): 70–78.

Kirby, John. 1980. *Black Americans in the Roosevelt Era*. Knoxville, TN.: U. of Tennessee Press.

Meier, August, Elliot Rudwick and Francis Broderick, eds. 1971. *Black Protest Thought in the Twentieth Century*, Indianapolis, In.: Bobbs Merrill Co.

Myrdal, Gunnar. 1942. *The American Dilemma*. New York, N.Y.: Harper & Row.

Outlaw, Lucius. 1983. "Philosophy, Hermeneutics, Social-Political Theory: Critical Thought in the Interest of African Americans." In Leonard Harris, ed. *Philosophy Born of Struggle* Dubuque, Iowa: Kendal Hunt.

Reed, Jr., Adolph. 1986. "The Black Revolution and the Reconstruction of Domination." In Adolph Reed Jr., ed. *Race, Politics and Culture*. Westport, Ct.: Greenwood Press.

_____. 1987. "DuBois and the Study of Afro American Political Thought," unpublished manuscript.

Shallhope, Robert. 1972. "Toward a Republican Synthesis: The Emergence of an Understanding of Republicanism in Early American Historiography." *William and Mary Quarterly*, 3rd Ser. XXIX: 49–80.

Walton, Hanes. 1970. "Black Political Thought: The Problem of Characterization." *Journal of Black Studies* 1.

West, Cornel. 1982. *Prophesy Deliverance!* Philadelphia, Pa.: Westminster Press.

_____. 1987. "Race and Social Theory: Towards a Geneological Materalist Analysis." In *The Year Left* 2. New York, N.Y.: Verso Press.

_____. 1983. "Philosophy, Politics and Power: An Afro American Perspective." In Leonard Harris, ed., *Philosophy Born of Struggle*. Dubuque, Iowa: Kendal Hunt.

Willingham, Alex. 1986. "Ideology and Politics: Their Status in Afro American Social Theory." In Adolph Reed Jr., ed., *Race Politics and Culture*. Westport, Ct.: Greenwood Press.

Political Movements in American Politics: An Essay On Concept and Analysis

Robert H. Salisbury

Washington University

Political movements are important phenomena in American political life. They are composed of core movement organizations plus those who identify and often work for the movement's cause. Movements often rest upon the support base of institutions, especially churches in the American case. They are highly dynamic, rising swiftly to prominence and, as swiftly, fading. The rhetoric of American movement politics tends to be apocalyptic and is often cast in religious terms.

American politics, past and present, is rich in political movements. The civil rights movement, the environmental movement, the student movement, and the labor movement are but a few of the phenomena to which the term is attached as a defining concept. And lest we suppose that movements come only from the left, the neoconservative movement of recent years or the Prohibition movement of an earlier time give witness to the contrary. The Progressive movement gave the dominant tone to an entire political era in the United States, and democracies elsewhere in the world have also experienced substantial impact from forces that both participants and observers designated as movements.

Among sociologists, social movements have long been of central concern, providing a standard subfield in the discipline and generating a considerable body of literature (Zald and McCarthy, 1987). The neighboring social sciences have less often incorporated the sociologists' work into their own analysis, however. Political scientists have quite generally failed to give explicit attention to movements, tending instead to divide their attention to movement phenomena between mass behavior (mainly electoral behavior), on the one hand, and interest groups, on the other. The one studies mobilization; the other looks at organization, but few political scientists examine the interaction—how organizations mobilize public support and thus build a movement. Recent scholarship has begun to incorporate social movement theory and research into political science, but there still is little or no attention to whatever might be distinctive about movements within the context of the political arena (cf. Morris and Herring, 1987).

In this essay, I propose to explore the conceptual elements involved in the study of political movements, drawing in part on the social movement literature to do so but focusing specifically on those movements that seek to enter the political arena and the impact that arena has on the dynamics of movement activity. I will argue that neither organizational nor individual behavior alone provides an adequate focus if we are to encompass the full range of what is politically important.

The Concept of a Political Movement

Let us consider the essential elements involved in the observables we call movements. The most common definitions of social movement begin by stressing the importance of a particular configuration of opinion that aims at "changing some elements of the social structure and/or reward distributions of a society" (McCarthy and Zald, 1977:1217). Immediately, however, we must restrict this definition. To include every desire to alter the reward distribution of a society would make *movement* virtually synonymous with *human striving*. What we call movements seek relatively major changes, and it seems preferable therefore to confine the term to those who advocate changes in the *structure* of the socioeconomic–sociopolitical order. Thus the civil rights movement encompasses all those who have worked to reconstruct the status relationships among racial groups, whereas the Urban League, a "mere" interest group, has generally confined its attention to enlarging job opportunities for blacks. An interest group as such typically seeks to achieve an optimum payoff from the existing structure. It hopes to win within the system, not to alter the system's structure. Particular groups may, of course become integral parts of movements in which their goals are linked to larger purposes. Thus the distinction between interest groups and movements can be shadowy, and often quite dynamic as groups shift their focus from narrow to broad "change" objectives and back again. Moreover, some discrete interest groups may couch their purposes in the encompassing rhetoric of systemic change without ever becoming part of a movement. Figure 1 expresses the movement–group distinction schematically.

Because they seek structural change, many movements are thought to be radical, critical of "the system" from the "outside," so to speak, rather than accepting the system as it operates and working to maximize advantage within it. Whether a structural change is regarded as truly radical depends a good deal on one's analytical perspective, of course, and also on the scope and magnitude of consequences likely to result from the movement's recommendations. Many a reform movement in American urban experience, for example, has discovered that the consequences of institutional change were much less significant than they had expected. Nevertheless, we commonly call these campaigns movements, as did the participants themselves, and we should therefore define the term to include them. The key is thus the movement's definition of goals in terms of structural change rather than simply redistribu-

Figure 1
Interest Groups and Political Movements

Scope of Policy Ojectives

Range of Inter-group and Mass Relationships		Extensive/Systemic	Narrow/Optimizing
	Extensive	Political Movement	Group Coalition; eg, farm organization, alliance of business groups.
	Narrow	Apocalyptic Isolate	"Classic" interest group; eg. American Legion, National Rifle Association

tion of valued outcomes. To be sure, at the margin that distinction becomes blurred. Many movements draw support from people who mainly want more of what there is, but their mobilization is predicated on the assumption that, in order to achieve meaningful redistribution of values, some structural/institutional change is required. In some cases, the rhetoric of protest so confounds structural change with redistribution that it becomes impossible to differentiate between them. Still, there is a difference between the quest for "more" and the effort to restructure social relations.

Movements themselves have structural characteristics; they are not mere aggregations of opinion. A movement includes one or more formal organizations (SMOs in the parlance of sociological usage) that act as the "carriers" and mobilizers of the movement. These organizational components often operate in ways that are very similar to other interest groups and are commonly included in most treatments of interest groups. Yet to define the civil rights movement solely in terms of the NAACP and other active organizations, even to equate the labor movement with the AFL-CIO, would lead us to misunderstand the special characteristics of movements. The latter embrace followers as well, identifiers who endorse the movement's goals and may take part in some or all of a considerable repertoire of supportive activities without formally joining any organized association. It was appropriate to refer to an American labor movement so long as the cause of enhanced working-class power and associated income redistribution evoked broadly sympathetic support from intellectuals, opinion leaders, and diverse other segments of the population. Once that support waned, the "movement" became a mere constellation of interest groups.

The extent to which people have come to identify with a movement is usually difficult to measure precisely, but that very uncertainty may serve to enhance the bargaining position of movement leaders who can claim a strong following that opponents cannot confidently disregard. A movement, then, has organizational components—and is thus different from a crowd—and an uncertain number of identifier-followers ready to act in concert with the organizations that lead the way.

Very often we employ the word *mass* in conjunction with movement, and although that word is no model of measurement precision, its central implication—that the scope of the movement's support is, actually or potentially, large—is one we embrace. It makes little sense to designate a neighborhood clean-up campaign a movement. Its potential support is too small for such promotional hype. Higher prices for soybeans likewise is a poor prospect for movement status. Indeed, most of the activities described by Lowi (1969) under the heading of interest group liberalism are clearly *not* movement material. Nevertheless, political/social entrepreneurs quite often will call their efforts *movements* in order to imply the existence of a mass support base, at least in potential. In part, this claim may stimulate a bandwagon effect among the previously uncommitted, but there is another implication as well. A movement, seeking structural change that will putatively benefit a large number of people, far in excess of the participants so far associated with the cause, can usually enjoy a more favorable moral position among intellectuals and publicists than the self-interested pursuit of benefits by interest groups and institutions. The prospect of a mass base confers a degree of democratic legitimacy on movements—what Useem and Zald (1982) call the legitimacy of numbers—that interest groups often lack.

There are other reasons for adopting the movement label as well. It implies dynamic growth and an optimism about the possibilities of collective action that are nontrivial assets in mobilizing support. The well-known arguments of Mancur Olson (1965) and others regarding the difficulty of recruiting members to an organization in order to strengthen a campaign for supraorganizational collective benefits is, as Moe (1980) and others have shown, considerably modified when the "rational individual" is unclear regarding what it would take to secure the collective purpose. One may well join a movement whose momentum promises to sweep away all obstacles, especially if refusing to join threatens to leave one isolated from one's peers. If everyone seems to be flocking to the movement's banner, the appeal is more persuasive. Calling a group of farmers the American Agriculture Movement (Cigler, 1986) conveys a good deal more of this dynamism than naming the same group with the same purposes the American Farmers Association.

A movement is thus characterized by the rhetoric and, when it prospers, the reality of dynamic growth. Closely related is the strong preference among movement tacticians for direct expressive action rather than, or at least prior to, bargaining and negotiation. Associations have conventions and speeches, but movements have songs and marches, sit-ins and picket lines. Associations are prosaic; movements are dramatic. Associations seek to secure and maintain access to decisionmakers, and the maintenance of friendly communication channels is of the highest priority. Movements accept a degree of risk, sometimes though not always great, that extant elites will be offended and authorities alienated by direct action tactics that may reach all the way to martyrdom.

From one perspective, the expressive emphasis of movement tactics reflects the heavy dose of moral self-righteousness that so often accompanies movement rhetoric. One ought not to compromise or bargain over what is morally right; rather, one should declare it forthrightly from the housetops and put the burden of compliance with rectitude on those in authority. From the more mundane perspective of detached analysis, however, dramatic expressive action has other advantages. It confers upon participants the "selective" benefit of personal excitement, the delights of enthusiasm for a noble cause, and the very real sense of solidarity with those of like persuasion. Moreover, dramatic expressive acts have a better chance than many more conventional tactics of gaining the attention of potential sympathizers, sometimes raising their consciousness that they are in fact sympathetic and sometimes persuading identifiers that this expressive core of "the movement" is actually "doing something" directly and not just sitting around the mimeograph machine. The combination of mobilization effects with the intrinsic pleasures to participants of being noticed go far toward explaining the tactical emphasis by modern political movements on media events with all the concomitant uncertainty about what is real and what is manufactured in this kind of tactical exercise.

A final element of definition can be disposed of quickly. It involves the distinction between political movements and social movements. The latter is clearly the broader term, for it encompasses all movements, whether or not they involve activity within the political arena. Movements are political whenever and insofar as they undertake actions intended to affect governmental officials, by persuading them to act in a particular way or indeed by determining who will hold office. Any movement whose goals require some governmental response is political. Many movements are almost entirely so; the Progressive movement, for example. The American labor movement, on the other hand, despite its extensive political agenda, finds its primary raisons d'être in the economic bargaining relationship with employers. In modern times, a very large share of the phenomena we call movements in the United States plainly have involved at least some action in the political arena and so may properly be included in the set of political movements. Sometimes an aggregation of groups and followers may largely abandon the political arena but maintain enough dynamism and sharpness of purpose to qualify as social movements. One might regard the feminist movement in the late 1980s in this light. Since the demise of the ERA, feminism has been an important social movement, but without very much immediate political presence. Again, the point is that a distinction between social and political movements, although often blurred in real life, is of analytic and descriptive utility.

Movements and Their Enemies

Movement rhetoric in American (and other democratic) politics is often filled with apocalyptic metaphors, emphasizing that the desired structural change can come about only through the destruction of hostile forces and stressing verbs of action, adjectives conveying great intensity, and adverbs of moral virtue. Interest groups, despite Truman's conception of them as adverse to others, often find themselves without visible opposition (Salisbury et al.,

1987; Walker, 1983) and to a large extent appeal to members in Olsonesque fashion by offering selective benefits unavailable except through the association. Movement organizations, those associations that are a movement's active agents, must likewise offer specific membership benefits. But the recognition of an enemy and a commitment to oppose are not selective organizational benefits, restricted to those who join. They are matters of attitude and conviction that anyone may come to share. Once the beliefs are in place, selective benefits to participants, especially of a solidary character, will more readily follow, but first there must be the shared belief in social structural change. Is conflict a necessary condition of such belief? Is it possible to be emotionally committed to changing the system without also being committed to the view that there are social forces or groups or elites or somebody on the other side, preventing the change, acting out of self-interest and perhaps corruption also to block the desired reform? Logically, it does not appear to be a requirement. Social systems and political institutions may be thought of in essentially impersonal terms in which no individual or group wills the undesired outcomes, but neither can anyone overcome the institutional barriers; hence the movement, born out of frustration. Such arguments are surely possible and sometimes employed, but it is clear that movement rhetoric is seldom content with such detached analysis. Instead, appeals for support are predicated upon opposition—to "the bosses," including those in charge of political machines, capitalist employers and hierarchical superiors both inside and outside of government, or to such other putative oppressors, exploiters and despoilers as have been defined by the movement's rhetorical foundations and proposed reforms.

The sense of embattlement carries a message of urgency; the stakes are great, and time is short. Armageddon is at hand; the battle is on, and failure looms unless potential members promptly and generously make a commitment of support. If we were to postulate a continuum of political rhetoric along which appeals for support may range from the most intensely apocalyptic to the mildest nonconflictual expression of group's policy desires, it is clear that those political formations we call movements would be bunched together toward the high-conflict end of the spectrum.

Movements and Movement Organizations

Discussions of political and social movements commonly separate out from the "mass of activity" those formal associations that have been constructed in support of the movement's goals. In some movements, there is a single core group. Often there are several. Sometimes organizations vie for movement leadership; sometimes they work out a kind of functional division of labor. Some movements are characterized as "reticulated," networks of organizations and more inchoate followings bound together by contacts among leaders who move back and forth across the landscape of both geography and political society (Freeman, 1983).

Movement organizations, as we have noted, must maintain themselves as viable enterprises against all the challenges of apathy, disappointment, and rival associations. In so doing, they face the free-rider problems that Olson outlined. Insofar as a movement organization seeks to attract and hold members primarily with selective benefits composed of expressive rhetoric—espousing the purest doctrine or the correct line—the association risks swift collapse. Expressive groups are easy to start but hard to maintain. And this is especially true if the costs of membership are at all burdensome, as, for example, they were when what Wilson (1973) refers to as redemptionist organizations in the civil rights movement required such sacrifices as going to jail or suffering physical beating.

The history of political movements in America is replete with examples of organizational failures, to be sure, but in a sense what is more surprising is how many movement organizations survive, at least for considerable periods of time. How is it that groups whose symbolic emphasis is on achieving structural changes in society and that typically couch their appeals in relatively conflict-centered language filled with moral outrage can last so long? A part of the answer lies in the findings of Walker and others (cf. Berry, 1977; Freeman, 1983; Salisbury, 1969) regarding subsidies granted to one group by another. Walker attributes a significant share of the success in organizing various kinds of public interest movement organizations during the 1960s and early 1970s to the infusion of financial aid from sympathetic groups already established and from foundations and government agencies. A similar story may be told of much union organizing and farm group development, among others.

It would not provide very dependable support for movement organizations if the subsidizers were themselves highly vulnerable to the vicissitudes of movement momentum, factional strife, or rapid decline in resources among potential members. In fact, however, a large share of the subsidizing agents are quite securely institutionalized. Foundations, churches, universities, and government agencies may decide to stop funding change agents or, if they do not, risk losing some of their own support, but they generally remain in existence, and movement organizations may be able to come back again and again for help. From the perspective of the movement entrepreneur, sympathetic institutions typically constitute a more dependable base of support than individual members or identifiers, however important the latter may be as indicators of the movement's broad appeal. In American experience, churches have played a particularly important role as institutional bases for such diverse movements as abolition, temperance, civil rights, peace and disarmament, and the "right-to-life." We will return to and elaborate on this theme later in this essay.

A second basis of movement survival, at least of its core, is to be found in the dedicated commitment of relatively small numbers of faithful adherents who do not accept defeat or bow to what others see as inevitable demise but continue on in the hope that success will yet crown their efforts. Minor political parties and many interest groups operate on essentially the same kind of slender foundation, of course. When such a fragmentary enterprise calls itself a movement, however, observers should not accept the designation at face value. It may again become one; the civil rights movement might well regain the momentum and broad support it had in the early 1960s. Until that happens, however, to give the interest groups seeking civil rights policy objectives, the label of *movement* would misrepresent their character and misread their short-term prospects.

Disruption and Organization: Can Movements Survive?

Piven and Cloward (1977) present in most explicit form the argument that political movements are inevitably robbed of their vital essence as change agents when they become institutionalized and the active movement entrepreneurs turn their energies away from leading direct action and concentrate on maintaining formal organizations. They contend that significant structural changes can sometimes be forced by means of disruptive protest, which so raises the cost to society of maintaining the status quo that dominant elites are forced to accept new arrangments. Once the protestants are organized and begin to negotiate, however, the momentum is lost, and "the system," either as it was or as modified, once more begins to function with the usual results of excluding the unorganized from its benefits.

This interpretation—that organization only means power *within* a given system and is thus antithetical to systemic change—is an interesting, if extreme, variation on the more familiar argument of Michels to the effect that bureaucratization and oligarchical dominance tend to affect all organizations, even those imbued with democratic dogma and revolutionary objectives. The needs of organizational maintenance supersede movement elan and momentum, and, as this happens, the possibility of dynamic growth itself fades very quickly. Thus it takes a feat either of memory or retrospective empathy to speak in the 1980s of the labor *movement* or the student *movement*. In 1984, Jesse Jackson's presidential campaign mobilized many previously inactive black citizens, but it did not reinvigorate the civil rights *movement*. It may well be, of course, that movements accomplish less policy change than more narrowly focused interest group pressure. The NAACP Legal Defense Fund litigation strategy was surely an important adjunct and perhaps even a necessary precondition to the marches of Martin Luther King. In the context of the legalistic culture of American politics, it is often helpful to have tested the possibilities and explored the limits of legal action before appealing to people to take to the streets. But test cases and *amicus* briefs are not the same as the direct-action tactics of a movement. They do not hold the potential for altering the consciousness of large numbers of people or of mobilizing them to action. And the political logic that underlies movements is that only large-scale action and demands can get beyond incrementalism to achieve fundamental changes in the structure of social relations, political power, or economic reward.

On the Origins of Movements

Samuel Huntington (1981) has argued that a cyclical pattern can be discerned in American political experience in which periods of "creedal passion," manifested in a burgeoning of movements and righteous causes, alternate with periods of relative quiescence. Albert Hirschman (1982) has advanced a somewhat similar argument, in which the cycles of movement and retreat result from the frustrations and disappointments of each phase as accomplishments fall short of promises. Related to these hypotheses is that considerable body of literature on party realignment that, in some versions at least, sees the rise of various political movements and third parties as the major signal of structural strain and upheaval that eventually force the major parties into departures from past coalition appeals and thereby bring about significant realignment and reinvigoration of voter loyalties. It is not entirely clear whether a new party alignment is expected to "solve" the structural crisis sufficiently to quiet the movement impulse. Clearly, the "System of 1896" did not; thereafter the congeries of Progressive, socialist, and Prohibition reform movements picked up speed. Nor was the 1928–1932 realignment followed by notable quiescence—labor organizers, the Townsend Plan, and others provided the "politics of upheaval" (cf. Schlesinger, 1960). Conversely, the movements of the 1960s—civil rights, antiwar, environmentalist, and so on—quieted down without any lasting party realignment taking place. The connections between party development and political movements are obviously important but would seem to present more complexity than either cyclical or realignment theories can well accomodate.

A useful clue to the conditions likely to generate movements as compared to those leading to the formation of conventional interest group associations may be found in David Truman (1951), who does not even mention movements as one of the "stages of technique" in organized group action. Truman locates the source of group foundation in the disturbance of an equilibrium of interactions. Although he is not very explicit about the distinction, he speaks of some disturbances in terms that involve quite large numbers of people and involve interactions that are best described in the language of social structure—labor versus capitalist management, for example, or wheat farmers against the banks and railroads. Other "disturbances," however, such as many of those resulting from technological changes, are discussed in terms of relatively small differentiations of detailed interests, such as those leading to the formation of trade and professional associations.

Neither large structural shifts nor lesser differentiations of interests generate political, relevant activity with complete spontaneity. Leadership and mobilization are necessary ingredients for anything beyond the fragments of anomic outbursts. But whereas entrepreneur–organizers are necessary, they are never sufficient. Their efforts must find responsive audiences, and responsiveness is conditioned in part by the more or less objective positions people occupy in the complex of social relations we call political society. When these "market conditions" are experiencing major shifts in status relations among social groupings, for example, movement entrepreneurs may find rich opportunities. And, inasmuch as American society has long been characterized by extraordinary dynamism and growth, with correlative status uncertainties, movement politics, for all its high risk, has generally been an enticing opportunity. Meanwhile, however, and often in almost unnoticed parallel through time, the processes of social fission and marginal differentiation of interests go on apace, creating new opportunities, without much melodrama or fireworks, for interest associations to be formed and for them, along with institutional representatives, to go about the business of pursuing their comparatively modest policy objectives in the corridors of power.

The Movement Market and Its Customers

If our social imagination permits us to envision potential movement entrepreneurs "raising capital" from sympathetic institutions and investing their own commitment as dedicated believers in the cause, where may we expect them to find their most likely adherents? What sectors of the population will most readily respond to a movement's appeal? Part of the answer depends of course on the existing distribution of beliefs, values, and preferences. One finds supporters among those who share the movement's values and believe in its goals. But that is not a very satisfactory answer for at least two reasons. One is that commitment is not simply a given. People can be converted; from unbelief to acceptance, from acquiescence to enthusiasm, from applauding spectator to dedicated, even fanatic, activist. A movement depends upon and, indeed, is defined by those whom it *moves*—those who are mobilized to act in ways they would not were it not for the movement's impact upon them. And this mobilization is problematic. It may be great, swiftly achieving momentum sufficient to effectuate major social change. Or it may fall short, lapsing into the petty wrangling that, for example, characterized left wing movements of the 1920s and after; perhaps settling into comfortable bureaucratization with meetings in Las Vegas and Key Biscayne, a la the present day labor movement; or, like the student movement of the 1960s, disappearing almost totally with only a faded bit of poster or graffiti to show it was ever alive.

Many movement markets are quite volatile. One might suppose that an effort to restructure some basic social relationship would draw a relatively stable level of latent public support, but, at least at the overt level, many movement causes have experienced quite wide and rapid swings in saliency and popularity. McAdam (1982) shows, for instance, that the issues of civil rights fluctuated greatly in their perceived importance in the period from 1963 to 1966 when they were, in effect, displaced by concern over Viet Nam.

There is another side to this same phenomenon. Movements tend to come in sets (Freeman, 1983), often only loosely connected but sharing a degree of sympathy, drawing on the same organizations and social strata, articulating values and espousing causes that occupy adjacent locations in the issue space of the day. Thus, in the three decades prior to the Civil War, abolition was political kin to feminism, prison reform, concern for the mentally ill, and public education (Fuller, 1944; Rothman, 1971). The New Right of today embraces a congeries of movements, some of them uneasy about their allies but caught up in a context, a "market" of potentially responsive opinion, that has been identified as offering the most promising route to rapid growth and effectiveness. Right-to-life demonstrators do not necessarily share the views of the economic conservatives or nuclear power advocates, and the elites of each movement component may be very different. Nevertheless, they function to some degree in common political harness because their most likely prospects of broad mass support, needed to enact or sustain their basic policy or structural change objectives, are found in the same social sectors.

Thus the "market" for movement organizers is often fluid and problematic, but there may be rather clear limits constraining conversion and mobilization. Predispositions can be identified. Sympathies are not randomly distributed.

The logic of modern mass mailing technique rests on the increased likelihood of a positive response to a second appeal tapping the same or a related social value. Movement entrepreneurs therefore tend to work primarily within particular value sectors of society (Salisbury, 1969, 1975), some of which have been revealed by past behavior and some even better illuminated by present affiliations.

Having said this, however, it remains true that movement leaders must take a further step to identify the most likely sources of people who, apart from their sympathy with the values espoused, will be willing to undertake the activity that specifically distinguishes a movement from "mere" interest group support, namely direct action (Judkins, 1983). Who are the people most likely to respond to exhortations to march, to sing, to sit down, or sit in? Surely they will tend to be people not otherwise engaged, with few existing commitments of time or dependent interests that might be placed at risk by disruptive direct action. Thus the young, the restless, the unemployed, and those who, like writers and entertainers, have some autonomous control over their working schedules are more promising movement material than those with families to support or with employers who might look askance at demonstrators. Farmers are more readily mobilized in winter than when crops require tending. Senior citizens seeking policy relief may not always be able to travel long distances or endure physical hardship, but, within limits, their very freedom from obligations makes of them an attractive market for movement recruits.

At the same time, however, the very condition that enables these people to undertake direct political action—the absence of competing obligations—greatly reduces their inclination to care very much about the cause to which the movement is devoted. Even when the movement's purpose is quite directly linked to the differentiated needs of the putative market—draft resistance for students, jobs for the unemployed, or better pensions for the aged—free riderism combines with inertia and, often, an absence of reinforcing social context to keep most potential participants far removed from the movement in question. And when the movement does not seek differentiated group benefits, as with the anti-nuclear-energy campaign, for example, it is especially difficult to exploit these markets of comparatively unattached, otherwise uncommitted people.

Just as the mobilization of "loose" voters—first-time voters and those previously not participating—is a key element of party and candidate strategy in elections, the mobilization of people with scanty networks of affiliation is of surpassing importance to movement development. We have stressed the short time frame within which movement mobilization must build if it is to have significant impact, and this has two interesting connections with what we have said about the attractiveness of the underaffiliated segments of society as the prime market for movement recruitment. The first is that these segments are composed of people for whom the appeal of movement participation is likely to have an especially short life. In part, this is because people with little to lose from risky direct action are also likely to be highly oriented toward the present, taking a short-term view of both gratification and adversity, and are less willing to remain committed to any group promising only long-run rewards. In part, however, it should be noted that, for many of the less densely affiliated, that condition itself is of rather short duration. The young get older and acquire more compelling responsibilities. Students eventually leave the care-free protected sanctuary of academe. (Faculty members, by contrast, remain in this institutional setting, permitted by tenure rules and academic norms to indulge their expressive fancies in all sorts of movements without much risk.) Some of the unemployed obtain jobs. And, even though new cohorts of individuals replace them, the problem of movement mobilization is nearly continuous. Movement causes typically are difficult to accomplish and hence frustrating to their supporters, and they draw support disproportionately from social sectors that themselves undergo rather rapid turnover of individual members.

A consequence of this is seen in the studies of student protest and civil rights movements of the 1960s in which "generational" change and inter-generational conflict developed in a remarkably brief period of time (Ross, 1983). In those movements, a generation lasted approximately five years, after which new recruits came in with different expectations and values, and the older generation gradually withdrew. The new cohort itself, however, was gone in another five years. This tendency to suffer frequent generational turnover and conflict reflects what might be called the "sunshine patriotism" of much movement support—it will be remembered that George Washington Plunkitt (Riordan, 1948) called reformers "morning glories"—and contributes to it as well. The result is that movements very often have brilliant but brief prominence, and fade very quickly, losing all but a hard core of deeply com-mitted activists for whom the cause remains important or appealing enough to keep them at work.

We come back then to the organizers, leaders, and core activists, upon whom must rest a very large share of any effort to understand movement growth and decay as well as the residual survivals of what might be called movement shells, once-prominent centers of political action now moribund save for the dedicated true believers who keep the faith against all the evi-dence around them of public indifference or even contempt. The WCTU and the American Council on Alcohol Problems are virtually all that remain of the Prohibition movement that, having achieved such success under the guidance of Purley Baker and Wayne Wheeler, fell quickly into disrepute and caricature when Bishop Cannon took over (Gusfield, 1969; Odegard, 1928). Antiwar movements, influential in the 1930s, quiescent from Pearl Harbor until the late 1950s, flowered again in the Viet Nam years, led by some of the same figures, such as David Dellinger and A. J. Muste (Hentoff, 1963), who had kept the flickering light of pacifism alive throughout the period (Wittner, 1984). These two examples remind us not only that movement leaders can, by their wrang-ling and internecine struggles, quickly bring a movement down, but that continued dedication to the cause may sometimes bring the reward of revived support and social impact. It is the latter lesson, of course, that sustains the optimism of those who remain committed to a movement that has ceased to move, losing its momentum, and finding its best rhetorical flourishes greeted with stony indifference. That same confidence, however, often encourages the very intramural conflict that speeds decline, as rival leaders, *knowing* that they are *right* and that the future will confirm it, refuse to yield or compromise.

Movements are concerned with causes, with matters of principle, defined in terms of moral, even theological, right and wrong. To adopt the wrong doctrinal position is not merely mistaken, therefore: It is sinful. Error must be combatted by every available means, especially within the family of movement sympathizers, for if they do not get things right, how can the larger world ever be expected to understand the truth? It would rarely be quite correct to say that a movement has been wracked by heresy, for that term implies the existence of an agreed-upon standard of truth and, usually, some degree of hierarchical authority to establish and enforce that standard. Politically interesting movements in America have not often or for long had such clearly established central leadership. Yet, if they have avoided heresy trials, they have been rife with schism. Abortionists, feminists, prohibitionists, socialists, right-to-lifers, participatory democrats, and on and on, virtually without exception, have shown a wonderful ability to find grounds for doctrinal dispute of sufficient seriousness to lead one faction to exit and found a new organization, still within the larger movement perhaps, but presenting a different interpretation of its moral purpose, its enemies, or the strategies of action that should be followed. In this respect, clearly, political movements in the United States closely resemble, just as they often have drawn vital organizational support from, American Protestantism.

The Institutional Foundations of Political Movements: The Case of the Churches

Social scientists have recently begun to discover that their assumption that religious beliefs and institutions would wither away in the face of postindustrial modernity was false, at least in the United States. Rather than fading away, religiosity has fully maintained its strength at the level of individual belief and practice, and churches, in the aggregate, are not only flourishing but displaying unwonted vigor with respect to political affairs. The specific importance of institutional religion to the study of political movements is enormous because, in both past and present, church organizations have provided major sources of support for political movements of many kinds.

The civil rights movement is a well-known example in which Southern churches came to constitute key elements in the organized infrastructure of the movement, providing leadership, workers, communication centers, funds, and even physical asylum for those active in the campaigns (Zald and McCarthy, 1987). A similar dependence on local congregations was exhibited by the classic campaign for Prohibition; the right-to-life movement has found wide support in Catholic parishes. New Right campaigns of various kinds have drawn resources from fundamentalist churches, especially some of the large Southern Baptist congregations, conservative Presbyterian churches, and Pentacostals. At the other end of the spectrum, various manifestations of peace movements throughout the twentieth century have rested on support from sympathetic church groups, such as the Methodist Church Washington office, or what Morris (1984) calls "halfway houses," groups such as the American Friends Service Committee or the Fellowship of Reconciliation, which themselves depend largely on churches for support, and which, in turn, provide organizational cadres for such campaigns as the nuclear freeze movement (Dwyer, 1983).

The importance of churches as institutional foundations of so many American political movements is twofold. First, they are relatively secure organizations with indefinite longevity. Unlike the volatile movements, the churches will continue to function for years to come, and even though one movement fades, another may soon rise up from the same resource base to pick up the campaign threads and try again. The peace movement, as we have noted, is a prime example wherein key leaders resurface again and again as new wars and threats of war raise once more the old questions. To the extent that political movements can build upon such stable institutional foundations, they can become permanent fixtures on the political scene. Despite the considerable ebb and flow of their strength, they never entirely disappear because their organizational core remains in operation. Thus we find the irony: Specific political movements tend to rise and fall within relatively brief spans of time, but many of what might be called movement streams, including peace, civil rights, and the moral reforms espoused by religious fundamentalists, are quite enduring parts of the political system.

A second consequence of the fact that church organizations constitute the core of so many political movements in the United States is rhetorical. Movements, by definition, must appeal to a far broader audience than can be made content with solidary or material selective benefits. The structural reform goals a movement pursues must be articulated in ways that first capture the attention and then the commitment of large numbers of people who have not previously been motivated to care. A movement must therefore fashion powerful rhetorical tools.

It may be a truism that, any time rhetoric can draw upon widely shared symbols and patterns of belief, its prospects of persuasion are enhanced. Certainly, it is true that the continued breadth of acceptance of Christian symbols and beliefs among Americans offers an attractive opportunity to many types of entrepreneurs, political and otherwise, and would-be movement leaders partake of this opportunity. Beyond this, however, the fact that churches themselves are so often the institutional core of movement action guarantees that goals and aspirations will be cast rhetorically in religious terms. Not content to argue in behalf of one social class against another or to urge the prudential advantages of a particular course of reform, all sorts of movement leaders in the United States state their cases in the language of moral principle, pitting sin against salvation, and either they draw upon Holy Writ for inspired justification or they endow more worldly documents such as the Constitution with quasi-divine qualities. We need not argue that this is the only reason for the importance of political rhetoric grounded in religious themes to recognize the role of American churches as institutional infrastructures serving political movements.

Conclusions

It may be inappropriate to label the final observations of this chapter as conclusions because their purpose is really to open some issues for discussion and enlarge the scope of both our theoretical and conceptual understanding and our descriptive accomplishments. By explicitly bringing the concept of movement into harness with interest group, association, institution, and so on, we can perhaps establish a sufficiently broad frame within which to discern more clearly the different organizational modes employed by people seeking political purposes, track more accurately the progress (and decay) from one mode to another, and map the interrelationships among these several forms of activities. Thus, we have suggested that movements typically encompass one or more movement organizations, which we would ordinarily call interest groups, and often depend upon the long-term support of institutions such as churches and other subsidizing agents for the survival of the movement shell or core.

One of the most important differences between a political movement and a "mere" interest group is in the language employed. Movement activists use a language of action. They stress the imminence of the crisis and the great magnitude of the stakes. Their characteristic rhetoric reflects the fact that they tend to have so little time in which to succeed. The language of interest group advocates, by contrast, tends to be circumspect in emotional tone and constrained by the particular norms of the institutional setting—congressional committee, regulatory agency, appellate court, and so on—in which their policy advocacy is expressed. Most of them will be back year after year to pursue their concerns, goals that are largely incremental and distributive rather than matters of basic structural change.

The term *movement* itself is often a political weapon, used in order to convey a sense of dynamic growth and prospective impact, as well as an analytic concept. Accordingly, we must be careful in according the analytic status of movement to activity simply on the basis of self-referencing rhetoric. It is important to pay close heed to political rhetoric, however, precisely because of this conflation of political with analytic usage. Any ambitious optimist may call a cause a movement; social scientists should always be clear enough about the meaning of their concepts to know the difference.

References

Berry, Jeffrey. 1977. *Lobbying for the People*. Princeton: Princeton University Press.

Cigler, Allan. 1986. "From Protest Group to Interest Group: The Making of American Agriculture Movement, Inc." In Allen Cigler and Burdett Loomis, eds., *Interest Group Politics* 2nd ed. Washington, D.C.: Congressional Quarterly Press.

Dwyer, Lynn E. 1983. "Structure and Strategy in the Antinuclear Movement." In J. Freeman, ed. *Social Movements of the Sixties and Seventies*, New York: Longman, pp. 148–161.

Freeman, J. 1983. "On the Origins of Social Movements." In J. Freeman, ed., *Social Movements*, pp. 8–30.

Gusfield, Joseph. 1969. *Symbolic Crusade*. Urbana: University of Illinois Press.

Hentoff, Nat. 1963. *Peace Agitator: The Story of A. J. Muste*. New York: Macmillan.

Hirschmann, Albert O. 1982. *Shifting Involvements: Private Interests and Public Actions*. Princeton: Princeton University Press.

Huntington, Samuel. 1981. *American Politics: The Promise of Disharmony*. Cambridge: Harvard University Press.

Judkins, Bennett M. 1983. "Mobilization of Membership: The Black and Brown Lung Movements." In J. Freeman, ed., *Social Movements*, pp. 35–51.

Lowi, Theodore. 1969. *The End of Liberalism*. New York: W. W. Norton.

McAdam, Doug. 1982. *Political Process and the Development of Black Insurgency*. Chicago: University of Chicago Press.

McCarthy, John D., and Mayer N. Zald. 1977. "Resource Mobilization and Social Movements: A Partial Theory." *American Journal of Sociology* 82:1212–41.

Moe, Terry, 1980. *The Organization of Interests*. Chicago: University of Chicago Press.

Morris, Aldon, and Cedric Herring. 1987. "Theory and Research in Social Movements: A Critical Review." In Samuel Long, ed., *Annual Review of Political Science*, Vol. 2. Norwood, N.J.: Ablex Publishing Corp., pp. 137–198.

Morris, O. D. 1984. *The Origins of the Civil Rights Movement*. New York: Free Press.

Odegard, Peter. 1928. *Pressure Politics: The Study of the Anti-Saloon League*. New York: Columbia University Press.

Olson, Mancur. 1965. *The Logic of Collective Action*. Cambridge: Harvard University Press.

Piven, Frances Fox, and Richard Cloward. 1977. *Poor People's Movements: How They Succeed, How They Fail*. New York: Vintage.

Riordan, William. 1948. *Plunkitt of Tammany Hall*. New York: Knopf.

Ross, Robert J. 1983. "Generational Change and Primary Groups in a Social Movement. In J. Freeman, ed., *Social Movements*, pp. 177–189.

Rothman, David J. 1971. *The Discovery of the Asylum: Social Order and Disorder in the New Republic*. Boston: Little, Brown.

Salisbury, Robert H. 1969. "An Exchange Theory of Interest Groups." *Midwest Journal of Political Science* 13:1–32.

————. 1975. "Interest Groups." In Fred Greenstein and Nelson Polsby, eds., *Handbook of Political Science*. (IV, pp. 171–228). Reading, Mass.: Addison-Wesley.

————, John P. Heinz, Edward O. Laumann, and Robert L. Nelson. 1987. "Who Works with Whom: Patterns of Interest Group Alliance and Opposition." *American Political Science Review*. 81:1217–1234.

Schlesinger, Arthur M., Jr. 1960. *The Politics of Upheaval*. Boston: Houghton, Mifflin.

Truman, David B. 1951. *The Governmental Process*. New York: Knopf.

Tyler, Alice Felt. 1944. *Freedom's Ferment: Phases of American Social History from the Colonial Period to the Outbreak of the Civil War*. Minneapolis: University of Minnesota Press.

Useem, Bert, and Mayer N. Zald. 1982. "From Pressure Group to Social Movement: Efforts to Promote Use of Nuclear Power." *Social Problems* 30:144–156.

Walker, Jack. 1983. "The Origins and Maintenance of Interest Groups in America." *American Political Science Review* 77:390–406.

Wilson, James O. 1973. *Political Organizations*. New York: Basic Books.

Wittner, Lawrence S. 1984. *Rebels Against War: The American Peace Movement*. Philadelphia: Temple University Press.

Zald, Mayer, and John D. McCarthy, eds. 1987. *Social Movements in an Organizational Society: Collected Essays*. New Brunswick, N.J.: Transaction Books.

Civil Rights and Liberties in the First Term of the Rehnquist Court: The Quest for Doctrines and Votes

Twiley W. Barker
Michael W. Combs

University of Illinois–Chicago
University of Nebraska–Lincoln

The most salient characteristic of Chief Justice Rehnquist's first term remains that of a court in search of both doctrines and votes. A review of major decisions in civil liberties and civil rights during this term suggests that neither the first year of the Rehnquist Court, nor some twenty years of the Burger Court, has brought about the conservative revolution in our law and jurisprudence that many conservatives had hoped for and some analysts had predicted. In view of the nature of judicial decision making and the overall political-social environment in which the court functions, it is quite plausible to suggest that the Rehnquist Court, not unlike the Burger Court, will perhaps remain a court in transition, one that will need to hone both doctrines and votes if it is to achieve the conservative revolution that some had expected.

After nearly two decades of decision making, the Burger Court simply did not develop into a bellwether of conservatism in the area of civil liberties and civil rights (Blasi, 1982; Lee, 1983). Rather, it remained a court in transition, even providing unexpected support for several important civil rights decisions, particularly in the area of sex discrimination. The Burger Court employed a case-by-case brokerage type approach in its decision making. This enabled the Court to satisfy at one time or another, competing claims of competing interests. Few bold precedents were established, and overarching legal principles or doctrines were absent. As a result, the state of the law in a number of areas became enmeshed with a large measure of ambiguity and uncertainty. Overall, however, the Burger Court seems to have left intact much of the general thrust of liberal policies developed during the era of the Warren Court (Wasby, 1976).

To be sure, the issues that came before the Burger Court were far more complex and subtle than those presented to the Warren Court. Although the Warren Court confronted questions of "should we?," the Burger Court dealt with questions of "how" and "to what extent should we?" In the area of rights of the accused, for example, the Burger Court had to come to grips with the implementation of broad policies announced by the Warren Court, for example, the application of the exclusionary rule of *Mapp* (367 U.S. 643, 1961) and of the *Miranda* warnings (see 384 U.S. 436, 1966). Although the Burger Court at times spoke with hostility and disdain and narrowed or modified the thrusts of certain distasteful precedents such as *Mapp* and *Miranda*, neither was overturned by the Court.

Thus, the years of the Burger Court did not constitute an extensive, principled swing to the Right; rather, the Court under Burger behaved like a court in transition. Clearly, it was to the right of the Warren Court, but the principled basis for a conservative revolution did not emerge with any degree of certainty. Nevertheless, the case-by-case brokerage approach of the Burger Court and its resulting uncertainty did leave the new Rehnquist Court ample room to chart the more conservative approach to the law that had long been predicted.

Not unlike the Burger Court, however, it is the personnel of the Rehnquist Court that remains the chief barrier that prevents it from taking definitive thrusts or trends in any direction. Consequently, presidents consider carefully the task of filling vacancies in the Supreme Court because changes in court personnel can alter decisional thrusts of the Court that in turn can affect overall policy and politics, including important presidential initiatives and programs. Although most justices tend to behave in an anticipated manner, just what decisional stance a justice will take remains somewhat of a gamble. Of the nine members of the Burger Court, Republican presidents appointed all but two—Justices Marshall and White. Except for Ford, Republican presidents since the 1960s sought nominees who would shift the Court toward the right, reflective of conservative policies that the presidents construed from their popular mandates.

President Nixon, for example, made four appointments to the Court, but over time, two of his appointees (Blackmun and Powell) began to move toward the Center, and on some issues, Blackmun was Left of Center. In fact, after a somewhat cautious start in which he sided with fellow Minnesotan Chief Justice Burger, Blackmun was in frequent agreement with the liberal bloc on the Court, Brennan and Marshall (e.g., *Roe v. Wade*, 410 U.S. 113, 1973; *Kaiser v. Weber*, 443 U.S. 193, 1979), and Justice Powell became a power broker in several major cases (e.g., *University of California v. Bakke*, 438 U.S. 265, 1978) successfully crafting opinions that received support both from liberals (Brennan and Marshall) as well as from Justices John Paul Stevens and Sandra Day O'Connor.

Perhaps contrary to what some conservatives had hoped, Justice Stevens (appointed by President Ford) did not become a consistent supporter of the conservative bloc. In fact, his voting record has been quite similar to that of

Justice Blackmun during the last two terms where he has often joined the liberal bloc of Justices Brennan and Marshall. Indeed, after Marshall and Brennan, Stevens provided the greatest level of support for civil liberties during the past two terms. Likewise, Justice O'Connor (appointed by Reagan) has not voted consistently with the conservatives (Burger and Rehnquist) on all major civil liberties issues. As the first woman justice, O'Connor's appointment portended the power of women as well as the salience of women's issues on the national agenda. This suggests that the same forces that gave rise to her appointment to the Court also form the basis for some of the major issues that now have prominent places on the Supreme Court's agenda.

The appointment of Rehnquist to the chief justiceship was hailed by conservatives as a crucial step in moving the Court in more appropriate directions. Much more than Burger, it was widely believed that Rehnquist possessed the intellectual stature, leadership ability, and overall respect needed to move the Court in a more definitive conservative direction. This conservative push was bolstered by President Reagan's simultaneous appointment of Judge Antonin Scalia to fill the seat left vacant by the elevation of Rehnquist as chief justice. Scalia, a former law professor at the University of Chicago, brought to the Court impressive credentials as a legal scholar and a proven record as a conservative jurist while serving on the Court of Appeals for the District of Columbia. This hope for a conservative breakthrough on the Court was certainly bolstered by the opportunity afforded President Reagan to fill the vacancy created by the unexpected resignation of Justice Powell in July 1987. Presumably the president's appointment would provide the fifth conservative vote needed to bring about the long-awaited conservative revolution. In the end, however, primarily due to the changed political complexion of the Senate, the president had to settle by appointing the more moderate conservative jurist, Anthony Kennedy of the Ninth Circuit, after being rebuffed in his attempt to fill the vacancy with archconservative jurist Robert Bork of the District of Columbia Circuit of the Court of Appeals and Douglas Ginsburg, a lesser known conservative judge of the same court. These efforts reflect the strength of the president's determination to steer the Court in a conservative direction (see, 87 *Columbia Law Review* 119, 1987).

In order to bring about a conservative revolution, we suggest that two conditions must exist: (1) There must be a principled basis for such a transformation, and (2) there must be the necessary votes to put the principles in place. By principled basis, we mean the development of the legal philosophical base and foundation sufficiently convincing and persuasive so as to offer legal rationale for changes in particular judicial policies and overall nature and direction of judicial decision making. In short, even though narrow and restrictive decisions and the hostile rhetoric of the Burger court have undoubtedly weakened important Warren court decisions, continuing moves toward uprooting and particularly for overturning existing precedents must be accompanied by well-reasoned legal basis for doing so. And, to put these legal foundations in place, requires more than legal rhetoric; they require the votes needed to make for a Court majority.

Clearly, to bring about such a revolution in our civil rights and civil liberties law is no small undertaking. Since Justice Stone's famous footnote no. 4 in

United States v. Carolene Products Co. (304 U.S. 144, 1938), the Supreme Court, with few exceptions, has pursued a course of protecting our civil rights and liberties providing important legal-political support for "discrete and insular" minorities and interests. The principled legal basis upon which this support has been forthcoming has been "equality" and "more equality." Clearly, President Reagan, with a good measure of popular support and through his many points of influence (e.g., the judicial nomination process), has sought to alter and change important decisional thrusts of the Warren Court in this regard. But a number of factors continue to frustrate and stifle the president's efforts. First, the incremental nature of policy change is strengthened by the importance and role of precedent in judicial decision making. Second, the continuing uncertainty that particular judicial nominees, once confirmed, will support policy positions envisioned by the president at the time of original appointment. Third, the shifts in the political environment such as changes in public opinion and personnel changes in political institutions occasioned by our system of regular and periodic elections (e.g., the change from a Republican to Democratically controlled Senate brought about in the 1986 elections).

Although these factors have thus far tended to frustrate and stifle President Reagan's efforts, the right combination or synchronization of these factors can, in time, bring about major changes in judicial policymaking. Even so, these factors pose continuous formidable barriers to revolutionary change in judicial policies, whether led by a Rehnquist, Burger, or by any chief justice no matter his or her legal or philosophical bent. More concretely, although the Burger Court may well be viewed as a court in "transition," a Rehnquist Court must still find both doctrine as well as votes to bring about revolutionary changes in judicial policy. Thus, even if he is so disposed, Chief Justice Rehnquist may not fare any better than Burger in leading the conservative revolution. At least this is strongly suggested by our review of the first term of the Rehnquist Court in four major issue areas of civil liberties: religion, rights of persons accused of crime, women's rights, and racial segregation and discrimination. To these discussions we now turn.

Religious Liberty—Toward a Reexamination of Establishment Clause Jurisprudence

Ever since the Supreme Court struck down prayer exercises in the public schools more than two decades ago (*Engel v. Vitale*, 370 U.S. 471, 1962; *School District of Abington Township v. Schempp*, 374 U.S. 203, 1963), there have been periodic attempts to overcome the Establishment Clause barrier to a range of public policies and get religion back into the public schools (see *Stone v. Graham*, 449 U.S. 39, 1980; *Stein v. Oshinsky*, 348 F.2d 999, 1965; *Wallace v. Jaffree*, 105 S.Ct. 2479, 1985). Supporters of a "narrow" construction of the Establishment Clause that would permit such activity were optimistic that the Rehnquist Court would be more sensitive to their interests. They had to be disappointed, however, with the initial Establishment Clause ruling of the Rehnquist Court in *Edwards v. Aguillard* (107 S.Ct. 2573, 1987). With only the new chief justice and Justice Scalia dissenting, the Court rejected the Louisiana legislature's effort to require the teaching of religious-based theory in public schools.

The act appears to embrace a rather simple subterfuge—requiring that instruction in "creation science" (the biblical story of the creation) be taught along with any other theories of evolution (La. Rev. Stat., Ann., sec. 17: 286.1–17: 286f.). The emphasis is on balanced examination of "competing" theories. In this sense, supporters of the legislation claimed that it has a secular purpose—the furtherance of academic freedom and inquiry. But seven members of the Court refused to accept such a characterization of the statute and found it unsupportable under existing Establishment Clause law.

With Chief Justice Rehnquist in dissent, the Court's senior member in the majority was Justice William J. Brennan who took this opinion for himself. For Brennan, the appropriate starting point was to assess the Louisiana statute under the three-pronged *Lemon* test that the Court had applied to church–state questions for the past sixteen years (*Lemon v. Kurtzman*, 403 U.S. 602, 1971). This succinct adherence to well-rooted precedent raised an insurmountable barrier for proponents of the "creation science" law. Finding constitutional support for the statute would have undoubtedly required abandoning *Lemon* or at least performing major surgery to carve out a distinction.

Brennan's opinion focused on the purpose prong of the test. Noting the usual judicial deference to the proclaimed purpose of a legislative enactment, Brennan could not accept the "sham" advanced by the legislature as the underlying purpose of the creation science law. A simple examination of the legislative history of the act made it clear that its sponsors and supporters had as their primary purpose a restructuring of the public school science curriculum to require instruction that advances the Biblical version of creation along with other theories of evolution. For Brennan, then, the legislature's purpose was clear—mandating the exposure of schoolchildren to the religious view of the divine creation of humankind. Furthermore, Brennan disdained the attempt to camouflage the purpose in the garb of academic freedom and inquiry. To him, the statute curtails academic freedom by conditioning the teaching of theories of evolution upon the "balanced instruction in creation science." Consequently, Brennan argued that such mandated arrangement does not protect academic freedom but restricts it because the failure to offer instruction in creation science triggers the elimination of all instruction of theories of evolution.

Justices White and Powell wrote short concurring opinions, underscoring the statute's religious purpose. White's opinion adds nothing of significance because Brennan focuses on the overriding religious purpose of the creation science statute. He does stress, however, the Court's usual deference to the lower court's conclusions on the meaning of state statutes because they (the lower courts) "are better schooled in and more able to interpret the laws of their respective states."

Justice Powell, joined by Justice Sandra O'Connor, appeared to be writing to blunt some of the criticism that is usually directed at the Court when its decision sets aside state educational policies. Powell emphasizes the broad latitude that state authorities possess in determining instructional subject matter and concludes that only when, as in this case, the state's purpose is *clearly to advance* religion should the Court raise the Establishment Clause barrier. In what appears to be a further effort to assuage the fears of some who are concerned with "oversecularization" of public school curricula, he made it clear that the clause is not abridged simply because some subject matter being taught in the classroom "happens to coincide with the tenets of some or all religions." Consequently, he argued that it is not constitutionally inappropriate to use religious materials in the public school classroom in secular courses such as history, ethics, and comparative religion.

Justice Antonin Scalia's dissent, which Chief Justice Rehnquist joined, focused on the proper role of the Court in reviewing such legislation. Although questioning the premise of the first prong of the *Lemon* test that the motivation of legislators can be the basis for striking down a statute, the new justice thought it appropriate for the Court to defer to the articulated secular purpose of the Louisiana legislature. He voiced astonishment at Brennan and the majority for disbelieving the secular purpose set forth by the legislators and for their characterization of that action as a mere "sham" to mask Christian fundamentalist beliefs. He could not believe that such a clearly articulated secular purpose should escape acceptance by the majority. His complaint here simply confirms the perspective that he brings to the Court—that of great deference to the articulated purpose of the legislature. What is more significant, however, is his questioning of the purpose prong of the *Lemon* test itself. In this connection, he indicated his agreement with the view expressed by Rehnquist in *Wallace v. Jaffree* (472 U.S. 38 at 112, 1985) that the purpose prong is "a constitutional theory [that] has no basis in the history of the amendment it seeks to interpret, is difficult to apply, and yields unprincipled results." Certainly, it is possible to conclude that his solution to what he characterizes as the "perilous enterprise" of ascertaining the subjective intent of legislators is to jettison the purpose prong from the *Lemon* test altogether. This position does not portend a change in Establishment Clause law in the immediate future, and the addition of Judge Anthony Kennedy will probably not bring additional support for it. It appears, then, that any Rehnquist–Scalia led effort to modify Establishment Clause law must await the outcome of the 1988 presidential electioin and subsequent changes on the Court.

No indication of a directional change was evident in a second religious liberty ruling during the initial term of the Rehnquist Court. In fact, the Court gave a resounding reaffirmation to a precedent set in the Warren Court era. The case brought to the Court involved a conflict between religious observance and employment demands, bringing into play guarantees underboth the Free Exercise and Establishment clauses. As in *Sherbert v. Verner* (374 U.S. 398, 1963), decided slightly more than two decades earlier, *Hobbie v. Unemployment Appeals Commission of Florida* (107 S.Ct. 1046, 1987) resulted from the denial of unemployment compensation benefits to a person who had been fired from her job for refusing to work on her Sabbath day. Just as it had held in the *Sherbert* case and had reaffirmed six years earlier in *Thomas v. Review Board of Indiana Employment Security* (101 S.Ct. 1425, 1981), the Court made it clear that the free exercise of religion is abridged when state policy forces a claimant to a choice of *abandoning* religious beliefs and practices in order to retain employment or of *adhering* to religious precepts and practices and forfeit compensatory benefits.

Chief Justice Rehnquist, who was the lone dissenter in *Thomas*, again found himself (even as Chief) without support in his dissent in *Hobbie*. He indicated a desire to begin to bring clarity to First Amendment jurisprudence, chiding his associates for "add[ing] mud to the already muddied waters of First Amendment jurisprudence." Acknowledging the considerable tension between the Free Exercise and Establishment clauses, he believed that the chief cause of such tension was the Court's "overly expansive interpretation" of them. Justice Potter Steward had voiced a similar concern in *Sherbert*, and Justice Arthur Goldberg had counseled in *School District v. Schempp* (374 U.S. 203, 1963) the need for the Court to strive for greater consistency in its rulings on issues that involve both the Establishment and Free Exercise clauses. Noting that the overarching purpose of the First Amendment is one of promoting and assuring the "fullest possible scope of religious liberty," he urged that both clauses must be read together to realize the objective.

So the Chief Justice, in dissent in *Hobbie*, sought to revive a concern raised more than two decades earlier. It could well be that he realized that, if his Court is to ever be successful in approving some of the religious programs of the Reagan agenda, a necessary first step is to get the Court to reexamine its First amendment jurisprudence that has evolved over the past twenty-five years. But having failed to convince even Justices O'Connor and Scalia, the accomplishment of such an objective, short of a massive turnover in the Court, appears to be farfetched indeed.

Criminal Law and Procedure

Justice Rehnquist's appointment as chief justice and the addition of Justice Antonin Scalia to the Court did not bring about immediate change in the Court's major decisions in the area of criminal law. With only an occasional departure of Justices Powell and O'Connor, the solid core of Chief Justice Rehnquist and Associate Justices White, Powell, O'Connor, and Scalia continued to support the interest of law enforcement officials and to show considerable deference to legislative policymakers. And Powell's replacement by Justice Anthony Kennedy is not expected to alter significantly the law in this area. There are strong indications that Justice Kennedy's view of criminal law is likely to resemble that of former Justice Powell; hence, the position of the prolaw enforcement bloc will essentially remain the same.

During the first term of the Renhquist era, the Court moved to dispose of several remaining challenges to the death penalty. In probably its most celebrated ruling of the term, the Court through a five-member majority (Rehnquist, White, Powell, O'Connor, and Scalia) rejected a statistically based racial discrimination challenge to capital punishment in *McClesky v. Kemp* (107 S.Ct. 1756, 1987). The case embraced the last-ditch effort of a black man (McClesky) to stop Georgia from executing him for the murder of a white police officer. Alleging that the Georgia capital sentencing process is infected with racial discrimination, the centerpiece of McClesky's argument was a major statistical study based on over 2,000 murder cases in Georgia during the 1970s. The Baldus study, as it was identified by the Court, attempted to show that there is a disparity in the imposition of the death penalty in Georgia that is correlated with the race of both the victim and the defendant. In simplistic terms, the data showed that black defendants who killed white victims have the greatest likelihood of being sentenced to death. Consequently, McClesky argued, the sentencing process was administered in a racially discriminatory manner and was thus violative of the Equal Protection Clause of the Fourteenth Amendment.

Justice Lewis Powell, who wrote for the Court, began dismantling McClesky's argument by requiring him to meet the more demanding intentional segregation standard to prove the equal protection violation alleged. The record below contained no such proof. Justice Powell then went to the heart of McClesky's statistical argument. He noted that even the author of the study did not contend that the statistics proved that race was the critical factor in the imposition of the death penalty on McClesky. He concluded that "statistics, at most, may show only a likelihood" that capital sentencing decisions may be influenced by racial prejudices. Furthermore, Powell would not accept the statistical racial disparity in the imposition of the death penalty in Georgia as proof that the state's capital punishment system is administered in an arbitrary and capricious manner. He rejected the notion that a constitutional violation results when a death sentence is not imposed on a defendant similarly situated to one who has been sentenced to death. Accepting such an argument would negate the traditional discretion of juries considered essential to the criminal justice process. Certainly, juries should have the opportunity to consider arguments for leniency as they weigh "particularized characteristics" of defendants. In the end, Powell contended if McClesky's race-disparity statistical argument is taken to "its logical conclusion," it could very well be "extended to claims based on unexplained discrepancies that correlate to membership in other minority groups and even to gender" (107 S.Ct. at 1779). So in the end, the argument that racial considerations carry considerable influence in Georgia's capital sentencing process (supported by a bevy of statistical evidence) was rejected as having no merit. To be sure, the decision all but turned the switch on a number of death row inmates with the admonition that these kinds of presentations should be taken to legislatures.

Justices Brennan and Marshall, who are opposed to the death penalty in all circumstances, were joined in dissent by Justices Blackmun and Stevens. The core of their disagreement with the majority was their differing views of the Baldus statistical evidence. In his opinion, Brennan thought the study at least made it unmistakably clear that arbitrariness in the imposition of the death penalty has not been eliminated in the enforcement of the "new" capital punishment statutes. They were convinced that the study was valid and showed that race was an influential factor in capital sentencing. Brennan would also assess the statistical conclusions in Georgia's and the nation's historical context. Consequently, he argued that "Georgia's legacy of a race-conscious criminal justice system underscores the significance of McClesky's claim" (107 S.Ct. at 1786). As Brennan put it succinctly, "McClesky's claim is not a fanciful product of mere statistical artifice" (107 S.Ct. at 1786). Noting that formal racial bias and intentional discrimination may no longer be prominent in Georgia, the "subtle, less consciously held racial attitudes" may well impact on the Georgia criminal justice system (107 S.Ct. at 1786). Hence, Brennan's conclusion that "McClesky's statistical evidence is consistent with the lessons of social experience" is plausible. In the end, though ample concerns were raised by the dissenters, the majority refused to come to grips with the reality of being black in the throes of the criminal justice system in a white society.

In a case decided one day before *McClesky*, the Court expanded the latitude of states to impose the death penalty on accomplices to a crime that resulted in murder though the accomplices did not inflict the lethal act. In *Tison v. Arizona* (107 S.Ct. 1676, 1987), the same five-person majority as in *McClesky* (Rehnquist, White, Powell, O'Connor, and Scalia) made it clear that the Court's decision five years earlier in *Enmund v. Florida* (458 U.S. 782, 1982) is not to be construed expansively as barring the imposition of the death penalty for all accomplices as had been done by some lower courts. On the contrary, Justice O'Connor's opinion for the majority focused on the "intent" requirement that the Court set forth in *Enmund*. In determining the culpability of an accomplice in a felony-murder case, the nature and character of his or her participation was crucial. In *Enmund*, she noted, the degree of participation was minimal. The accomplice was certainly a key participant in the robbery plan—remaining in the car outside the robbery scene to aid in the escape of the robbers. However, it could not be inferred from this degree of participation in the robbery that Enmund was a substantial participant in the murder that took place in the course of the robbery. Hence, the *Enmund* Court concluded that to impose the penalty of death on such an accomplice was indeed disproportionate to his minimal participation in the felony murder.

But Tison's participation in the Arizona felony murders was far more substantial. Although not firing the fatal shot, the accomplice's actual participation in the series of criminal activities that eventually led to the killing of four victims, where he was physically present at the site of the murders, was considered distinctively different from the "minimal" involvement of the *Enmund* accomplice, thereby justifying the imposition of the death penalty. The critical test, as Justice O'Connor put it, is whether the accomplice possessed the "culpable mental state of reckless indifference to human life" (107 S.Ct. at 1682). Thus, in such a context, the more demanding "intent" test is not necessary for the imposition of the death penalty.

In dissent, Justice Brennan, joined by Justice Marshall and, in part, by Justices Blackmun and Stevens, complained of the majority's approval of a felony-murder doctrine that permits the execution of a felon who neither committed murder not intended to do so. Certainly, for them, this represented a return to a legal era where capital punishment was routinely imposed for all kinds of felonies. Furthermore, such policy was contrary to the doctrine adhered to currently "in most American jurisdictions and in virtually all European and Commonwealth countries" (107 S.Ct. at 1689). Consequently, Brennan reiterated that he would follow the rule announced in *Enmund* and that to impose the death penalty on a nontriggerman accomplice, there must be proof of an "intent" to kill.

The acceptance of this expansive application of a felony-murder statute portends increased discretion of states in imposing the death penalty. In the context of this case, it would appear that prosecutors needed to find some way to exact retribution on the Tisons when the triggerman's father died from exposure in the Arizona desert before he could be captured and brought to justice. Hence, an expansive application of the state's felony-murder statute resulted in the sins of the triggerman's father being visited upon the son. Though one of the members of the Court majority that accepted the expansive application of the felony-murder statute (Jusice Lewis Powell) has since retired, it is expected that his replacement (Justice Kennedy) will weigh the competing interests in cases like *Tison* fairly similar to Justice Powell. (Note, for example, Kennedy's opinion in *Neushafer v. Whitley*, 816 F.2d. 1390, 1987, C.A.9.)

Both the *McClesky* and *Tison* rulings serve to enhance the discretion of the states. But in a third death-penalty ruling during the term (*Hitchcock v. Dugger*, 107 S.Ct. 1821, 1987), all the justices agreed that sentences in capital cases must be held to the "core" requirements for imposition of the death penalty enunciated in its prior rulings. Here the unanimous court reversed the imposition of a death sentence where instructions to the advisory jury precluded its consideration of nonstatutory mitigating evidence and where the sentencing judge himself also refused to do so. Justice Antonin Scalia's opinion for the Court cited rulings in *Skipper v. South Carolina* (106 S.Ct. 1669, 1986) and *Lockett v. Ohio* (98 S.Ct. 2954, 1978) that underscore the convicted person's right at the sentencing hearing to present "any and all relevant mitigating evidence that is available" (107 S.Ct. at 1824).

In another major ruling during the term, the Court was presented with the question of whether judges violate constitutional rights of convicted persons by cautioning the jury not to be "swayed by sentiment, sympathy, passion, public opinion, etc." on weighing evidence of mitigating circumstances. Again, in *California v. Brown* (107 S.Ct. 837, 1987), a bare majority of the Court (Rehnquist, White, Powell, O'Connor, and Scalia) did not think so. They held that a judge's instruction in the penalty phase of a murder trial admonishing the jury not to be swayed by "mere sentiment, conjecture, sympathy, passion, prejudice, public opinion or public feeling" (107 S.Ct. at 1840) did not amount to a constitutional violation of the Eighth or Fourteenth amendments. The California Supreme Court had reversed the death sentence, apparently accepting the defendant's contention that the instruction in question was constitutionally defective because it withdrew from jury consideration any "sympathy factor" that might flow from the evidence of mitigating circumstances that he had presented. But the Chief Justice rejected this interpretation of the instruction. He argued that a "reasonable juror" would also reject that view of the instructions. Instead, he would construe it "as a directive to ignore only the sort of sympathy that would be totally divorced from the evidence adduced during the penalty phase" (107 S.Ct. at 840). He concluded that the instructions do no more than caution jurors not to allow "*extraneous emotional factors*" to enter their consideration of the evidence.

Although clinging to his view that the death penalty can never be constitutionally imposed, Justice Brennan would have rejected the instructions to the

Brown jury because not only could they be construed as precluding jury consideration of the defendant's character and other mitigating factors, but they could confuse the jury. Hence, it was possible that the jury was not "fully aware of the scope of its sentencing duties" (107 S.Ct. at 849). Justice Blackmun went a step further and complained because he felt that the instruction accepted by the majority so circumscribed the jury's discretion that it could negate a response to a mercy plea. He noted, for example, "when a jury member is moved to be merciful to the defendant, an instruction telling the juror that he or she cannot be 'swayed' by sympathy, may well arrest or restrain this humane response, with truly fatal consequences for the defendant" (107 S.Ct. 850).

Death penalty proponents are undoubtedly pleased with the Rehnquist Court's initial response to the issues presented. With the appointment of Justice Kennedy to the Court, any remaining arguments designed to limit the imposition of the death penalty are likely to have the same fate as those put forth in *McClesky, Tison,* and *Brown.* Hence, we could see the Rehnquist Court in its second term, ignoring considerable world opinion, approving state statutes that permit the imposition of the death penalty on minors.

In another aspect of the death-sentencing process at issue in *Booth v. Maryland* (107 S.Ct. 2529, 1987), a sharply divided Court rejected the introduction of victim-impact statements for consideration of the sentencer as a violation of the Eighth Amendment. Justices Brennan, Marshall, Blackmun, Powell, and Stevens agreed that the statements that describe the emotional impact of the crimes on surviving family members are irrelevant to a capital sentencing decision. What is more, they held that to allow consideration of such information could well lead the sentencer to the kind of capricious and arbitrary imposition of the death penalty that was condemned in *Furman v. Georgia* (408 U.S. 238, 1972).

The dissenters—Chief Justice Rehnquist and Justices White, O'Connor, and Scalia—speaking through Justice White, argued deference to the Maryland legislature's determination that such information was useful to the sentencer in making its determination of the degree of punishment that is appropriate for the crime. From their perspective, impact statements are appropriate evidence for the prosecution in order to counteract the mitigation evidence that a defendant is entitled to present.

The resignation of Justice Powell and the appointment of Justice Kennedy indicate that victim-impact statements such as those in *Booth* could once again come before the Court in the immediate future. Kennedy, not unlike Powell, could well prove the pivotal vote in crucial cases. Thus, the five-to-four majority rejecting the use of victim-impact statements in *Booth* could well become a five-to-four majority upholding the use of such statements in the future.

Many observers expect a further erosion of *Miranda v. Arizona* (384 U.S. 436, 1966) and *Mapp v. Ohio* (367 U.S. 643, 1961) in a Rehnquist Court. But such changes might be very slow in coming about. To be sure, during the seventeen-year Burger Court era, a number of exceptions to both *Miranda* and *Mapp* were approved. Even so, however, the core objectives of both cases were never threatened. In fact, Chief Justice Burger, who often led majorities in carving out such exceptions, indicated a willingness to "live" with *Miranda* in his concurring opinion in *Rhode Island v. Innis* (446 U.S. 291) in 1980. There he expressed the view that the meaning of *Miranda* had become "reasonably clear" and that because law enforcement officers had adjusted their practices to conform with the requirements without significant hindrance to their work, he saw no need to overrule it.

Likewise, Justice Sandra Day O'Connor, agreeing for the most part with the contraction of *Miranda* by carving out certain exceptions, expressed her concern in a disent in *New York v. Quarles* (104 S.Ct. 2626) in 1984 that the particular exception at issue (public safety) would "unnecessarily blur the edges" and lessen the rule's clarity. Consequently, Justice O'Connor is not likely to join an effort to overturn *Miranda*.

It is not surprising, then, that in its first two *Miranda* actions, the Rehnquist Court gave no indication that it was going to forge new directions that would lead to rejection of *Miranda*. Its decision in *Colorado v. Spring* (107 S.Ct. 851, 1987), considered only a technical question in the waiver of the right of the accused to remain silent. A seven-to-two majority did not find that the *Miranda* rule was abridged merely because the police did not inform the suspect of all the crimes about which he might be questioned. Justice Powell, who spoke for the Court, indicated that such an omission did not hamper the suspect in arriving at the decision to make a "knowing" and "intelligent" waiver of his or her right to remain silent.

Justice Thurgood Marshall's dissent (supported by Justice Brennan), however, emphasized that it is essential for the suspect to know the "scope and seriousness of matters under investigation" (107 S.Ct. at 860) in determining whether to waive the privilege to remain silent. He reminded the majority of the state's heavy burden in proving that a suspect's waiver was "knowing," "intelligent," and "voluntary." He further cautioned his brethren that as a matter of jurisprudential principle, the Court is to "indulge every reasonable presumption against waiver of fundamental rights" (107 S.Ct. at 861).

In a second ruling during the term, seven justices refused to construe *Miranda* as negating the fruits of oral interrogation where a suspect indicated only his or her refusal to give a written statement (without consulting counsel) but a willingness to talk about the incidents that led to this arrest. Speaking for the majority in *Connecticut v. Barrett* (107 S.Ct. 828, 1987), Chief Justice Rehnquist argued that the oral statements should not be suppressed because *Miranda* only guaranteed a suspect the choice between "speech and silence" and this suspect had decided to talk. Furthermore, the chief justice made it clear that a limited invocation of the counsel guarantee with respect to any written statement should not be construed as an invocation of it broad enough to proscribe the oral-discussion dimension of the interrogation in which the suspect had indicated a willingness to participate. Thus, the message to suspects undergoing interrogation is clear—*Miranda* will not be construed expansively by the Rehnquist Court and a *Barrett*-type waiver could have adverse consequences for suspects, but neither does it seem that there will be an attempt to overturn *Miranda*.

The exclusionary rule controversy was not raised in the Rehnquist Court's first term, but if the Court's position on warrantless searches is indicative of its approach to Fourth Amendment construction, the rule could well be in for further contraction. Early in the term, the chief justice led the seven-to-two majority in the ruling in *Colorado v. Bertine* (107 S.Ct. 738, 1987) that re-affirmed warrantless "caretaking" searches of automobiles. His opinion em-phasized the automobile inventory search as a "well-defined exception to the warrant requirement" (107 S.Ct. at 741). In such cases, he argued, considerable deference is accorded police officers because the search is not undertaken in a criminal investigation. Rather, its purpose is to safeguard the vehicle's con-tents.

But Jusices Marshall and Brennan disagreed. Marshall complained of the unfettered discretion allowed the police under the Boulder, Colorado, care-taker-inventory procedures. Certainly, he felt that "preservation" of the ar-restee's automobile and its contents by impoundment and search is not an interest sufficient to outweigh the Fourth Amendment privacy rights raised. In the end, Marshall felt obliged to remind the majority of the assertion put forth by the plurality in *Coolidge v. New Hampshire* (403 U.S. 443 at 461, 1971) that "[t]he word 'automobile' is not a talsiman in whose presence the Fourth Amendment fades away and disappears" (107 S.Ct. at 749).

In a second case, the Court approved a New York statutory procedure that authorized warrantless inspection of commercial establishments engaged in dismantling automobiles (*New York v. Burger*, 107 S.Ct. 2636, 1987). And, in a third case (*O'Connor v. Ortega*, 107 S.Ct. 1492, 1987), a narrow five to four majority (Rehnquist, White, Powell, O'Connor, and Scalia), though recogniz-ing the applicability of Fourth Amendment search and seizure guarantees to government employees, supported some contraction of them by approving warrantless searches by supervisors in work-related contexts (desk drawers, files, etc.) subject only to a standard of "reasonableness."

Justice O'Connor's plurality opinion underscored the "operational realities of the workplace" (107 S.Ct. at 1498) to support supervisor investigation of work-related misconduct that she felt outweighted employee privacy claims. In approving this additional governmental restraint on employee privacy rights, O'Connor recognized the Fourth Amendment implications of man-datory drug testing for employees but indicated in a footnote that the Court was not addressing the issue in the context of *Ortega*. To be sure, however, that issue will find its way to the Court at an early date, and it may well be that the *Ortega* ruling portends a majority position on it.

In probably the strongest evidence to support a progovernment stance on criminal procedure issues, Chief Justice Rehnquist led a six-to-three majority in upholding the controversial preventive detention provision of the 1984 federal Bail Reform Act in *United States v. Salerno* (107 S.Ct. 2095, 1987). Under the act's terms, courts may detain (by denying bail) persons accused of serious felonies when the government demonstrates with "clear and con-vincing evidence" that release of the accused would pose a threat to safety of the community and/or individuals. The chief justice, writing for the majority, took judicial notice of the problem of serious crimes being committed by persons free on bail and gave deference to the Congress' effort to remedy the problem through changes in the bail process.

In rejecting arguments that preventive detention abridges guarantees pro-tected by both the Due Process Clause of the Fifth Amendment and the Eighth

Amendment's bail provision, the chief justice emphasized two points: (1) Preventive detention invoked under careful procedural safeguards is a permissive regulatory procedure and not a form of pretrial punishment violative of substantive due process and (2) the government's interest in providing for preventive detention (public safety) can "outweigh an individual's liberty interest" (107 S.Ct. at 2102) in particular circumstances without abridging Eighth Amendment guarantees.

The major difficulty posed by the majority's position in upholding the statute is, as Justice Thurgood Marshall complained in dissent, the subversion of the well-entrenched jurisprudential principle of the *presumption of innocence*. Furthermore, Marshall thought that the preventive detention tool was a dimension of unbridled governmental power against which the Constitution provides a shield. In approving this congressional action to strengthen law enforcement efforts in combating crime, he was concerned that the majority may well have contributed to the "demolition" of that constitutional shield.

Prison inmates got the message rather quickly that the Rehnquist Court would not depart from the well-established path of considerable deference to the determinations of prison administrators in the management of those facilities. Emphasizing this principle, Chief Justice William Rehnquist, writing the Court's opinion in *O'Lone v. Estate of Shabaz* (107 S.Ct. 2400, 1987), noted "the respect and deference that the Constitution allows for the judgment of prison officials" (107 S.Ct. at 2405). Consequently, in a five to four decision reversing a court of appeals ruling, the Court did not consider a general prison work detail regulation that had the effect of preventing Muslims from attending a weekly afternoon religious ceremony an abridgment of the free exercise of religion guarantee. "Legitimate penological objectives" of the regulation were considered sufficient to justify dismissal of the First Amendment claim.

In what was probably a more pointed message to prisoners and their advocates, the Rehnquist Court, speaking through Justice O'Connor, rejected an expansive construction of the leading prisoners' rights case decided by the Burger Court more than a decade earlier (*Procunier v. Martinez*, 416 U.S. 396, 1974) and concluded that ordinary scrutiny was the appropriate standard of review for judicial resolution of prisoners' constitutional claims. The examination of the proper standard of review was presented in the context of *Turner v. Safely* (107 S.Ct. 2254, 1987) where regulations limiting interinmate correspondence and inmate marriages were at issue. Stressing judicial restraint on the subject of prison administration as well as the need to protect constitutional rights of prisoners, Justice O'Connor noted that, in this case, the penological objectives sought through enforcement of the interinmate correspondence regulation were of sufficient governmental importance to justify the burden on First Amendment rights. In the end, the Court engaged in a simple balancing of the conflicting interests at stake. But in the process, the justices did back away from the ban on inmate marriages because they concluded that such a regulation was not reasonably related to a legitimate governmental interest—prison security.

Underscoring the consequence of the standard of review advanced in *Safely* for determining the constitutionality of prison regulations and practices, the future portends a heightened judicial deference to policymakers in this area.

Under the less-demanding *Safely* standard of review, inmates will be hard pressed to establish the "exaggerated response" to the legitimate governmental concerns now necessary for a successful challenge to regulations alleged to impinge on their constitutionally protected rights. And not unlike Justice Powell, Justice Kennedy's position on these matters could well determine the outcome of litigation in this and other areas.

Affirmative Action: Blending Diversed Philosophy

The affirmative action controversy contains sharp disagreements over fundamental principles. The opponents contend that such measures do irreparable harm to many basic and cherished values (i.e., individualism, merit, and equality). They also contend that affirmative action undermines both the value system and the Constitution. On the other hand, the proponents of affirmative action argue that such measures are necessary to remove the many disadvantages and barriers that have fenced out blacks and other minorities in their pursuit of educational and employment opportunities and that group-based remedies are within constitutional limits. Without such plans, they argue, equality for blacks and other minorities will continue to be elusive and beyond their grasp [see Combs and Gruhl, 1986].

In addition to generating disagreements over fundamental principles and values, the affirmative action controversy has produced a plethora of legal issues, focusing on the meaning of Title VII of the Civil Rights Act of 1964 and the Equal Protection Clause of the Fourteen Amendment. These two grounds provide the underpinnings for affirmative action remedies. Some of the major issues are: Are Title VII and the Equal Protection clause coterminous? Do they permit appropriate race- and sex-conscious remedies? Is the purpose of Title VII to facilitate the entry of blacks into the work force? Or is the purpose of Title VII to prohibit the taking of race (and sex) into consideration in hiring and promotion decisions? Are district courts permitted to award relief that may benefit individuals who were not actual victims of the employer's discrimination under Title VII? Under what circumstances may "innocent" whites be required to bear the burden of affirmative action relief? What legal standards should courts employ to determine whether or not an affirmative action plan encroaches upon statutorial and constitutional rights of "innocent" whites under Title VII and the Equal Protection clause? Finally, does Title VII preclude the voluntary imposition of race- and sex-conscious remedies absent discrimination on the part of an employer? If so, what conditions must be satisfied?

The ambiguous language of Title VII coupled with the powerful influence of the Reagan presidency in the affirmative action debate has added to the vituperative nature of the legal controversy. Several of the aforementioned legal questions seemed to have been implicitly or explicitly resolved in earlier cases, for example, *Fullilove* and *Weber*. But they are being contested. The increased saliency of these questions, however, points to how issues are redefined and given new life under favorable political climates. This section of the essay focuses upon how the Burger and Rehnquist courts, particularly the

Rehnquist Court, have come to terms with many of these and other pivotal legal issues.

First, let us look at the Burger Court that endeavored to blend diverse points of view in its decisions. In so doing, under Burger, the Court has left a legacy of ambiguity and weak precedents in the critical area of affirmative action. Except for its last term, the Burger Court framed its holdings so as to satisfy both the opponents and proponents of race- and sex-conscious measures in education and employment. In *Regents of the University of California v. Bakke* (438 U.S. 265, 1978) for example, the Burger Court was asked to determine the permissibility of affirmative action as a principle and the use of quotas to implement such remedy. The Court's ruling contained elements that would appeal to both foes and supporters of affirmative action. First, the Court concluded that raw quotas, under normal circumstances, were not within the ambit or bounds of the Constitution. The Court also held the Bakke was to be admitted into the University of California–Davis Medical School because the affirmative action plan did not allow the individual consideration of each student and that white applicants were prevented from competing for positions protected by quotas. At the same time, the Court did not outlaw numerical measures that would insure the effectiveness of affirmative action. Additionally, it held that race could be a consideration in bestowing a benefit without embracing entirely the principle of group-based remedies for past and societal discrimination. The principal motivation for the decision seemed to be the benefits of pluralistic representation in the student body. To be sure, however, the *Bakke* decision was pregnant with confusion and ambiguity. It was not clear at all as to how the Burger Court would decide subsequent decisions. There was no real definitive opinion or majority.

The Burger Court's next two rulings on affirmative action also sought to blend the two sets of diametrically opposed principles. In *Kaiser v. Weber* (443 U.S. 193, 1979), the Court held that Title VII permitted the establishment of voluntary affirmative action programs by private sector companies provided (1) that the measures are temporary and (2) that they do not unnecessarily trammel the rights of innocent persons. Then one year later in *Fullilove v. Klutznick* (448 U.S. 448, 1980), the Court sustained the constitutionality of a congressional statute that set aside 10 percent of a $4 billion public works program for "minority business enterprises" to benefit companies in which blacks, Hispanic-Americans, Oriental-Americans, American Indians, Eskimos, or Aleuts controlled at least 50 percent. In a manner of speaking, the Burger court accepted the overriding purpose of the enactment of Title VII of the Civil Rights Act of 1964—the amelioration of the economic plight of blacks. Speaking for a divided court, Chief Justice Burger noted that the administrative apparatus of the set-aside program provided for each company to be considered on an individual basis. Each company had to substantiate that it was an actual victim of discrimination on the construction. As in the *Weber* case, the Court found persuasive the temporary nature of the set-aside program and the legislative concern that the program would not unnecessarily trammel the rights of innocent whites.

Even after the Reagan administration indicated that it would pursue the abrogation of affirmative action, the Burger Court continued its "alchemist" approach in deciding such cases. According to the Reagan administration, if affirmative action measures were to remain operative, each beneficiary should be required to establish that he or she was an actual victim. To be sure, acceptance of the actual victim standard would limit the coverage of race-conscious remedies, would severaly undermine the usage of past and societal discrimination as a rationale for affirmative action, and would completely bar the usage of group-based remedies. For the Reagan administration, this was the appropriate standard to be followed in testing the constitutionality of both voluntary and court-imposed affirmative action programs.

Although the Court has not fully embraced the Reagan administration's position, the Burger Court did initially seem to provide precedential support for the actual victimization standard. In *Firefighters v. Stotts* (467 U.S. 561, 1984), the Court's language indicates tacit approval of the standard. "Each individual must prove," the Court stated, "that the discriminatory practice had an impact on him" (Ibid. at 574). Thus, the *Stotts* decision intensified litigation on the use of remedies that benefit individuals who were not the actual victims of discriminatory practices.

During Burger's last term, the Supreme Court spoke with both a clearer and more emphatic voice on the question of actual victimization and more generally on the parameters of affirmative action. In *Firefighters v. Cleveland* (106 S.Ct. 3063, 1986), the Court held that Title VII did not preclude the "voluntary adoption [in a consent decree] of race-conscious relief that may benefit non-victims" of discriminatory practices (Ibid. at 3077). And in *Sheet Metal Workers v. EEOC* (106 S.Ct. 3014, 1986), the Court, focusing on the powers of district courts to fashion affirmative action remedies, held that the language of section 706(g) of Title VII is not so restrictive that it could be construed to limit remediation to actual victims. As Justice Brennan noted, Title VII does not say that a court may order relief only for the actual victims of past discriminations. Consequently, the justices rejected the allegation that *Stotts* prohibits a lower court from ordering any kind of race-conscious affirmative (action) relief that might benefit nonvictims. With unusual definitiveness, the Court held that "the purpose of affirmative action is not to make identified victims whole but rather to dismantle prior patterns of employment discrimination and to prevent discrimination in the future" (106 S.Ct. at 3049). "Such relief," the Court continued, "is provided to the class as a whole rather than to individual members; no individual is entitled to relief and beneficiaries need not show themselves victims of discrimination" (106 S.Ct., at 3049). Here the Court supported the principle that the group provides the moral and legal motivations or basis for affirmative action rather than the exoneration of the *specific* rights of *specific* individuals. At the same time, the Court accepted the district court's use of numerical goals and its directive that the necessary funds be provided to finance portions of the affirmative action program.

The last two affirmative action cases of the Burger court produced its most bold and definitive statements on the issues of actual victimization and the use of quantitative measures as a remedial tool. And these meanings were certainly not what the Reagan administration wanted to hear. The liberal bloc had, for the time being, been successful in blunting the effort to move away from group preference to individual remediation.

But all was not lost for the Reagan administration. A Court under the vigorous leadership of Justice William Rehnquist could be expected to take a decisional stance that would aid the administration's commitment to dismantle affirmative action programs. Of course, the appointment of additional conservative justices as vacancies of the Courts occurred would make the effort much easier.

That Rehnquist would need additional support among the justices if there was to be a successful rewriting of affirmative action law was underscored in the first two affirmative action decisions handed down by the Rehnquist Court. They afforded the Court the opportunity to address affirmative action programs in both race and gender contexts. In *United States v. Paradise* (107 S.Ct. 1053, 1987), racial considerations in employment were at issue. There a class of black plaintiffs alleged in prolonged litigation that the Alabama Department of Public Safety had followed racial discriminatory employment policies in the state police force. Their relentless effort eventually produced relief in the district court that required "one-black-for-one-white promotion" as an interim measure. Eventually, the Rehnquist Court was asked to determine if the "one-black-for-one-white" promotion requirement abridged the Equal Protection clause of the Fourteenth Amendment. And, in a five to four decision with Rehnquist, Scalia, White, and O'Connor dissenting, the Court concluded that this court-imposed race-conscious remedy did not. Because the relief ordered was "'narrowly tailored' to serve a 'compelling governmental interest,'" the majority refused to apply the strict scrutiny test. As Justice Brennan put it: "The persuasive, systematic and obstinate discriminatory conduct of the Department [of Public Safety] created a profound need and a firm justification for the race-conscious relief ordered by the district court." Accordingly, the protracted failure of the department made the remedial decrees of the district court necessary.

To determine whether race-conscious remedies are appropriate, Brennan pointed to several factors. These include:

> the necessity for the relief and efficacy of alternative remedies, the flexibility and duration of the relief, including the availability of waiver provisions; the relationships of the numerical goals to the relevant labor market; and the impact of the relief on the rights of third parties (107 S.Ct. 1067).

Using these factors, the majority concluded that the "one-for-one" promotion relief of the district court passed constitutional muster. Justice Brennan emphasized that

> the remedy imposed . . . is an effective, temporary and flexible measure. It applies only if qualified blacks are available, only if the Department has an objective need to make promotions, and only if the Department fails to implement a promotion procedure that does not have an adverse impact on blacks. The one-for-one requirement is the product of the considered judgment of the district court which, with its knowledge of the parties and their resources, properly determined that strong measures were required in light of the Department's long and shameful record of delay and resistance (106 S.Ct. 1074).

In a dissenting opinion, joined by Chief Justice Rehnquist and Justice Scalia, Justice O'Connor complained that the "one-for-one" promotion relief imposed by the district court would have failed the strict scrutiny standard. She thought that the court "imposed a racial quota without first considering the effectiveness of alternatives that would have a lesser effect on the rights of non-minority troopers" (107 S.Ct. 1082).

In *Johnson v. Transportation Agency* (107 S.Ct. 1442, 1987), the Rehnquist Court was asked whether in making the promotion of a female employee who was rated slightly lower than a male applicant, there was an unlawful consideration of her sex in violation of Title VII of the 1964 Civil Rights Act. The agency's affirmative action plan "provides that in making promotions to positions within a traditionally segregated job classification in which women have been significantly underrepresented, the agency is authorized to consider as one factor the sex of a qualified applicant" (107 S.Ct. at 1446). Unlike in *Bakke*, the plan did not provide for the setting aside of a specific number of positions for minorities or women but rather allowed for the "consideration of ethnicity or sex as a factor when evaluating qualified candidates for jobs in which members of such groups were poorly represented."

In a six to three decision, the Court sustained this sex-based promotion plan. First, Justice Brennan's opinion for the Court inquired whether or not the "consideration of the sex of applicants for skilled craft jobs was justified by the existence of a manifest imbalance that reflected underrepresentation of women in traditionally segregated job categories" (107 S.Ct. at 1452). Next, Brennan considered how a manifest imbalance "that would justify taking race or sex into account" is to be determined. Initially, he asserted that the employer should compare

> the percentage of minorities or women in the employer's work force with the percentage in the area labor market or general population [and] . . . where the job requires special training, [and] the comparison should be with those in the labor force who possess the relevant qualifications (107 S.Ct. at 1453).

Brennan, however, did not speak to what constitutes an "area labor force." But he did emphasize that in order to protect the interests of employees not benefiting from the plan and to make sure "that sex or race will be taken into account in a manner consistent with Title VII's purpose of eliminating the effects of employment discrimination," (107 S.Ct. at 1452) *manifest imbalance* must be related to a "traditionally segregated job category" (107 S.Ct. at 1452). The Court made certain that, indeed, "blind hiring" was not to be the case. In fact, the Court took judicial notice that the agency's affirmative action plan "expressly directed that numerous factors be taken into account in making hiring decisions, including specifically the qualifications of female applicants for particular jobs" (107 S.Ct. at 455).

Next the Court considered whether the agency's plan "unnecessarily trammeled the rights of male employees . . . or created an absolute bar to [their] advancement" (107 S.Ct. at 1451). On that issue, Brennan noted that, whereas the plan authorized the consideration of the applicant's race and/or sex, it still provided for the individual consideration of each applicant. "No persons," said Brennan, "are automatically excluded from consideration; all are able to have their qualifications weighed against those of other applicants" (107 S.Ct. at 1455). He also noted that the promoted applicant was one of several qualified applicants and that the nonpromoted applicant retained his employment. To be sure, he continued, the purpose of the "agency's plan was intended to attain a balanced work force, not to maintain one" (107 S.Ct. at 1455). In the final analysis, the plan was a manifestation of both judicial and congressional recognition of " 'the value of voluntary efforts to further the objective of the law'" (107 S.Ct. 1457).

On this issue, Justice O'Connor joined the liberal bloc. In a concurring opinion, she took issue with both Brennan's opinion for the Court and Justice Scalia's dissenting opinion. For her, Brennan's majority opinion "follows an expansive and ill-defined approach to voluntary affirmative action" by public employers (107 S.Ct. at 1461). And she contends that Scalia's dissenting opinion "rejects the Court's precedents and addresses the question of how Title VII should be interpreted as if the Court were writing with a clean slate" (107 S.Ct. 1461). Next, O'Connor argues that before a voluntary affirmative action plan is put in place under Title VII by a public employer, there should be evidence to support a prima facie case of discrimination. To do so, she would require the employer "to point to a statistical disparity sufficient to support a prima facie claim under Title VII by the employee beneficiaries of the affirmative action plan of a pattern or practice claim of discrimination" (107 S.Ct. at 1461). According to O'Connor, the prima facie requirement is the same under Title VII as it is under the Equal Protection clause. O'Connor takes judicial notice that the absence of women or minorities in a work force cannot be subsumed under "societal discrimination" (107 S.Ct. 1462) alone and that remedial action is appropriate in such circumstances. O'Connor concluded that "Joyce's sex was simply used as a 'plus' factor" (107 S.Ct. at 1465).

In a dissenting opinion joined by Chief Justice Rehnquist and, in part, by Justice White, Scalia argues that the majority has completed the process of converting Title VII from a prohibition against sex or race discrimination into a guarantee that such discrimination shall take place. Among other things, he argues that the agency's plan was not to remedy prior sex discrimination by the agency; rather this assertion turns upon the premise that there had been no proof of such discrimination. Scalia rejects the position that affirmative action plans are permissible to eliminate societal discrimination. He would have overruled *Weber*.

Johnson v. Transportation Agency is perhaps the Court's most important statement on affirmative action since *Bakke* and *Weber*. In a real sense, *Johnson* fills in much of the puzzle that was left unsolved by *Bakke* and *Weber*. First, we now know with some certitude that public employers may establish affirmative action programs when there has not been a judicial, administrative, or legislative determination of discrimination or where there is no proof of prior discrimination, on the part of the employer. Thus, employers need not make a showing of previous discrimination. This means that employers may adopt voluntary affirmative action plans to address the underrepresentation of blacks, ethnic minorities, and women "caused not only by their own and society's proven employment discrimination, but also by the effects of unconscious discrimination and internalized sexual and racial stereotypes that discourage women and minorities from seeking certain kinds of employment" (Harv. L. Rev., 1987: 301).

Women might benefit from this decision enormously. The unconscious sexual (or racial) discrimination that encourages or silently instills in women (blacks and other minorities) the attitude that certain jobs or careers are not for them might form the basis for a voluntary affirmative action. Public employers have received the green light to establish voluntary plans without the imminent fear of suits alleging reverse discrimination.

Additionally, *Johnson* might reduce the litigation burden of litigious interest groups. The number of suits filed may be reduced. *Johnson* has also diluted tremendously the force of the Reagan administration's attack on affirmative action as well as made it more difficult for the Rehnquist Court to void affirmative action completely.

The Rights of Women: O'Connor's Dilemma

The women's rights movement has been viewed with concern by conservatives who connect the weakening of the family to the increased integration of women in the workplace and the overall expansion of the women's rights movement. Consequently, these conservatives would downplay and would be supportive of Court decisions contracting such rights. (This poses an interesting dilemma for the Rehnquist Court as it did for the Burger Court.) Justice Sandra Day O'Connor, generally considered to be a key vote for the conservative bloc on the Court, would appear to have almost a "vested" interest in the advancement of the civil rights of women. Her appointment to the Court points to the vitality and political influence of supporters of women's issues among conservatives and moderates alike. And, although she had consistently sided with conservatives on the rights of the accused and capital punishment, for example, she has resisted the administration and conservative's overtures on abortion, hostile environments in the workplace, and affirmative action for women. Whereas the Burger Court worked with almost a clean slate on women's rights issues (*Goesaert v. Cleary*, 335 U.S. 464, 1948, the women's bartender case was the major exception); it left several important rulings on women's rights issues to confront the Rehnquist Court. Among these are *Craig v. Boren* (429 U.S. 190, 1976), where the Court provided the standard by which classifications on the basis of gender would be evaluated; *Reed v. Reed* (404 U.S. 71, 1972), where the Court employed strict scrutiny to strike down a state statute that gave a preference to males in the administration of estates; and *Meritor Downing's Bank v. Vinson* (106 U.S. 2399, 1986), where the Court determined the scope of sexual harassment under Title VII of the 1964 Civil Rights Act.

The Rehnquist Court's initial consideration of women's rights issues came in *California Federal Savings and Loan Association v. Guerra* (107 S.Ct. 683, 1987). At issue was whether a California statute that required employers to provide female employees an unpaid pregnancy disability leave of up to four months was preempted by Title VII of the Civil Rights Act of 1964. It should be noted that the statute did not require the employer to provide paid leave to pregnant employees; rather the only benefit provided pregnant workers "is a qualified right to reinstatement."

Although Justice O'Connor did not write the opinion for the six-to-three majority, she did join the liberal bloc in sustaining the constitutionality of the statute. Chief Justice Rehnquist and Justices White and Powell dissented. Speaking for the Court, Justice Marshall argued that "this would be erroneous to infer congressional intent to pre-empt state laws from the substantive provisions of Title VII." Having examined the relevant sections (708 and 1104), Marshall took judicial notice of the "importance Congress attached to state antidiscrimination laws in achieving Title VII's goal of equal employment opportunity" (107 S.Ct. at 690). Next Marshall focused on whether the California statute permits an employer to violate Title VII, as amended by the Pregnancy Discrimination Act. That Congress amended Title VII with the Pregnancy Discrimination Act, according to Marshall, underscores the fact that "Congress intended . . . to provide relief for working women and to end discrimination against pregnant workers" (107 S.Ct. at 692). "'By taking pregnancy into account,' California's pregnancy disability leave statute allows women, as well as men," Marshall insisted "to have families without losing their jobs" (107 S.Ct. at 694). The pregnancy disability leave statute is part of the state's overall effort to bring about equal employment opportunities for women, particularly those who wished to have families. With this in mind, Marshall concluded that the California pregnancy disability leave statute "does not compel California employers to treat pregnant workers better than other disabled workers, it merely establishes benefits that employers must, at a minimum, provide to pregnant workers (107 S.Ct. at 695).

Chief Justice Rehnquist and Justice Powell joined Justice White's dissenting opinion. In it, White argued that the California pregnancy disability statute constituted a violation of Title VII, as amended by the Pregnancy Discrimination Act. He cited as the statute's principal defects: (1) the requirement that employers institute a pregnancy disability leave policy even if there was no leave policy for any other disability and (2) the statutory preference provided for pregnant workers. In addition. White raised the preemption issue, asserting that the California statute was preempted by Title VII.

In *Board of Directors of Rotary International v. Rotary Clubs* (107 S. Ct. 1940, 1987), the Rehnquist court dealt a blow to all-male clubs and in the process removed another barrier in the path of the women's equality movement. At issue was the constitutionality of a California statute that required Rotary Clubs in the state to admit women as members. The contention was that the statute abridged freedom of association protected by the First Amendment. Speaking for an unanimous Court (Justices O'Connor and Blackmun did not participate) sustaining the constitutionality of the statute, Justice Powell observed that, whereas previous court cases have recognized constitional protection for freedom of association, "the relationship among Rotary Club members is not the kind of intimate or private relation that warrants constitutional protection." (107 S. CT. at 1946). Consequently, Powell concluded that application of the statute to California Rotary Clubs did not abridge any associational rights protected by the First Amendment.

Ethnic Discrimination: Who Is Protected?

In *Saint Francis College v. Al-Khozraji* (107 S. Ct. 2022, 1987), the Court was asked to determine whether or not the Civil Rights Act of 1870 (Sections 1981 and 1983) protected persons who are discriminated against on the basis of ethnicity or ancestry. The Reconstruction statute provides that

> all persons within the jurisdiction of the United States shall have the same right in every state and territory to make and enforce contracts, to sue, be parties, give evidence, and to the full and equal benefit of all laws and proceedings for the security of persons and property as is enjoyed by white citizens . . . (107 S. Ct. at 2026).

The respondent, a citizen of the United States born in Iraq, was an associate professor at Saint Francis College. He applied for tenure, but his tenure request was denied, and subsequently, the respondent filed a complaint in federal court, alleging a violation of Title VII and discrimination on account of national origin, religion, and/or race.

The petitioners contended that the respondent is a member of the Caucasian race and thus cannot turn to section 1981 for relief. Speaking for a unanimous court, Justice White rejected the contention. White argued that at the time the statute was adopted, the understanding of race was different. Many ethnic groups today are considered members of the Caucasian race, those groups were not in the 1870s. He noted that in the middle of the nineteenth century, dictionaries and encyclopedias described race in terms of ethnic groups rather than the broader concept of race. The legislative history of the statute also has this understanding of race and ethnicity. White went on to conclude that "Congress intended to protect from discrimination identifiable classes of persons who are subjected to intentional discrimination solely because of their ancestry or ethnic characteristics" (ibid. at 2028). See *Shaare Jefila Congregation v. Cobb* (107 S. Ct. 2019, 1987).

Discrimination and Infectious Disease: Portents for AIDS

In *School Board of Nassau County v. Arline* (107 S. Ct. 1123, 1987), the Court considered the question of infectious disease and the discrimination that is directed against such patients. Specifically, the issue was whether or not

> a person afflicted with tuberculosis, a contagious disease, may be considered a "handicapped individual" within the meaning of section 504 of the [Rehabilitation Act of 1973, as amended], and if so, whether such an individual is "otherwise qualified" to teach elementary school (ibid. at 1125).

The respondent suffered several relapses of tuberculosis. In 1957, she was hospitalized for tuberculosis, and positive cultures were taken in 1977, March 1978, and November 1978. Her tuberculosis was in remission from 1957 to 1977. Following the 1978–1979 school year, after a hearing, the school board discharged her. The district court held in favor of the school board, but the court of appeals reversed.

Sustaining the court of appeals, a seven-to-two majority of the Supreme Court found that the respondent was a handicapped individual within the meaning of the Rehabilitation Act of 1973, as amended. Writing for the Court, Justice Brennan turned to the legislative history of the statute and the regulations promulgated by the Department of Health and Human Services for guidance. The regulations provide that a person must have a physical impairment that affects major life activities to satisfy the statutory definition. Brennan noted that the respondent was physically impaired with "a physiological disorder . . . affecting [her] . . . respiratory system" (107 S. Ct. at 1127) and that this condition, in turn, affected her major life activities. The school board's contention that Arline was not dismissed because of "her diminished physical capabilities, but because of the threat that her relapses of tuberculosis posed to the health of others" (107 S. Ct. at 1127) was rejected by Brennan as a superficial distinction to justify discriminatory treatment. He went on to argue that Congress did not intend such a distinction because "Congress was as concerned about the effect of an impairment on others as it was about its effects on the individual" (107 S. Ct. at 1128). "Allowing discrimination based on the contagious effects of a physical impairment," Brennan retorted, "would be inconsistent with the basic purpose of section 504 which is to ensure that handicapped individuals are not denied jobs or other benefits because of the prejudiced attitudes or the ignorance of others" in the workplace (107 S. Ct. at 1128, 1129).

Brennan also focused on whether or not the respondent is "otherwise qualified" for the job of elementary schoolteacher. Regarding "otherwise qualified" inquiry, he provided some fairly specific instructions to the district court. Agreeing with the American Medical Association, Brennan stated that inquiry should include "'[findings of] facts, based on reasonable medical judgments given the state of medical knowledge, about (a) the nature of the risk (how the disease is transmitted), (b) the duration of the risk (how long is the carrier infectious), (c) the severity of the risk (what is the potential harm to third parties) and (d) the probabilities the disease will be transmitted and will cause varying degrees of harm'" (107 S. Ct. at 1131). Brennan posited that the next step in the "otherwise qualified" inquiry is to determine how and to what extent, in light of the medical findings, the employer could reasonably accommodate the employee.

In a dissenting opinion joined by Justice Scalia, Chief Justice Rehnquist argued that the majority's decision rested on "its own sense of fairness and implied support from the Act" (107 S. Ct. 1132). According to Rehnquist, the earlier decisions of the Court clearly indicated that conditions can be placed upon the receipt of federal funds only when Congress speaks "with a clear voice." This principle also applied to the Rehabilitation Act. Taking issue with Brennan, Rehnquist insisted that a separation can be made between the reactions of others and the effect of the condition upon the claimant. Finally, he argued that the majority did not make its case that "Congress contemplated that a person with a condition posing a threat to the health of others may be considered handicapped under the Act" (107 S. Ct. at 1134).

Arline has important ramifications for the treatment of victims of other communicable diseases in the workplace and the abrogation or the preservation of their civil rights. The Reagan administration has endeavored to have mandatory testing for AIDS for all government employees. The Centers for Disease Control, also, encourage widespread testing for AIDS. And to compound the political and legal climate, in 1986, the Justice Department issued a memorandum taking the position that federal antidiscrimination laws may not apply to persons who test positive for the AIDS antibodies. This is particularly the case if employers can show that fellow employees have a "real or perceived" fear of contagion. Thus, the fate of AIDS victims in the workplace could, in part, be determined by how *Arline* is interpreted and applied in future cases.

Conclusion

The first term of the Rehnquist court did not produce any major surprises. The selected areas of civil liberty/civil rights reviewed here indicate that the issues were decided about as expected. With respect to religion, for example, a comfortable majority of the justices remained committed to the underlying principles of Establishment Clause law. Only Chief Justice Rehnquist and Justice Antonin Scalia gave any indication that modification is in order. Only the Chief Justice called for a full-scale reexamination of FIrst Amendment jurisprudence. Nor did the Court forge new directions in the criminal law/procedure area. As expected. Justice Antonin Scalia's voting behavior on such issues was very similar to that which would have been expected of retired Chief Justice Burger. Hence, on most criminal law issues, a simple majority of justices was in place to support the law-enforcement interests. And on some occasions, the majority of five (the Chief Justice and Justices White, Powell, O'Connor, and Scalia) became a majority of seven as Justices Blackmun and Stevens joined them.

Only rarely out of forty-six such cases decided with full opinions did members of the conservative bloc move to the "liberal" position and support the claims of the individual against the prosecutorial forces of the government. On one such occasion, for example, Justices O'Connor and Powell joined the "liberal" bloc (Brennan, Marshall, Blackmun, and Stevens) to strike down a Nevada mandatory death penalty statute for prison inmates (*Summer v. Shuman*, 107 S. Ct. 2716, 1987) because of its departure from the "individualized capital sentencing" doctrine. In other instances in the criminal law area, Justice O'Connor departed from the company of the chief justice and Justice Scalia on six occasions, whereas Justice Scalia broke ranks four times. Chief Justice Rehnquist, however, departed from his other two conservative colleagues (O'Connor and Scalia) only once on the criminal law decisions.

In the area of affirmative action, Chief Justice Rehnquist and his general view of the law were in the minority. Once again, it is quite evident that if there is to be a successful rewriting of affirmative action law in the "Rehnquist image," the chief justice needs additional votes on the Court. And moreover, the continuation of the building of precedents in support of affirmative action will certainly further delay the Rehnquist revolution even if the necessary votes are present on the Court.

This reality emerges in both the race and gender contexts. In *United States v. Paradise*, a five to four majority approved an interim remedial plan that required "one-black-for-one-white" promotion. This sharply focused remedy underscores the majority's willingness to give unusually strong support for affirmative action, establishing the precedent that demanding measures may be taken in instances in which public employers have a clear history of "pervasive, systematic and discriminatory conduct." Similarly, a six-to-three majority, over Chief Justice Rehnquist's objection, sustained a sex-based promotion plan. As we suggested, O'Connor joined the liberal bloc of the Court there. This proclivity is also seen in her vote in *California Savings and Loan Association v. Guerra*, sustaining a California statute that provides female employees an unpaid pregnancy disability leave of up to four months.

Finally, the Court's handling of the question of infectious diseases in the workplace holds enormous significance for the AIDS pandemic. In holding that workers as victims of infectious diseases are covered by the Rehabilitation Act of 1973, antidiscrimination policies are made applicable to them. One protection is against the dismissal of victims who are "otherwise qualified" from their jobs. Here is yet another example where the posture of the Court majority ran counter to that of the Reagan administration.

Overall, it is clear that Chief Justice Rehnquist and his views of the law are in a minority on the Court on most issues with the possible exception of rights of the accused. This suggests that unless the Republican party nominee wins the 1988 presidential election and then as president succeeds in appointing conservative justices whose views of the law are similar to those of the Chief Justice, the Rehnquist court is not likely to develop into that bellwether of conservatism that some had predicted or hoped for. Neither does the replacement of Justice Powell with Justice Anthony Kennedy portend major shifts in any particular direction.

This overall calculus, however, could obviously be changed by changes in the behavior of individual justices.[1] For example, it remains to be seen as to whether, how, and to what extent Rehnquist's role as chief justice might influence his behavior and participation in the work of the court. Additionally, of course, there is the view that Justice O'Connor may well pursue a more independent role that could move her more to the center. Even with these circumstances, however, and given the nature of judicial decision making and the overall political-social environment in which the court functions, it is quite plausible to suggest that the Rehnquist Court, not unlike the Burger Court, will perhaps remain a court in transition, one that will need to develop both doctrines and votes if it is to achieve the conservative revolution that some had expected.

Note

1. In *Patterson v. McLean Credit Union* (48 CCHS. Ct. Bull. 1682, 1988) the Supreme Court voted five-to-four to reargue *Runyon v. McCrary* (427 U.S. 160, 1976). The Court held in *Runyon v. McCrary* that the Civil RIghts Act of 1866 reached some

private acts of discrimination against blacks.

In a per curiam decision supported by White, O'Connor, Scalia, and Kennedy, Rehnquist expressed the majority's desire to have Runyon reargued, even though neither the plaintiff nor the defendants had raised the issue. This might suggest that the Rehnquist Court has found both doctrines and votes.

Selected References

Baum, Lawremce. 1987. "Explaining the Burger Court's Support for Civil Liberties." *PS,* (Winter):21-28.

Blasi, Vincent. ed. 1983. *The Burger Court: The Counter-Revolution That Wasn't.* New Haven, CT: Yale University Press.

Combs, Michael W., and John Gruhl. 1986. *Affirmative Action: Theory, Analysis and Prospects.* Jefferson, NC: McFarland & Co., Inc.

Fiss, Owen, and Krauthammer, Charles. 1982. "The Rehnquist Court." *The New Republic* (March 10): 14-21.

Lee, Francis Graham. 1983. *Neither Liberal nor Conservative: The Burger Court on Civil Rights and Liberties.* Malaboo, FL: Krieger Publishing Co.

Lawrence. 1982. "The Id, the Ego, and Equal Protection: Reckoning with Unconscious Motivation." 39 *Stan. L. Rev.* 317.

Noble, Kenneth B. 1987. "Not Many Judges Practice What the President Preaches." *New York Times* (November 29) Sec. 4:2-3.

O'Brien, David M. 1987. "The Supreme Court: From Warren to Burger to Rehnquist." *PS* (Winter): 12-20.

Rabkin, Jeremy. 1986. "The New Chief, the New Justice and the New Court." 19 *The American Spectator* 20 (October).

Wasby, Stephen. 1976. *Continuity and Change: From the Warren to the Burger Court.* Pacific Palisades, CA: Goodyear Publishing Co.

Witt, Elder. 1986. "The Rehnquist Court: Right Turn?" *Editorial Research Reports* (September 26): 711-728.

Getting Out the Black Vote: The Party Canvass and the Black Response

Michael A. Krassa

University of Illinois

This essay examines patterns in and the impact of campaign canvassing on blacks in the United States. Using data from the American national election studies, the paper demonstrates the failure of either of the parties to fully include blacks in their campaign strategies, at least in this one way. It also demonstrates that substantial increases in both black voter participation and the Democrats' share of the two-party vote are possible through increased canvassing.

The patterns in contacting have remained relatively stable over a considerable time frame. This is true in spite of a number of public pronouncements (especially by Democratic candidates and party officials) that blacks are an important part of both the party in general and electoral strategies in particular. A small number of elite interviews underscore this position, though other interviews with activists show at least one reason for a difference in the rate at which blacks and whites are contacted by the parties.

Wolfinger and Rosenstone (1980:91) bluntly state the common wisdom that "blacks are less likely to vote than whites." This finding is nearly universal in the literature on turnout and is often attributed to the long period of black disenfranchisement in the United States, to legal, social, and practical barriers that were erected after the passage of the Fifteenth Amendment, and to the failure of the political parties to appeal to black voters in any meaningful way (see, among others, Key, 1949, 1964; Berelson, et al., 1954; Lazerfeld et al., 1968; Miller, 1971).

This paper examines black turnout and party (and candidate) efforts to mobilize blacks using the neighborhood canvass. First, using adjustments for various social-demographic characteristics, black voting rates are examined; then the effect of the partisan canvass on the chance that a black votes is considered; and finally the actual patterns of party canvassing are investigated, and its implications considered.[1]

Black Turnout

In the aggregate, blacks do vote at rates lower than either the rate for whites or the national average. This is well known and is shown in Table 1, which draws on data from the national election studies. Though these statistics rely on self-reports of voting and are therefore subject to overreporting, the social desirability bias inflates the rates for the entire sample only slightly less than it does within the black subsample (Traugott and Katosh, 1979). However, even with the slightly higher overreporting by black respondents the depressed black turnout rates (vis-à-vis the national) are evident in the aggregate, though there is evidence that the differences have declined somewhat since the passage of the Voting Rights Act.

Further, there has been some suggestion that much of the differential in aggregate statistics is due to aggregate differences in important social demographic factors such as income distributions, educational attainment, and social class. Zipp (1983), for example, has found that since the late 1970s

Table 1. Black and National Sample Turnout Rates, 1952–1984

Year		Blacks	National	Difference
1952	% Voting:	41.5	76.1	34.6
	N:	171	1899	
1956		42.4	75.8	33.4
		170	1854	
1960		44.1	76.7	32.6
		312	1821	
1964		70.8	78.5	7.7
		422	1834	
1968		61.0	67.6	6.6
		315	2011	
1972		53.6	61.4	7.8
		267	2705	
1976		54.2	60.0	5.8
		271	2107	
1980		53.8	58.8	5.0
		198	2891	
1984		56.4	65.9	9.5
		250	2257	

Note: Percentages are percentages of NES respondents who reported voting. N's are numbers on which the percentages are computed. All differences are significant at alpha 0.05 or less.

working-class blacks have been voting at higher rates than have whites of comparable income, education, and occupational status. Though he finds that non-working-class blacks seem to continue to have lower turnout rates than whites, a portion of the difference is eliminated when the educational, economic, and class differences are accounted for.

Education and income are often seen as important elements in determining whether or not a person will go to the polls on election day. Indeed, Wolfinger and Rosenstone (1980) find that education is the single best indicator of the chance that a person will vote, arguing that the time spent in school increases one's interest in political life, improves one's skills for understanding both politics and the voting process, and increases the chance that one will have economic resources that enhance both the ability and willingness to bear the various costs of voting. Others have argued that income is more important, but the significant theme of all of these inquiries is that social status and its related measures are all strongly correlated with the chance that a person votes (see for example, Bennett and Klecka, 1970; Milbrath and Goel, 1977; Verba and Nie, 1972). Because, in the aggregate, the social status of blacks is lower than that of most Americans, lower voting rates among blacks are not unanticipated.

Thus, to understand the degree to which black turnout is depressed, one must account for the social difference between blacks and whites in the United States. Using data from the 1984 American National Election Study, Figure 1 shows probability estimates of the chance of voting from separate logistic regressions for blacks and whites with education (in years) and income (in dollars) used to predict voting behavior. (Logistic regression is used because, in this individual-level data, the dependent variable, whether or not a person voted, is a dichotomy, and hence does not meet the assumptions necessary for OLS regression.)

In 1984 black turnout was higher than it had been in a decade, due in part to the efforts of Jesse Jackson and the Rainbow Coalition. Even in that year, however, black turnout was lower than that of whites at almost all education and income levels except among those with less than six years of schooling. Among this low-education population segment, these estimates, like those by Zipp (1983), show that blacks have slightly higher turnout rates than whites (whether or not one adjusts for income differences).

In Figure 1, there are two lines tracing black turnout, one that adjusts for the income differential between blacks and one that does not. It is important to note, however, that the two lines follow each other quite closely; because income is apparently not as strong an influence on black voting rates (note the coefficient), the adjustment has only a minor impact on the turnout estimates. From this figure, we see that with education and income differences controlled, black and white turnout rates are rarely as far apart as the overall statistics indicate they might be, which suggests that much of the total difference may be due to differences in distributions on important social characteristics.

Though turnout for all groups in the United States has declined to the point where it is relatively low, blacks especially provide an enormous potential voting block to any politician who should effectively gain the lion's share of their support and votes. However, because of a traditionally low overall turn-

Figure 1. Probability of Voting in the 1984 Election for Blacks and Whites.

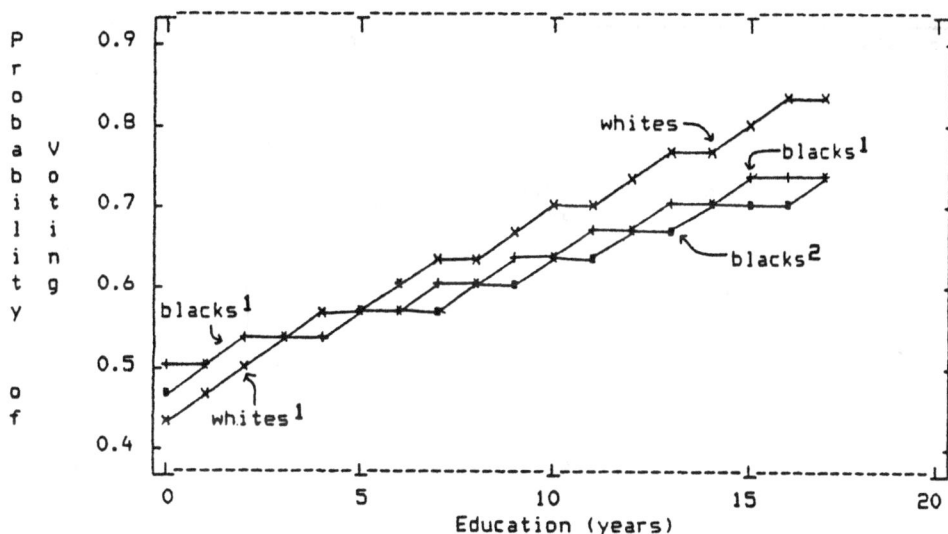

[1] Black turnout adjusted for black–white income differential (+).
[2] Black turnout using black mean family income ($15,243) (■).

$$p(\text{vote}) = 1/1 + e^{-f}$$

whites: $f = -1.15 + 0.10*\text{education} + 0.000027*\text{income}$
(SE)   (0.23) (0.02)   (0.000004)

blacks: $f = -0.50 + 0.06*\text{education} + 0.00001*\text{income}$
(SE)   (0.32) (0.03)   (0.00001)

Note: Data are from self-reported behaviors from the 1984 American Election Study. Expected average probabilities from separate estimates with family income held constant at means ($24,127). N of whites: 1708; N of blacks: 241.

out, black support has been seen as less beneficial (electorally) than the support of other social and ethnic groups, with many candidates making little more than token appeals to black Americans. Mobilizing black nonvoters, therefore, must be a prime concern of a candidate who depends on blacks for election.

The Effect of the Canvass

One of the important means by which the parties attempt to mobilize voters is through their canvassing efforts: going door-to-door asking supporters to vote for their candidate. This has proven to be an effective means of getting people to vote, increasing turnout by several percentage points, but having little impact on the direction of the vote (for discussions on the importance of

Table 2. Impact of the Canvass on Black and White Turnout, 1984

Education		Percent Voting		Difference	
(years)	Race	Contacted	Not Contacted	Pct.	Adj.
Less than	Black	78.6	44.6	34.0	61.4
H.S. Grad	N:	14	67		
	White	67.9	43.1	24.8	43.6
	N:	53	376		
H.S. Grad	Black	66.7	50.6	16.1*	32.6*
	N:	12	79		
	White	92.2	55.8	36.4	82.3
	N:	142	572		
Some Coll.	Black	85.7	62.5	23.2	61.9
or more	N:	14	64		
	White	92.0	73.2	18.8	70.1
	N:	225	639		

Note: Data are self-reports from the 1984 American National Election Study, for persons answering all four questions only (race; whether or not they voted; whether or not they were contacted; and education). All contacted-not contacted differences are significant at alpha 0.025 or less unless indicated with an asterisk (*).

the canvass, see Cutright, 1963; Kramer, 1970; or the classic work by Katz and Eldersveld, 1961). The canvass provides a direct contact with someone from one of the candidate or party campaign organizations, and such interpersonal contacts prove to be one of the most effective means of getting people to the polls.

People differ in their responsiveness to the canvassing efforts of campaign organizations, and many of the same factors that determine whether or not a person will vote also have an impact on the degree to which the person will react to being contacted. Income, education, and general social status, for example, all mediate the impact of the canvass, with the greatest impacts (measured as changes in percent voting) being among those with lower social standing.

Using data from the 1984 American National Election Study (NES), Table 2 reports on the impact of the canvass for blacks and whites and is presented by educational attainment to control for possible differences in either the patterns of contacting (by class) or predisposition to vote. In any one of the election surveys, the number of blacks is often insufficient for subgroup analyses; however, as Table 2 shows, the effect of being contacted is so sizable that the difference in turnout between contacted and noncontacted individuals is significant at the 0.025 level for two of the three black educational groupings, and is significant for all white groups.

The difference percentage column of Table 2 shows that the simple neighborhood canvass has a sizable impact on the chance that a person will vote, increasing that chance by as much as 36.4 percentage points. Note, too, that the effect is present even for those initially most favorably predisposed toward voting: The turnout of contacted blacks with at least some college is 23.2 percentage points higher than noncontacted blacks, and the same difference for whites is 18.8 points. Similarly, using the NES preelection question about whether or not a person expects to vote as a different type of indicator of predisposition toward voting, we find a similar trend: The turnout rate among those who did not expect to vote was 8.8 percent ($n = 320$), but the turnout rate for persons not expecting to vote but who were later contacted by a campaign worker was 21 percent ($n = 30$). Further, turnout for persons who did expect to vote was 72 percent ($n = 1,410$), and 93.2 percent for persons who both expected to vote and were contacted ($n = 427$). Thus, the canvass provides a powerful tool for mobilization and, properly targeted, may have a considerable impact on both turnout and candidate vote totals. Regardless of one's predisposition toward voting, the canvass is a potent means of converting nonvoters to voters.

Examinations of other election studies show that the effect of the canvass has been consistently large over time and that the largest absolute effects are on those least initially least predisposed toward voting, at least as measured by the various social demographic correlates of turnout (such as education). One reason for this, of course, may be a ceiling effect where the turnout of those with a high propensity to vote has little room for improvement. One way to reformulate the question of the impact of contacting without the ceiling effect problem is to measure the additional mobilization as a proportion of the maximum possible change in turnout. Generously assuming that turnout is limited to 100% voting, we can rewrite the 34-point canvass-produced increase in the turnout of blacks with less than a high school diploma as (78.6-44.6)/(100-44.6), or 61.4 percent of the maximum possible increase in voting. The adjusted column of Table 2 presents the impact of contacting calculated in this fashion and shows that the canvass has a very large impact on individuals at all levels of education.

Although they are most likely of less interest from a campaign management vantage point because large adjusted differences do not necessarily translate directly into large numbers of new voters, these figures do show that persons at all social status levels are highly susceptible to the influence of the canvass. Being contacted presents the recipient with a powerful and highly effective stimulus that motivates him or her to vote. The interpersonal interaction has an impact that mobilizes large percentages of those who would otherwise have stayed at home on election day. Further, when calculated in this fashion, the tendency for a declining impact to coincide with increasing initial propensities to turn out is no longer present (either in the 1984 study or other years).

It is well known that being contacted has little impact on the direction of the vote (see, for example, Cutright, 1963; Kramer, 1970). The effect is largely one of mobilization and not persuasion, and this holds for the 1984 NES data as well. Table 3 presents data for individuals who both voted and were contacted and shows that an individual's partisanship has a much greater impact on the

Table 3. Impact of the Canvass on the Direction of the Vote, 1984

Respondent Party ID	Which Party Contact R	Who did R. Vote for? Mondale	Reagan
Democrat	Dem.	77.1	19.3
	N:	64	16
	Both	80.0	9.1
	N:	44	5
	Rep.	70.7	24.3
	N:	29	10
Independent	Dem.	16.7	66.7
	N:	1	4
	Both	33.3	50.0
	N:	2	3
	Rep.	0.0	60.0
	N:	0	3
Republican	Dem.	3.9	94.2
	N:	2	49
	Both	2.0	95.9
	N:	1	47
	Rep.	3.1	94.0
	N:	2	61

Note: Data are for persons who were contacted and voted. Cell entries are row percentages; percentages may not add to 100 due to rounding, third-party votes, and respondents who could not recall how they voted.

direction of the vote than does the party canvass. Indeed, in Table 3 no difference within a party ID–candidate column is significant at alpha less than 0.10, indicating that Democrats voted for Mondale or Reagan at the same or nearly the same rates regardless of which party contacted them. Democrats contacted by Republican canvassers were not statistically less likely to vote for Mondale than were Democrats contacted by Democrats, or even noncontacted Democrats. Similarly, Republicans contacted by Democrats were no less likely to vote for Reagan than those contacted by Republican canvassers. In short, the canvass appears to have no statistically discernible influence (at alpha 0.10 or less) on the vote.

Although a similar table with an additional strata for race would yield cell sizes too small to make inferences, there is no reason to believe that blacks and whites react any differently to the canvass. No ethnic group should show greater sensitivity (in vote direction) to being contacted than any other. Indeed, because many ethnic groups are more strongly partisan than the general population, ethnics generally may be *even less* likely to change their vote intention as a result of being contacted than the general population statistics show.

Thus the canvass can have a large impact on who votes but not a very large impact on who votes for whom. The data presented in Table 2 are indicative of the magnitude of the mobilization effect of canvassing, showing a large effect across the three education categories used. Similar analyses in other years and using other controls show very similar results: The nearly universal finding is that the canvass has only the effect of mobilization. The most obvious strategy for any party or candidate campaign organization, therefore, would be to target canvassing efforts toward party or candidate loyalists and "leaners." Rather than a potentially counterproductive "blanket effort" that may mobilize more opponents than supporters, a candidate should seek to contact those who can be expected to at least lean toward voting for him or her, thereby mobilizing more allies than opponents, allowing the enormous resources that are sometimes devoted to canvassing to yield a net gain in support for the candidate.

Party Canvassing and the Black Vote

The 1984 NES shows that 84.2 percent of black respondents who voted reported casting their ballot for Mondale, the Democrat, with less than 10 percent voting for Reagan. By contrast, the Democrats captured only 35 percent of the white vote. Other Democratic candidates in other years have received similar shares of the black vote, although almost continuously losing more and more white voters every year since 1968.

Figure 2 shows that over time, though the canvass has become more comprehensive and inclusive, a much higher proportion of whites than blacks is contacted in any given year. In most years since the mid-1960s nearly 30 percent of the respondents to the NES surveys report being contacted by someone representing one of the political parties. However, as the line for blacks in Figure 2 shows, the proportion of blacks reporting a contact is roughly half as large.

Of course, one possible explanation for the lower rate of contacting of blacks would be if only the Democratic party and its candidates made a concerted effort to canvass blacks. Because as noted earlier, blacks vote overwhelmingly Democratic (and because the canvass has mainly a mobilization effect), there appears to be little reason for Republican organizers to target poor black neighborhoods (though there is some suggestion among Republican leaders that middle-class blacks should be targeted). If this sort of

Figure 2. Campaign Contacting by Race, 1952–1984

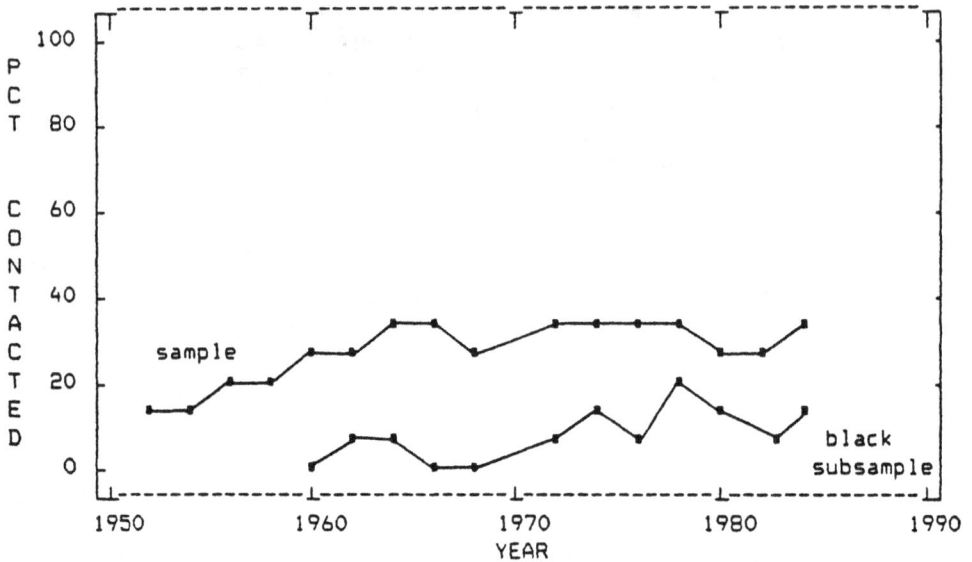

Note: Data are percentages of NES respondents who report that they were contacted by someone representing one of the parties or candidates during the campaign.

rationale guides canvassing, then Republicans will not invest heavily in the canvassing of black neighborhoods, whereas Democratic organizers will split their resources among blacks and non-blacks. If the Democratic organizers will split their manpower relatively evenly, then we can expect blacks to be contacted about half as frequently as whites, much as Figure 2 shows.

Such a rationale appears not to guide the canvassing efforts of the two parties, however. Although Democratic candidates do contact blacks more often than do Republican candidates, candidates of both parties are substantially less likely to contact blacks than whites. Figure 3 traces the percentages of black and white NES respondents reporting that they were contacted by either the Democratic or the Republican candidate organizations. It shows the comparatively low rate at which the parties and candidates attempt to contact blacks directly and that there is a clear but inconsistent trend among Democratic candidates toward increased coverage of black neighborhoods. However, due to the small black subsamples in the NES, the differences in percentages of blacks contacted by the Democrats are generally not significant except at extremes.

Moreover, blacks at almost all status levels are less likely to have been contacted than are similar whites, although as their statuses increase, both blacks and whites are more likely to have found a party worker at their door at some point during the campaign. One simple indication of this comes from a basic logistic regression using race and education (as a status indicator) to predict the probability of being contacted, as in Equation 1. In this regression,

Figure 3. Contacting by Race and Party, 1960-1984

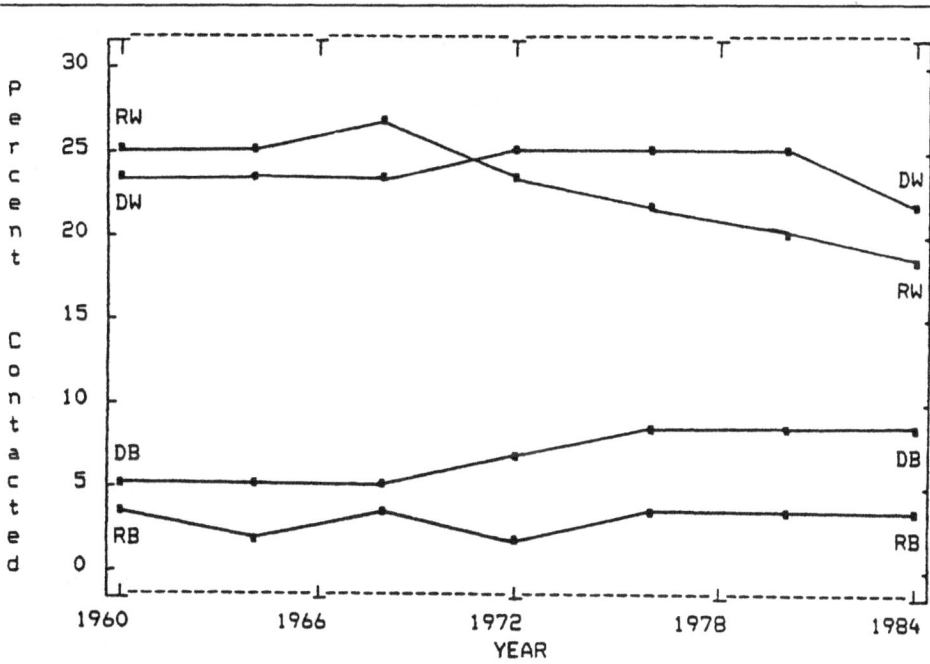

Note: Data are percentages of NES respondents who report that they were contacted by someone representing one of the parties or candidates during the campaign. RW are the percentages of whites contacted by Republicans; RB are blacks contacted by Republicans; DW and DB are white and black percentages contacted by Democrats.

the test for the differences in the chance of being contacted as one achieves different status levels is in the size, direction, and significance of the coefficients on the education variables, and the coefficient on the dummy variable for blacks tests whether or not race continues to explain contacting rates even with status controlled.

$$p(\text{contacted}) = 1/1 + e^{-f}$$

(Eq. 1)

$$f = -2.80 + 0.12^{*}\text{education} - 0.11^{*}\text{education}^{*}\text{black} - 1.13^{*}\text{black}$$
$$(0.28)\ (0.02)\qquad (0.5)\qquad\qquad (0.54)$$

Equation 1 shows that even with education included as a measure of status, race remains a significant predictor of the probability that an individual was contacted. Though its significance is somewhat smaller when one accounts for the effect of social status, the fact that the coefficient on the dummy variable for blacks remains both sizable and significant indicates that the difference in canvassing rates is not entirely due to status differences but rather may stem directly from the racial factor itself.

This finding is particularly surprising given images put forth by the candidates and party organizations. In 1984, the leadership of the Democratic party argued that blacks were an important part of the party and that the black vote was an important, even critical, element of their electoral strategy. Issues and positions meant to improve their appeal among blacks were incorporated into the stated party platform, and advertising and public statements by both the Mondale and the party leadership throughout the campaign were intended to court the black vote. Mondale sought partnership with Jesse Jackson for these same reasons.

The desires of the Democratic leadership were incorporated to some degree into policy proposals and even into campaign strategy. They voiced a desire to improve the standing of the party and the candidate among blacks and to "bring blacks into the mainstream" of the party. Further, these desires are echoed by the state Democratic Party chairmen of five major midwestern states and one northeastern state interviewed during the summer of 1987, who proposed that they were very concerned with both appealing to and mobilizing blacks—and four volunteered that they were less successful on both counts than they had wished, indicating that organizational and resource constraints as well as Mondale's selection of a white running mate all limited their ability to make a strong and effective appeal to and mobilization effort among the black communities.[2] One also attributed part of the failure to the execution of campaign tactics as well as to his perception that many blacks seemed to feel that many of the policies and tactics were "a 'half-hearted' attempt to capture some of the activism and enthusiasm that began with the Jackson campaign." Although quick to assert that the policies were indeed not simply strategic, he indicated that their late incorporation into the Mondale effort left many blacks feeling that the Democrats simply wanted their votes without making black concerns central to their agenda. This, he suggested, translated into a practical inability to mobilize blacks substantially more than in the past.

Campaign activists at county and local levels somewhat corroborate the stories of the state chairmen.[3] Fifteen county and local Democratic leaders in three midwestern states were also interviewed during the summer months of 1987. From both rural and urban areas, these activists, both black and white, suggested that they saw little carryover of commitment or enthusiasm from the Jackson campaign. Unlike their state chairmen, however, seven of the fifteen proposed that they felt the Mondale effort to appeal to blacks was calculated to win votes rather than representing the genuine policy prefer- ences of the candidate. A former Jackson activist who joined the Mondale effort stated the view that seemed to underlie the comments of several others by suggesting that during the primaries black issues "barely had a place on the Mondale agenda."

Perhaps what is more important is that when asked about whether or not there were pressures to appeal to, contact, or mobilize blacks from the state or national organizations, the fifteen local activists, all of whom had experience in past presidential campaigns, indicated that they felt no greater pressure from the Democratic organization "than usual" to try to mobilize or appeal to blacks in their localities or counties. Only one recalled a special effort to "go into the black community" in the 1976 campaign.

Practical problems also influence the coverage of canvassing efforts, es- pecially because the work force is largely volunteer. Two of the activists from large urban areas indicated that they saw urban areas as having special problems canvassing some black neighborhoods. One Chicago-area activist described the bulk of his volunteers as "middle aged and middle income" and largely female and said that he had difficulty leafleting and canvassing certain precincts for which his office was responsible because his volunteers were reluctant to go to some poor, black, high crime areas—regardless of their own race.

Such practical problems as these are not limited to the very large urban areas in the United States. A campaign worker from a relatively small downstate Illinois SMSA reported a similar reluctance on the part of some of her workers to canvass some predominantly black neighborhoods.[4] Thus, some black neighborhoods, though targeted for canvassing, receive only minimal coverage for two very significant reasons. One involves the apparent failure of the goals of the national organization to be made clear to the bulk of the volunteer force. Though the state chairmen implied that appealing to and mobilizing the black community was an important goal, the importance of this goal was not made clear to the local-level workers. Second, the practical problems of implementation were minimized or even overlooked by the party leadership.[5]

Thus, Equation 1 and the local party workers are telling us essentially the same thing: that race remains a factor in who is contacted by the parties. Both inform us that blacks, in particular blacks who have other blacks as neighbors, are less likely to be contacted by either party than whites (except perhaps those whites who have mostly black neighbors). Further, though there has been some change in the levels of direct contact between blacks and the parties, the amount of change has been small, and the slight increases have only somewhat narrowed the gap between the races. One should note, too, that the apparent narrowing rate of contacting by the Democratic party between 1980 and 1984 may be just that—apparent. It may be significant that this narrowing is as much a result of (a possibly temporary) downturn in the contacting of whites over the four-year interval as it is of any long-term trend in their canvassing of blacks.

We have already seen that the neighborhood canvass is a potent mobilizing force. We have also seen that there is an overwhelming tendency for blacks to vote for Democratic presidential candidates. Despite this, it is also clear that the Democratic party not only puts less effort into contacting blacks than whites but that blacks are also less likely to be included in the party's canvass. One obvious implication of this is that blacks are underrepresented in the actual implementation of the Democratic Party's campaigns; contacting blacks in proportion to their population proportion, as would be accomplished through "race-neutral" canvassing efforts, would result in increased numbers of blacks contacted, and, by extension, in greater black turnout and most likely an increase in the vote for the Democratic candidate.[6]

Even without an increased turnout, blacks contributed more than 20 percent of the vote received by Mondale in 1984—despite the fact that they comprised only about 10 percent of all voters in that year. Strength within the party in excess of that which would be indicated by population proportions shows a loyalty to the party greater than almost any other group even in this era, often characterized by declining partisanship and increasing independence. Therefore, a "rational" or *vote*-maximizing campaign strategy would use this advantage as fully as possible—and certainly should not include a reduction in attempts to mobilize probable loyal partisans. As noted, however, the data do show that implementations of Democratic campaign strategies do not show blacks being contacted even at a rate equal to their population proportion.

Further, survey evidence indicates that blacks are omitted from other aspects of the campaign as well. Though data on the distribution of general campaign literature and telephone contacting are not available, the 1984 survey data show that blacks were far less likely than whites to receive any sort of solicitation for donations—from either party. Whereas 38 percent of whites report receiving a request for money by mail, only 12 percent of blacks recall receiving such a mailing ($t = 11.0$ with $df = 2255$). Similarly, 5.4 percent of white respondents reported that they had someone ask them for a political contribution in person, whereas only 2.3 percent of blacks report such a personal solicitation ($t = 2.75$; $df = 2255$).[7]

Discussion

The failure to fully include blacks in the campaign has important consequences for both theoretical and practical representation issues; it raises questions for democratic theory as well as about electoral outcomes—each issuing challenges about the character of representation in America. Without doubt, greater black participation would influence the character of campaign debate and impact on issues. An additional but related question, of course, is whether greater black participation would influence electoral outcomes more directly, for as the black vote becomes a more critical determinant, the tenor of debate will also change.

Reagan's large victory margin suggests that a greater black turnout in 1984 would not have changed the outcome of that presidential election. However, it is not so clear that elections for other offices, or in other years, would not have been affected more dramatically. One possible test of this proposition is to estimate the expected mobilization due to the canvass and to examine the change in both the number of blacks voting and the Democrat's share of the two-party vote across differing levels of effort devoted to the canvassing of blacks.

One formulation considers simply the effects of an increase in the level of contacting directed exclusively at prospective black voters, noting only how additional canvassing might influence black turnout. Simple multiplication of average probabilities will provide information on the expected turnout for a given level of contacting. For example, according to estimates from the 1976 NES, 12.7 percent of blacks were canvassed in that year—almost all by Democrats; those contacted had a turnout rate that was 18.5 points greater than that of the noncontacted blacks, yielding a total turnout rate for blacks (contacted and noncontacted combined) of 66.1 percent in the sample. Doubling the contacting effort in the black community, making it almost equal with that for whites, may be expected to increase turnout by five percentage points, to 71 percent (a turnout rate that is nearly the same as that for whites).[8] If blacks cast 100 percent of their ballots for the Democrat, the Democratic vote share would increase by two percentage points, assuming that 20 percent of voters would be black. However, the Democrats receive "only" about 80 percent of votes cast by blacks, so the Democrats' vote share would increase by just 1.8 points. Thus a race-neutral canvass, where the canvassing is done without regard to race (so blacks and whites are contacted in equal proportions) would result in both an increased total turnout and an improvement in the Democrats' share of the two-party vote.

Of course, because Democratic candidates appear to have such an extraordinary advantage in capturing the vote of those blacks who do vote, it may make sense to put greater, not less, effort into attempts to mobilize that vote. Obviously, this, among other things, means that there is a greater payoff to canvassing (and otherwise targeting) black neighborhoods than white ones. Such targeting may indeed improve both total and black turnout and the Democrats' vote share even further. If, for example, blacks were contacted at a 30-percent rate rather than the 25-percent rate in the previously mentioned example, the logic of the preceding calculation leads to the conclusion that black turnout will improve to 72.3 percent,[9] and the Democrats' vote share improve by slightly more than two points.

Other means of assessing the impact of alternative canvassing strategies also exist and may provide even greater insights into the possibilities. For example, using multivariate estimation methods to estimate turnout as something akin to a production function, one may consider not only the aggregate effects of changes in canvassing but also the effects of specific types of targeting.

For example, if one uses a logistic estimate for the probability of voting, the probabilities of voting may be calculated for contacted and noncontacted individuals with specific characteristics. This will allow the consequences of a more finely targeted campaign to be assessed.

Equation 2 produces expected probabilities for black voting and is based on a logistic regression that controls for the racial composition of the neighborhood (PCblack), respondent education (red), and whether or not the person was contacted (contact).[10] The racial composition of the neighborhood is an important factor to include because it can provide campaign officials with a useful means of targeting a canvassing effort to populations that may be either influenced by the effort or overlooked in existing efforts.

$$p(\text{vote}) = 1/(1 + e^{-f})$$

$$f = -2.07 + 1.16 \text{*PCblack} + 0.179 \text{*red} + 2.01 \text{*contact}$$
$$\quad\ (0.89)\ \ (0.52) \qquad\quad (0.060) \qquad (0.77)$$

(Eq. 2)

Equation 2 shows that the three factors (neighborhood racial composition, respondent education, and whether or not the person was contacted) all significantly contribute to the chance that a person votes and jointly explain nearly 40 percent of the variance in black turnout in 1976. Using this to estimate the impact of canvassing is easily accomplished by computing a simple difference in turnout perentages (PDI) between contacted and noncontacted blacks. For example, the calculation yields a PDI of 19 when the neighborhood is 95 percent black (and education is held at the mean value of 11); this PDI may be interpreted as predicting that turnout in a 95-percent black neighborhood would increase by 19 percentage points if that neighborhood were targeted for canvassing such that all households were contacted. In an integrated neighborhood, split evenly between blacks and whites, canvassing would produce a 27-point increase in turnout among the blacks. Thus the efficacy of contacting would be even greater if integrated neighborhoods were targeted and the blacks in those neighborhoods were approached by the party and candidate campaign workers.

Two major but related points have been addressed in this chapter. In spite of repeated assertions to the contrary by party officials, especially Democratic officials, there is little evidence that either of the parties has attempted to mobilize black support or to approach them in the same way that they approach potential white supporters. Even into the mid-1980s, blacks were canvassed at lower rates than whites. Logically, this appears to be a reality that not only fails to conform to the image that Democratic party officials wish to convey but is also counterproductive, given the strong tendency for blacks to support Democratic candidates. The evidence also suggests that blacks are less likely to be contacted by telephone or through the mail than whites,[11] which makes the otherwise relatively persuasive arguments of campaign activists slightly more questionable. Although the overall pattern of contacting conforms to the activists' assertions that it is difficult to find volunteers to canvass some areas or neighborhoods (out of fear of crime, for example), any tendency to ignore similar areas in mail and telephone campaigns must be explained in other ways.

Thus if, as Wolfinger and Rosentone (1980) suggest, black citizens vote at rates lower than whites even after allowing for income and education discrepancies, then perhaps a portion of the blame may lay with the parties and candidates. For, in spite of an increasing secular turnout trend and a substantial loyalty to the Democratic Party, both the Republican and Democratic party campaigns underemphasize the black voter in practice by failing to direct resources and attention to mobilizing blacks—a fact that has both political and social consequences.

Clearly, Democratic candidates may improve their electoral chances by devoting greater effort to mobilizing black voters. The payoff, in vote terms, is greater for this than for almost any other campaign activity. This chapter has shown that if blacks were canvassed at the same rate as whites, there would be a sizable increase in the Democrats' vote share, even at the national level. Obviously, the gains may be greater if even more resources were devoted to contacting and mobilizing blacks. Thus one consequence of the failure to fully incorporate blacks into the political process is reflected in election returns.

Other consequences, although possibly not as dramatic, are perhaps more important and may help explain the lower black turnout. There is substantial evidence indicating that interest, efficacy, psychological involvement, and participation are all highly interrelated (Milbrath and Goel, 1977; Conway, 1985; Verba and Nie, 1972). Thus one explanation of the lower turnout rates among blacks may revolve around the parties' continued underemphasis of black voters. By failing to make blacks full partners in the electoral process, the party organizations may contribute to the feelings of anomie and lower efficacy found among blacks, which, in turn, may depress both interests in the campaign and participation rates.

Though voicing concerns about black involvement in elections, neither party devotes much real effort to mobilizing black supporters. Thus, as some of the party activists suggested, blacks may feel that, although both parties would like their vote, neither is willing to make a substantial effort to obtain it. Such a perception, whether valid or not, will increase voter apathy and decrease participation (Berelson et al., 1954; McCloskey and Schaar, 1965). In short, the parties may themselves be a contributing factor in the general tendency for blacks to turn out at lower rates than whites.

Overall, this research demonstrates that greater efforts by the parties might substantially increase black turnout and that, despite the fact that such efforts might provide a greater electoral payoff to the Democrats than similar efforts directed at whites, the Democratic candidates have failed to devote even proportional efforts at the prospective black voters. Thus, regardless of the apparent change in the public position of party officials, there has been little improvement in the way that blacks are included in campaign strategies.

References

Bennett, Stephen E., and William R. Klecka. 1970. "Social Status and Political Participation: A Multivariate Analysis of Predictive Power." *Midwest Journal of Political Science* 14:355-82.

Berleson, Bernard, Paul Lazarsfeld, and William McPhee. 1954. *Voting.* Chicago: University of Chicago Press.

Cutright, Phillips. 1963. "Measuring the Impact of Local Party Activity on the General Election Vote." *Public Opinion Quarterly* 27:374-86.

DeNardo, James. 1980. Turnout and the Vote: The Joke's on the Democrats." *American Political Science Review* 74:406-420.

Katz, Daniel, and Samuel Eldersveld. 1961. "The Impact of Local Party Activity upon the Electorate," *Public Opinion Quarterly* 25:1-24.

Key, V. O. 1949. *Southern Politics.* New York: Knopf.

_____ . 1964. Politics, Parties, and *Pressure Groups.* 5th edition. New York: Thomas Crowell.

Kramer, Gerald H. 1970. "The Effect of Precinct-Level Canvassing on Voter Behavior": *Public Opinion Quarterly* 34:560-72.

Lazersfeld, Paul, Bernard Berelson, and Hazel Gaudet. 1969. *The People's Choice: How the Voter Makes Up His Mind in a Presidential Campaign.* 3rd edition. New York: Columbia University Press.

McClosky, Herbert, and John Schaar. 1965. "Psychological Dimensions of Anomy." *American Sociological Review* 30:14-40.

Milbrath, Lester W. and M. L. Goel. 1977. *Political Participation.* 2nd edition. Chicago: Rand McNally.

Miller, Abraham. 1971. "Ethnicity and Political Behavior: A Review of Theories and an Attempt at Reformulation," *Western Political Quarterly* 24:483-500.

Traugott, Michael, and John Katosh. 1979. "Response Validity in Surveys of Voting." *Public Opinion Quarterly* 52:359-77.

Verba, Sidney, and Norman Nie. 1972. *Participation in America: Political Democracy and Social Equality.* Evanston, IL: Harper & Row.

Wolfinger, Raymond, and Steven Rosenstone. 1980. *Who Votes*? New Haven: Yale.
Zipp, John. 1983. "Race, Social Status, and Nonvoting in the U.S., 1952-1980." Unpublished mimeo. St. Louis: Washington University Department of Sociology.

Notes

1. The data utilized in this chapter were made available, in part, by the Inter-University Consortium for Political and Social Research. The data for the American National Election Study, 1984, were originally collected by the Center for Political Studies of the Institute for Social Research, the University of Michigan, for the national election studies, under the overall direction of Warren E. Miller. The data were collected under a grant from the National Science Foundation.

   Other data and comments presented in the paper are from interviews with twenty state and local Democratic party officials and activists, conducted during June and July of 1987.

   The author is responsible for all analyses and interpretations presented here.

2. Five past or present state party chairmen were interviewed in the summer of 1987; one was interviewed in a face-to-face setting, whereas the remainder were contacted by telephone. In every case, the person interviewed chaired the party during the 1984 campaign. Averaging about two to two and one-half hours in length, the interviews elicited information on the state chair's opinions of pressures from the national party and candidate organizations, the activities of local-level efforts and their attempts to influence the local efforts, the organization of the party, and their perceptions of the roles of various political actors in the campaign. Of the six contacted during the summer of 1987, one refused an interview. Three former Republican party state chairmen were also interviewed during this period.

3. Eighteen Democratic "activists" were contacted and fifteen were subsequently interviewed during the summer of 1987. Activists included paid and volunteer workers in county and local campaign offices. The names and addresses of local activists were solicited from the country chairmen if they had access to such information; otherwise they were asked to identify the person who would have information on who was active in the 1984 campaign.

4. These comments suggest another possible structural problem in the campaign organizations, relating specifically to the base of volunteer workers. Though such information was not directly sought in the "elite" interviews, it is apparent that campaign volunteers were not recruited (at least successfully) from the residents of those neighborhoods that are difficult to canvass. A logical assumption is that the residents of those neighborhoods would be more willing to canvass and leaflet around their homes. This, of course, would most likely require that resources be expended in these areas for the establishment of local offices and networks to serve these areas explicitly.

5. The small number of "elite" interviews prevents us from knowing whether or not the impressions of either the state or local activists were prevalent across the nation. The NES data, however, show a trend in contacting that is compatible with the statements by the local-level activists who did not feel an unusually strong pressure to canvass black areas and who saw the practical problems first hand.

   Note also that many of the practical problems would be minimized if blacks had seen the Mondale appeals as sincere—something that the state chairmen did not believe was the case.

6. As has been noted, blacks who vote cast their ballots for Democratic candidates at much higher rates than do whites who vote. This occurs at all status levels. Thus,

although there is some controversy, it is highly probable that increasing black voter turnout would result in an increased Democratic vote. For a dissenting view, arguing that increasing turnout would harm Democratic candidates, see De Nardo (1980), who looks at defection rates among all nonvoters rather than focusing on blacks alone.

7. When the aim is to solicit contributions for the campaign effort, it may not be irrational to solicit them from a smaller percentage of blacks than whites, given the inequities in the income distribution. Indeed, one does find that it is the higher income blacks who receive such solicitations. The mean income of blacks receiving any request or a donation to a political party was $22,318; the mean for whites receiving any solicitation was $28,626. This difference, although statistically significant ($t = 2.1$; $df = 700$), is not large and shows that it is clearly the "better-off" segments of both groups that receive the bulk of the solicitations.

8. This estimate is computed from simple probabilities according to the following formula for the proportion voting:

$$\frac{[N \text{ contacted}* \ p(\text{vote:contact}) + N \text{ not contacted} * p(\text{vote:no contact})]}{\text{total } N}$$

Although this estimate uses self-reports of voting behavior from the survey, which are known to be somewhat overreported, there is no difference in overreporting among contacted or noncontacted populations. Thus, whereas the two estimated turnout rates may be slightly exaggerated, the differences in the two estimates should be accurate (i.e., in this case, the five-point increase in total turnout should accurately reflect the population dynamic).

9. Estimated from the survey data; because of overreporting in the survey, this estimate is also inflated. However, the six-point difference between this and the turnout reported in the survey should remain constant, as noted in End-note 6.

10. The neighborhood composition data were drawn from the 1970 Census data and were made available by John D. Sprague and Louis P. Westefield. Neither Sprague nor Westefield bears any responsibility for the uses or interpretations presented here.

11. Note, however, that this evidence was only suggestive, as the data referred specifically to solicitations for contributions. However, it may be a reasonable extension that other mailings/telephone calls are targeted in a fashion similar to requests for contributions.

Second-Generation Educational Discrimination and White Flight from Public Schools

Kenneth J. Meier
Joseph Stewart, Jr.
Robert E. England

University of Wisconsin–Madison
West Virginia University
Oklahoma State University

Selective use of ability grouping, tracking, and discipline has been used to resegregate formerly desegregated public schools. This research demonstrates that the use of such within-school educational practices, termed "second-generation educational discrimination," attenuate white student enrollment losses. The results illustrate the goal displacement of school desegregation whereby policies intended to benefit black students are translated into policies designed to inconvenience white students the least.

Providing equal access to educational opportunities has been a long arduous political battle. Laws that made it illegal to educate blacks were replaced with policies of separate but definitely unequal schools and finally with desegregated education. The movement to desegregated schools was rarely voluntary and often delayed until sufficient coercion forced compliance with the Supreme Court's decisions (Rodgers and Bullock, 1976). Desegregating the nation's schools, however, did not provide blacks access to equal educational opportunities. Educational opportunities can be denied, and schools can be resegregated by selective use of ability grouping, tracking, and discipline (Bullock and Stewart, 1978; Eyler, Cook, and Ward, 1983; Hochschild, 1984; Rodgers and Bullock, 1972). Collectively, racial disparities in ability grouping, tracking, and discipline that have been used to limit black students' educational opportunities have been termed "second-generation educational discrimination."

Policies of second-generation educational discrimination are grounded in local politics. School districts that do not elect black school board members, have few black administrators, and few black teachers, also have higher levels of second-generation discrimination (England and Meier, 1985; Meier and England, 1984). Second-generation educational discrimination can be viewed as a political system's policy effort to extend segregation when more blatant discrimination is no longer possible (Rodgers and Bullock, 1972). By using less visible, yet equally effective, second-generation discrimination techniques, school systems can limit interracial contact and equal educational opportunities.

This research extends the growing political literature on second-generation educational discrimination (England and Meier, 1985; Eyler, Cook, and Ward, 1983; Fraga, Meier, and England, 1986; Meier and England, 1984; Stewart and Bullock, 1981) by linking such practices to school district efforts to limit declines in white student enrollment. The research question is: Can desegregation be made more tolerable to white parents by denying black students' access to quality education though second-generation discrimination? The analysis proceeds in several parts. First, the level of second-generation educational discrimination is reviewed for the nation's largest urban school districts. Second, a brief review of the white enrollment-decline literature is used to construct a model of white student enrollment. Third, measures of second-generation discrimination are incorporated into this model to probe the relationship between second-generation discrimination and white flight. Fourth, the rarely addressed topic of declining black school enrollments is examined in relation to second-generation discrimination. Finally, the implications of this study for equal educational opportunity are discussed.

Measuring Second-Generation Discrimination

Second-generation educational discrimination can be divided into two parts—ability grouping/tracking and discipline. After the desegregation of Southern school districts in the late 1960s, scholars noted that many schools were formally desegregated but blacks and whites were not attending classes together (Arnez, 1978; Rodgers and Bullock, 1972). School districts limited interracial contact with ability grouping and tracking. Ability grouping concerns the assignment of individuals to classes or to groups within classes on the basis of some measured ability. Tracking is the practice of designing curricula based on occupational or educational objectives such as college preparation or vocational training. Both processes separate students into groups with unequal status.

Racial inequities in ability grouping and tracking are fairly stark. Black students are far more likely to be assigned to special education classes and more likely to be funneled into vocational rather than college prep tracks. Similarly, black students are frequently denied access to gifted classes, reserving such quality education for a primarily white clientele. Racial disparities are of concern because ability grouping/tracking has harmful effects on low-ability groups and only a mixed effect on high-ability groups (Epstein, 1985:30; Findley and Bryan, 1975:13). In addition, assignments to ability groups are often made in error; yet once made, assignments usually become permanent (Gallagher, 1972:529; Garrison and Hammill, 1971:18).

This study uses three measures of ability grouping collected by the federal Office for Civil Rights—placement in classes for the educable mentally retarded (EMR), placement in classes for the trainable mentally retarded (TMR), and placement in gifted classes. To measure racial disparities, a ratio is calculated by dividing the percentage of blacks in a specified class (e.g., EMR classes) by the percentage of blacks in the student body. This ratio, sometimes called the "odds ratio," has some distinct interpretation advantages. It equals 1.0 when blacks are represented in an ability group in exact proportion to their numbers in the student body. Numbers larger than 1.0 indicate overrepresentation, whereas numbers less than one show underrepresentation.

Table 1 shows the black and white ability-grouping ratios for 141 urban school districts with at least 15,000 students and 1 percent black enrollment.[1] Black students are overrepresented in EMR classes by 117 percent, whereas whites are underrepresented by 26 percent.[2] TMR class assignments show smaller inequities (black ratio = 1.37; white ratio = 1.02), but gifted classes show major racial disparities. Blacks are underrepresented by 59 percent in gifted classes.

Punishment is a second dimension of second-generation educational discrimination. Research shows that black students are more likely to be punished for offenses permitted white students and their punishment is more severe (Children's Defense Fund, 1974:130; Eyler, Cook, and Ward, 1983:142). A student who is repeatedly punished, suspended, or expelled is likely to become discouraged and leave the educational system, a process called stu-

Table 1. Second-Generation Educational Discrimination:
Representation Ratios for Blacks and Whites*

Action	Blacks Mean	Standard Deviation	Whites Mean	Standard Deviation
EMR Classes	2.21	.93	.67	.22
TMR Classes	1.37	.51	.91	.23
Gifted Classes	.41	.30	1.38	.56
Corporal Punishment	1.72	.63	.84	.26
Suspensions	1.73	.49	.79	.20
Expulsions	2.49	1.50	.61	.53
Dropouts	1.11	.31	.95	.18
Graduates	.83	.15	1.12	.19

*All differences between blacks and whites are significant at .0001 or less.

dent pushout (Arnez, 1978:31). Three measures of racial disparities in discipline will be used; ratio measures similar to the ability grouping ratios were calculated for corporal punishment, suspensions, and expulsions.

The discipline ratios shown in Table 1 show striking differences between black and white students. In every case, the discipline ratios for blacks are at least twice as large as those for whites. The worst situation is the most severe action—expulsion. Black students are two and one-half times more likely to be expelled.

The sum effect of racial disparities in ability grouping and discipline is a lower level of educational quality for black students when compared to their white classmates. As a result, black students are more likely to drop out of school and less likely to graduate. The black and white ratios for dropouts and graduation from high school are also shown in Table 1. The black dropout ratio (1.11) is higher than the white dropout ratio (.95), and the black graduation ratio (.83) is much lower than the white ratio (1.12). Such inequities have a permanent impact on blacks. Black students who fail to complete high school will be more likely to be unemployed, earn lower incomes when employed, live in less desirable housing, and raise children who remain in poverty (Cohen and Tyree, 1986; Duncan, 1984; Smith and Welch, 1986).

Goal Displacement and Declining White Enrollment

Declining levels of white enrollment in urban schools, generally referred to as "white flight," is one of the more controversial issues in urban education. A frequently expressed fear is that school desegregation *causes* whites to flee school systems, reducing the overall white enrollment and thus frustrating the intent of desegregation. This fear has caused what Willie and Fultz (1984:164) call goal distortion: "A court order that gave local school authorities primary responsibility for developing plans *that protect the rights of blacks* was transformed into a primary responsibility to develop school desegregation plans *that are least offensive to whites.*" This goal distortion explains why the initial efforts to desegregate schools focused primarily on voluntary desegregation strategies such as open enrollment, voluntary magnet schools, and majority to minority transfers.

Viewed in this light, second-generation discrimination may well be a political choice by local school officials to make desegregation as tolerable to whites as possible. By grouping individuals by ability, not only are whites separated from most blacks, but middle-class whites are also separated from lower-class whites.[3] Disproportionate disciplinary practices in turn have a greater impact on black students and further limit interracial contact by pushing black students out of the educational system. Second-generation educational discrimination, as a result, has the potential to make public schools more attractive for white students. An hypothesis consistent with the goal displacement view is that second-generation discrimination should be negatively related to white flight. Because white enrollments respond to a wide variety of forces, the other determinants of white enrollment decline must be specified to provide a fair test of this hypothesis.

Previous Research on White Enrollment Decline

The issue of white flight was first sensationalized by James S. Coleman (see Coleman et al., 1975; Coleman, 1976; 1981). He argued that a substantial desegregation effort (that is, a reduction in the Taeuber[4] index of 20 or more) would result in a 6 percent loss of white enrollment during the year of implementation in districts with 25 percent or more black students. As Rossell (1978:48) noted, this would be double the normal white enrollment loss for such districts.

Several studies disputed Coleman's findings (e.g., Farley, 1975; Pettigrew and Green, 1976). This "white flight debate" degenerated into a series of charges and countercharges with individuals labeled everything from *racist* to *incompetent* (Rossell, 1978:46). Eventually, a consensus supporting some of Coleman's original claims emerged (Farley, Richards, and Wurdock, 1980). The consensus was that desegregation resulted in "an additional white enrollment loss of 8 to 10 percentage points in the year of implementation in school districts above 35 percent black" (Rossell, 1983:38). Such losses were conditional on a variety of factors, including distance of busing, type of school, type of desegregation plan, local publicity, and other factors (Rossell, 1983:38–9).[5]

A Model of White Enrollment Loss

Our intent is not to participate in the debate over the influences of white student enrollment; rather we are interested only in the relationships between white enrollment loss and second-generation discrimination. The model presented here is not intended to resolve any of the academic debates; we simply wish to incorporate as many possible determinants of white enrollment decline as our data permit and then proceed with our own analysis.

Franklin Wilson (1985:138), in his study of white enrollment decline, argues that "the policy implications of the impact of school desegregation can best be addressed by focusing on the long-term effects rather than on any implementation year effects that may be compensated for later." White enrollment fluctuates far more than one would expect; short-term declines are often compensated for by long-term effects in the opposite direction (England and Morgan, 1986; Wilson, 1985). Accordingly, we will not model white flight on an annual basis as is the custom in the literature because this can produce misleading findings. Our attempt will focus on long-term declines in white enrollment using the time period 1968 to 1986.[6]

Our model will begin by simply predicting white student enrollment in 1986 with white student enrollment in 1968. Both variables are subjected to a log transformation to eliminate problems of heteroscedasticity and extreme values. This initial model is consistent with the consensus approach used to model white enrollment decline (see Welch, 1987; Wilson, 1985).

That white enrollment has declined over this eighteen-year time period is beyond dispute. The average white student enrollment for the school districts in this study dropped from 35,162 in 1968 to 19,672 or 44 percent. Nowhere near all of this decline is attributable to desegregation. White enrollments have declined for a variety of reasons, including the decline in birth rates, migration patterns from cities to suburbs, economic patterns, crime, and countless other factors.

To the basic model of white enrollment, we will add several additional variables. If these variables have negative coefficients in the resulting regression, then they increase the rate of white enrollment decline. Positive slopes indicate that the variables attenuate the rate of white enrollment decline.

The first variable is, of course, desegregation, measured as the change in the Taeuber segregation index from 1968 to 1976.[7] Since the early white-flight studies, estimates of desegregation's impact have become more precise. Giles (1975) found a tipping point of 35 percent black; in districts greater than 35 percent black, desegregation results in white outmigration (see also Wilson, 1985). To measure this conditional impact, we created a dummy variable for those districts more than 35 percent black. We used both this variable and a second variable that was the interaction between desegregation and black enrollment (or the amount of desegregation multiplied by the black enrollment dummy variable). Such a procedure is consistent with previous work in this area (see Wilson, 1985).

White withdrawal from a school system, according to Giles and Gatlin (1980), is a function of both attitudes toward desegregation and the ability to act. We cannot, with our current data set, measure attitudes toward desegregation, but we can measure whites' abilities to leave the public school system. White students who leave urban public schools, the research suggests, do not usually transfer to suburban schools (Rossell, 1983:38). Escaping students are more likely to enroll in private schools. The opportunity to enroll in a private school is significantly limited by the availability of private schools. In a city without a developed private school system, a white student may have no choice other than to remain in public schools. To tap this dimension, the percentage of school-aged children enrolled in private schools in 1980 will be used.[8]

The existence of private schools is not a sufficient condition for leaving a public school system. Private schools charge tuition, and many individuals who would like to attend private schools may lack the financial resources. Our second measure of the capacity of whites to leave the public school system, then, is the white median family income in the district.

The group power thesis of desegregation (Feagin, 1980; Giles and Evans, 1985, 1986) holds that social class is linked to desegregation. The thesis contends that both racial and class differences contribute to intergroup hostility. Some white students, therefore, might leave public schools not because desegregation exposes them to black students per se but because it exposes them to lower-class black students. To tap this potential social-class-aversion view of white flight, the percentage of blacks with a high-school education will be used.

Finally, Southern region is associated with a decreased ability for whites to leave public schools (England and Morgan, 1986). Many Southern school districts are large, countywide districts covering more than one incorporated area. In such a district, moving to the suburbs is not an option because the school district includes the suburbs. To tap this and other elements of the

Table 2. Determinants of White Enrollment Decline
Dependent variable = Log [White Enrollment 1986]

<u>Regression Coefficients</u>

Independent Variables	Full Model	Reduced Model
Log (White Enrollment 1968)	.89682*	.88961*
Desegregation Change	.00311*	.00319*
Southern Region	.12824*	.14841*
Private School Enrollment	-1.26967*	-1.12030*
Desegregation * Percent Black	-.00462*	-.00470*
White Median Income	.00001	---
Black Education	-.00163	---
R^2	.76	.76
Adjusted R^2	.75	.75
F	52.74	74.21
N	122	122

*$p < .05$.

unique Southern educational patterns, a dummy variable for Southern districts will be included.

The regression model for white enrollment decline appears in Table 2. An initial glance at the model reveals that two variables are not statistically significant, white median income and black education. To avoid estimating a misspecified model, these two variables were deleted, and the model was reestimated (second column, Table 2). All coefficients in the second model are statistically significant and in the predicted direction. The model itself predicts fairly well with a coefficient of determination of .76.[9]

Second-Generation Discrimination and White Enrollments

If ability grouping and discipline can be used as techniques to limit white enrollment declines, we would expect to see positive relationships among practices that adversely affect black students and overall white enrollments. The measures of ability grouping and discipline are multiple-year averages because our concern is with long-term rather than short-term impacts.[10] To

Table 3. The Impact of Second-Generation Discrimination on White Flight Dependent Variable = Log [White Enrollment 1986]

| | Regression Coefficients | | | | |
Variable	Slope	t-value	R^2	F	N
EMR Classes	.711*	7.04	.83	96.02	122
TMR Classes	.380*	3.26	.78	67.86	119
Gifted Classes	-.266*	5.37	.81	81.49	122
Expulsions	.094	1.26	.77	60.95	116
Suspensions	.314*	2.29	.77	64.97	122
Corporal Punishment	.255*	2.02	.75	54.13	115
Dropouts	.212	1.59	.76	58.47	120
Graduates	-.556*	2.81	.78	66.84	122

Note: The Partial regression coefficients reflect controls for white enrollment 1968, desegregation, Southern Region, private school enrollment, and the interaction of desegregation and percentage of black enrollment.
*$p < .05$.

eliminate problems of heteroscedasticity, the ability grouping and discipline ratios are also subjected to a log transformation.

The regression coefficients resulting from the addition of black ability grouping and discipline ratios to the white enrollment decline model are shown in Table 3. A clear, consistent pattern exists for ability grouping. Districts that disproportionately assign blacks to EMR and TMR classes and disproportionately limit black enrollments in gifted classes experience smaller white enrollment declines. Each relationship is statistically significant and in the correct direction. Ability-grouping procedures that separate blacks from whites attenuate white flight from the school district.

The relationships between punishment of black students and white enrollment decline are not as strong as the relationships for ability grouping. Although only the relationships for suspensions and corporal punishment are statistically significant, districts that disproportionately discipline black students, as predicted, have smaller declines in white enrollments. In addition, a higher black dropout rate is associated with smaller declines in white enrollment, and higher black graduation rates are significantly correlated with larger declines in white enrollments.

The results suggest even stronger linkages of ability grouping and discipline to racial discrimination. The pattern that we have found is consistent with a postdesegregation strategy to resegregate schools. Via administrative actions, school districts are able to translate a court-ordered policy to benefit black students into a policy that provides the least inconvenience to white students by reducing the amount of interracial exposure. School districts have successfully traded black access to equal educational opportunities for continued white enrollments.

Declining Black Enrollments

Lost in the debate over white flight has been the phenomenon of decreasing black enrollments. In our survey districts, the average black enrollment dropped from 19,671 in 1968 to 18,231 in 1986. Although the black enrollment decline of 7.4 percent is nowhere near the white enrollment decline of 44 percent, it represents a significant demographic trend. In some districts, the drop has been much higher; Los Angeles, for example, lost 28.4 percent of its black enrollment during this time period, and Baltimore lost 31.2 percent.

Black enrollment declines should not come as a surprise. The black birth rate has dropped in the past 20 years, and black families follow many of the same migration patterns as white families. As Katzman (1983) argues, black flight is probably caused by the same factors that result in white enrollment decline. The presence of black enrollment decline suggests that the relationship between ability grouping and discipline may also affect black student enrollment. If such actions motivate blacks to leave the school system, those blacks who withdraw will likely be those with the ability to move or to send their children to private school. As a result, a district might lose enrollments from the middle-class black community.

To determine if ability grouping and discipline affect black enrollments, a model of black enrollment decline was constructed similar to the white enrollment model with some modifications to reflect black interests rather than white interests. The basic model remains the same; the dependent variable is the log transformation of black enrollment in 1986. The independent variables are black enrollment in 1968 (to tap the decline), Southern region, desegregation interacting with percentage of black enrollment, black median income, and private school enrollment. The latter two variables measure the capacity of blacks to leave the school system (see Table 4).

The decline in black enrollments follows a pattern different from that for white enrollments. Only two variables are significant—previous black enrollments and Southern region. Particularly interesting is the lack of relationships between black enrollments and the capacity to withdraw from the school system. Our findings may reveal the absence of such a capacity. Private schools do not offer the same opportunity to blacks as they do to whites. In the North, many private schools are Catholic, and most Northern blacks are not.[11] In the South, many of the private "Christian" schools were established to provide education for whites only. Only 5 percent of private school students are black, compared to 15 percent of public school students (Taeuber and James, 1982:134). In addition, black median family income is approximately only 70 percent of white median family income. Large numbers of blacks may not have the financial capacity to move to the suburbs or pay private school tuition.

The black enrollment model was then reestimated, using only previous black enrollment and Southern region. This simple model suggests that black

Table 4. Determinants of Black Enrollment Decline
Dependent Variable = Log [Black Enrollment 1986]

	Regression Coefficients	
Independent Variable	Full Model	Reduced Model
Log (Black Enrollment 1968)	.806*	.853*
Southern Region	.076*	.060*
Private School Enrollment	.672	---
Black Median Income	-.000	---
Desegregation * Percent Black	.000	---
R^2	.90	.90
Adjusted R^2	.90	.89
F	208.88	515.44
N	122	122

*$p < .05$.

enrollment declines are more consistent across school districts than are white enrollment declines. This supposition is further supported by the higher co-efficient of determination (.90) for the simple model of black enrollment than for the more complex model of white enrollment (.76). This consistency also suggests that ability grouping and discipline might not affect black enrollment because black students do not have as many options to avoid discriminatory educational practices.

The pattern of relationships between ability grouping, discipline, and black enrollments (Table 5) is consistent with this interpretation. None of the relationships except the one for black high-school graduates is statistically signifi-cant. In the case of graduation rates, more black graduates are associated with smaller declines in black enrollments. Exactly this relationship is expected because more black graduates means more blacks remain in school until they finish.

Ability grouping and discipline, then, do not appear to affect aggregate black enrollments. A school system that disproportionately assigns black stu-dents to lower-ability group classes, limits black enrollments in higher-ability group classes, and disproportionately punishes black students can induce more white students to remain in the school system. Because blacks lack the same capacity to leave the school system, they face a Hobson's choice of unequal education or no education.

Table 5. The Impact of Second-Generation Discrimination on Black Flight
Dependent Variable = Log [Black Enrollment 1986]

Variable	Slope	t-value	R^2	F	N
EMR Classes	.07	.60	.90	341.89	122
TMR Classes	.04	.87	.90	328.73	119
Gifted Classes	.02	.44	.90	341.36	122
Expulsions	.00	.00	.89	313.17	116
Suspensions	-.16	1.05	.90	344.26	122
Corporal Punishment	-.04	.36	.90	348.33	115
Dropouts	-.12	.90	.89	323.88	120
Graduates	-.84*	4.67	.91	410.86	122

Partial regression coefficients control for Black Enrollment 1968
and Southern Region.

*$p < .05$.

Conclusion

This study examined large U.S. urban school districts with at least 1 percent black enrollment. The practices of second-generation educational discrimination were linked to levels of white enrollment. The finding that blacks had their access to quality education limited by ability grouping and disciplinary practices was consistent with previous research on the topic. Racial disparities in ability grouping and discipline were then linked to white enrollment declines. In school districts that placed more blacks in lower-ability groups, restricted the access of blacks to higher-ability groups, and punished proportionately more blacks, white flight from the school district was reduced. Such practices did not affect the level of black enrollments because black student do not have the same potential to leave public schools as white students do.

This research suggests that school administrators have the potential to displace the goal of school desegregation by trading off black students' access to equal education for increased white enrollments. The unanswered question is whether school administrators are making this decision consciously. With the current data set, we cannot tell if such policies are made consciously; however, two factors suggest that they might be. First, second-generation education discrimination has been strongly linked to the discretion of school administrators and teachers (England and Meier, 1985). Second, the pattern of actions taken limits interracial contact among students, thus minimizing the impact of desegregation on white students. The data presented here and previous research, although they do not prove that school officials consciously limit black access to education in exchange for higher white enrollments, are consistent with conscious efforts to do so.

Viewed in this light, second-generation educational discrimination can be seen as a political decision adopted by school district officials. School district officials can maintain their positions of authority by maximizing support from the most powerful interests in the district. What are described as "professional" decisions regarding student placement and discipline thus become political decisions to gain the support of white parents. In this way, racial disparities in ability grouping, tracking, and discipline become this generation's segregated schools and compulsory illiteracy laws.

Notes

1. The list of school districts included in the sample is available from the authors. The school districts were surveyed with approximately 67 percent returning surveys. This survey information was then merged with OCR data on second-generation discrimination and census data on school district demographics. The measures are average scores for the district for all years between 1973 and 1982 for which OCR reported data.
2. Percentages for whites and blacks do not balance each other out because students of other races, primarily Hispanic but also Asians, American Indians, and numerous others, also attend these schools.
3. For a discussion of the class basis of second-generation educational discrimination, see England and Meier (1985). Class will be directly incorporated in our model later on this chapter.
4. The Taeuber index of dissimilarity measures the percentage of black students that would have to be moved to different schools so that the racial distribution in every school is equal to the racial distribution of the entire school district. A Taeuber index has a theoretical range of 100 for a totally segregated school system to 0 for a totally desegregated system.
5. The conditional nature of white enrollment loss is still controversial. Wilson (1985), in an elaborate pooled time series model, does not find that the type of desegregation plan affects white enrollment loss. His position on this issue has been criticized by Welch (1987).
6. To our knowledge, no other work has estimated white enrollment decline over such a long period of time. Normally, the estimates are made annually for the years 1968 through 1976. The preponderance of estimates of this type are a function of the availability of data on enrollments, levels of segregation, and so forth. The primary data set (part of which is used in our study) has become known as the Wilson–Taeuber data set because it was compiled by Franklin Wilson and Karl Taeuber of the University of Wisconsin, Madison.
7. Having segregation scores up to 1976 only is not as serious a problem as it seems. Very little desegregation occurred in the United States after 1976. A recent article (Berlowitz and Sapp, 1987) is highly critical of the Taeuber index as a measure of segregation. Three shortcomings are raised: (1) the index may overrepresent the amount of desegregation, (2) it is insensitive to access to quality education, and (3) it ignores second-generation resegregation efforts. The last two criticisms are consistent with our focus on second-generation discrimination.
8. This measure contains both Catholic schools and other private schools that were in existence before desegregation. It also contains those schools that we term

"Honky Christian Academies," schools that were established for the sole purpose of avoiding desegregated public schools.

9. Because our intent in this modeling process is not to explain white flight per se, we will not discuss this model. The one interesting finding, though, concerns private school enrollment because no one has ever included such a variable in a white flight model. The model shows that a 1 percent increase in private school enrollments is associated with a 1.12 percent decline in white public school enrollments.

10. The ideal way to study the use of second-generation techniques to resegregate school would be to measure ability grouping, tracking, and discipline both before and after desegregation. One would expect to find an increase in the technique after desegregation. Unfortunately, such a study is not possible. OCR did not gather any second-generation discrimination data until 1973 and did not gather a complete set of indicators until 1976. Because most school desegregation was implemented before 1976, the before-after comparison cannot be made. We can only argue that, logically, the use of ability grouping, tracking, and discipline cannot have segregative purposes in a segregated school system because a segregated school system does not permit interracial contact.

11. We are aware from anecdotal evidence that some Protestant black parents send their children to Catholic schools in Northern cities. We are also aware that some Catholic schools have made a concerted effort to attract black students by offering scholarships. The overall numbers involved, however, are fairly small.

References

Arnez, Nancy L. 1978. "Implementation of Desegregation as a Discriminatory Process." *Journal of Negro Education* 47:28-45.

Berlowitz, Marvin J., and Martin L. Sap. 1987. "A Critique of the Taeuber Index as a Measure of School Desegregation." *Journal of Negro Education* 56:475-484.

Bullock, Charles S., and Joseph Stewart. 1978. "Complaint Processing as a Strategy for Combating Second Generation Discrimination." Paper presented at the annual meeting of the Southern Political Science Association, Atlanta.

Children's Defense Fund. 1974. *Children Out of School in America*. Washington: Children's Defense Fund of the Washington Research Project.

Cohen, Yinon, and Andrea Tyree. 1986. "Escape From Poverty: Determinants of Intergenerational Mobility of Sons and Daughters of the Poor." *Social Science Quarterly* 67:803-813.

Coleman, James S. 1976. "Liberty and Equality in School Desegregation." *Social Policy* 6:9-13.

Coleman, James S. 1981. "The Role of Incentives in School Desegregation." In Adam Yarmolinsky, Lance Liebman, and Corinne S. Schelling, eds., *Race and Schooling in the City*. Cambridge, MA: Harvard University Press.

Coleman, James S., Sara D. Kelly, and John A. Moore. 1975. *Trends in School Segregation, 1968–73*. Working Paper 722-03-01. Washington: Urban Institute.

Duncan, Greg J. 1984. *Years of Poverty Years of Plenty*. Ann Arbor, MI: Institute for Social Research, University of Michigan.

England, Robert E., and Kenneth J. Meier. 1985. "From Desegregation to Integration: Second Generation Discrimination as an Institutional Impediment." *American Politics Quarterly* 13:227-247.

England, Robert E., and David R. Morgan. 1986. *Desegregating Big City Schools: Strategies, Outcomes, and Impacts*. New York: Associated Faculty Press.

Epstein, Joyce L. 1985. "After the Bus Arrives: Resegregation in Desegregated Schools." *Journal of Social Issues* 41:23-43.

Eyler, Janet, Valerie J. Cook, and Leslie E. Ward. 1983. "Resegregation: Segregation Within Desegregated Schools." In Christine H. Rossell and Willis D. Hawley, eds., *The Consequences of School Desegregation*. Philadelphia: Temple University Press.

Farley, Reynolds. 1975. "Racial Integration in the Public Schools, 1967 to 1972: Assessing the Effects of Governmental Politics." *Sociological Forces* 8:3-26.

Farley, Reynolds, Toni Richards, and Clarence Wurdock. 1980. "School Desegregation and White Flight: An Investigation of Competing Models and Their Discrepant Findings." *Sociology of Education* 53:123-139.

Feagin, Joe R. 1980. "School Desegregation: A Political-Economic Perspective. In Walter G. Stephan and Joe R. Feagan, eds., *School Desegregation: Past, Present and Future*. New York: Plenum Press.

Findley, Warren, and Miriam Bryan. 1975. *The Pros and Cons of Ability Grouping*. Bloomington, IN: Phi Delta Kappa Educational Foundation.

Fraga, Luis R., Kenneth J. Meier, and Robert E. England. 1986. "Hispanic Americans and Educational Policy: Limits to Equal Access." *Journal of Politics* 48:850-876.

Gallagher, James J. 1972. "The Special Education Contract for Mildly Handicapped Children." *Exceptional Children* 38:527-535.

Garrison, Mortimer, and Donald D. Hammill. 1972."Who Are the Retarded?" *Exceptional Children* 38:13-20.

Giles, Micheal W. 1975. "Black Concentration and School District Size as Predictors of School Segregation: The Impact of Federal Enforcement." *Sociology of Education* 48:11-19.

Giles, Micheal, and Douglas S. Gatlin. 1980. "Mass Level Compliance with Public Policy: The Case of School Desegregation." *Journal of Politics* 37:917-36.

Giles, Micheal W., and Arthur S. Evans. 1985. "External Threat, Perceived Threat, and Group Identity." *Social Science Quarterly* 66:50-66.

Giles, Micheal W., and Arthur S. Evans. 1986. "The Power Approach to Intergroup Hostility." *Journal of Conflict Resolution* 30:469-486.

Hochschild, Jennifer L. 1984. *The New American Dilemma: Liberal Democracy and School Desegregation*. New Haven: Yale University Press.

Katzman, Martin T. 1983. "The Flight of Blacks from Central City Public Schools." *Urban Education* 18:259-283.

Meier, Kenneth J., and Robert E. England. 1984. "Black Representation and Educational Policy: Are They Related?" *American Political Science Review* 78:392-403.

Pettigrew, Thomas F., and Robert L. Green. 1976. "School Desegregation in Large Cities: A Critique of the Coleman 'White Flight' Thesis." *Harvard Education Review* 46:1-53.

Rodgers, Harrell R., and Charles S. Bullock. 1972. *Law and Social Change*. New York: McGraw-Hill.

Rodgers, Harrell R., and Charles S. Bullock. 1976. *Coercion to Compliance*. Lexington, MA: D. C. Heath.

Rossell, Christine H. 1978. "Assessing the Unintended Impacts of Public Policy: School Desegregation and Resegregation." Report prepared for the National Institute of Education.

Rossell, Christine H. 1983. "Desegregation Plans, Racial Isolation, White Flight, and Community Response." In Christine H. Rossell and Willis D. Hawley, eds., *The Consequences of School Desegregation*. Philadelphia: Temple University Press.

Smith, James P., and Finis R. Welch. 1986. *Closing the Gap: Forty Years of Economic Progress for Blacks*. Santa Monica, CA: Rand Corporation.

Stewart, Joseph, and Charles S. Bullock. 1981. "Implementation of Equal Education Opportunity Policy." *Administration and Society* 12:427-446.

Taeuber, Karl E., and David R. James. 1982. "Racial Segregation among Public and Private Schools." *Sociology of Education* 55:133-143.

Welch, Finis. 1987. "A Reconsideration of the Impact of School Desegregation Programs on White Public School Enrollment, 1968–1976." *Sociology of Education* 58:215-221.

Willie, Charles V., and Michael Fultz. 1984. "Do Mandatory School Desegregation Plans Foster White Flight?" In Charles V. Willie, ed., *School Desegregation Plans that Work*. Westport, CT: Greenwood Press.

Wilson, Franklin D. 1985. "The Impact of School Desegregation Programs on White Public-School Enrollment, 1968–1976." *Sociology of Education* 58:137-53.

Doin' the Cincinnati
or
What Is There about the White House That Makes Its Occupants Do Bad Things?

Theodore J. Lowi

Cornell University

I wrote the first draft of this article in a frenzy within forty-eight hours of the revelation of the Iran-Contra affair in late November 1986. I revised it shortly after the *Tower Commission Report* but it was too long for current newspaper publication. I decided rather than cut it, I would postpone revisions until more facts were in and then seek to publish it in a more academic journal as an application of my 1985 book, *The Personal President*. When I went back in response to this invitation to revise the article, I found there was nothing to revise in light of the summer's investigations except the verb tenses.

Not long after the 1984 election, it appears that President Reagan had committed himself to certain international goals that (1) were contrary to Reagan's own previously stated and very popular positions; (2) were unpopular with a large segment of the American people as well as Congress; and (3) were in some respects illegal. White House and National Security Council (NSC) staff were acutely aware of Reagan's goals and were convinced that Reagan's goals were consistent with the highest and most vital national interests—laws and public expectations to the contrary notwithstanding. Driven by patriotism and their own sense of what their president wanted, they agreed to take whatever personal risks were necessary to pursue these goals. No matter that their selfish interests might also have been advanced. For example, McFarlane made clear that his vision was far above arms for hostages: Rapprochement with Iran through secret diplomacy was his chance to gain a place in history equal to that paragon of national security advisors—Henry

91

Kissinger. McFarlane himself compares it to China. Freeing hostages would be incidental, merely a way of keeping score. Lt. Col. North also made perfectly clear that hostages were incidental to the much larger goal of making the Contras and all "freedom fighters" a successful part of the Reagan Doctrine through Project Democracy. Casey always operated on the assumption that we were already at war with the Soviet Union. Severe restrictions on the CIA, arising out of Watergate, made it necessary to run this particular operation out of NSC staff. Others, such as Gen. Secord, may have had a stronger pecuniary interest, but their military careers proved beyond doubt that they shared with North and the others a larger vision of America that they felt was being endangered by compromise and confusion.

They all drew inspiration or justification from such conservative luminaries as Whitaker Chambers and Aleksandr Solzhenitsyn as preached by William Buckley, Irving Kristol, Jeanne Kirkpatrick, and others who fear that the West is going to lose to communism not because communism has greater strength or virtue but because the West has become too soft and self-indulgent to put up the right fight and make the appropriate sacrifices. People of the West might eventually be made ready to receive the stronger dose of patriotism. But until then, some things might have to be done secretly *for* the American people, even if not of, by, and with them. This is nicely encapsulated by the title of conservative George Will's book, *Statecraft as Soulcraft*.

Operating with the strong, though implicit, blessing of President Reagan, the main characters of the story—centering on a very junior man in the White House, whom Reagan called a national hero—formed some kind of a group. What kind of group? A conspiracy? A conspiracy is an agreement among two or more people to do something illegal. But *conspiracy* seems inappropriate for the people here, who felt sincerely that they were above the law or that the laws were contrary to the national interest. There is another concept that might better capture the character of the agreement among these people and the network they formed. That concept is the Society of the Cincinnati, and discovery of its revival was especially appropriate during the year of the bicentennial of the American Constitution.

The Cincinnati was an organization of officers of the Revolution, founded in 1783 on the eve of their being sent home at the end of hostilities with Great Britain. The purposes of its formation were both patriotic and pecuniary—to promote national union through perpetual friendship of officers of the American army and "their eldest male posterity" and at the same time to lobby Congress for four years of back pay and for redemption of the promise made by Congress in 1780 for half pay for life for officers who continued in service to the end of the war. They named themselves for Cincinnatus, the patriot who left his plow to save Rome in the fifth century B.C.; their insignia was naturally in Latin, translated as "He relinquished everything to serve the republic." Once the Society of the Cincinnati went public with its commitment to union through an hereditary membership group, it was immediately denounced as an effort to create an American aristocracy and to impose a national system contrary to the spirit of the Articles of Confederation.

Like the original, the new Cincinnati was at its core an organization of officers who refused to be dispersed after the last war, in this case the Vietnam

War. The core of the modern Cincinnati was the middle rank of career military people who felt betrayed by politicians after Vietnam and were inspired by Reagan's effort to ennoble not only the Vietnam participants but the war itself. Generating outward from this core group and their White House cubby were the more senior officers, many of whom were forcibly and prematurely mustered out because of their dissenting views during the more pacifist presidencies of the 1970s. This punishment was surely an inspiration to their successors. These military officers were joined by two sets of civilian officers: the civilian staff people of roughly equal rank in State and Defense, equally if not more intensely inspired by neoconservatism. Significant examples are Elliott Abrams and Richard Perle. A second group of officers were intelligence officers, especially in the CIA, who had felt alienated and circumscribed as early as Watergate and the Church Committee investigations. Then there were at least two important sources of membership outside the government altogether. The first of these is the neoconservative intellectuals—many of whom had themselves once been of the far Left. A second group is an indeterminate number of capitalists who have been willing quietly (and sometimes noisily, like Ross Perot) to subscribe to what is now being called the "privatization of foreign policy." Some of these private capitalists are of course not U.S. citizens, and yet they shared top secret and extremely sensitive information that ordinarily requires highest security clearance *plus* the "need to know." Although a mixed bag, the dominating force of the new Cincinnati was, from the start, the group of middle-level career military and civilian officers in the government, operating out of the White House.

Although middle in rank and status, this inner core of the new Cincinnati enjoyed great power through their access to the higher circles and through their greater dedication to Reagan's go-it-alone conservative foreign policy. Like the butler reminding his lordship of his place and duties, so these middle folk were able to shame the less dedicated into submission and permissiveness—with Ollie North behind John Poindexter running a fantastic network of international gun running, with Richard Perle managing a large chunk of the key elements of the defense budget, with Elliott Abrams colonizing Central America policy, and Robert McFarlane dominating a momentarily emergent Iran policy. (It is hard to resist the hypothesis that McFarlane left the government in order to have a freer hand to manage this aspect of the president's policies.)

But it is not their individual dedication that counts; what is significant is their togetherness in a new Cincinnati society and their achievement: a coup d'etat that almost succeeded—to control and reorient U.S. policy toward two highly sensitive and strategic regions and, through that, to rededicate overall American foreign policy toward the bipolar definition of the world from which we had departed (or retreated) after Vietnam and after the belated discovery that China is not a Soviet satellite. For them, the world may be objectively multipolar, but it is morally bipolar.

If the new Cincinnati has not as yet been recognized as a coup d'etat plot, it is only because we generally define coup d'etat as an effort to replace an existing ruling group with an entirely new ruling group. But there can be other kinds, such as a partial or specialized coup d'etat, where only one domain or region is taken over. We also know from Latin American experience that one part of the government, especially the military, can stage a coup against another part of the government. And we know from Chinese experience that a coup d'etat can be staged by an existing regime against part of its own governing apparatus. That is exactly what Mao tried to do when he unleashed the Cultural Revolution. Watergate itself can be understood as revelation of a coup by President Nixon's own group of plumbers and others against those parts of the government thought to be out of control or less than loyal to what President Nixon was trying to achieve. In this respect, the Cincinnati coup of 1985–87 is shockingly like the Nixon coup to the extent that a White House-centered group took over a large chunk of foreign policy without the knowledge of, and once discovered, against the wishes of other less ideological parts of the national government.

It is almost certain that President Reagan was ignorant of the Contra diversion. But it was planned ignorance, not the genuine ignorance implied by the criticisms of Reagan's co-called mismanagement. Many lies were exposed in the investigation, and there will be other lies before the affair is over. But probably the biggest lie of all was "presidential mismanagement." At best, mismanagement was a gigantic plea bargain: The president agreed to plead guilty of mismanagement if all other charges were dropped. This helps explain why many of President Reagan's allies were so quick to jump on him with what appeared to be such a severe criticism. But genuine conservatives have a very interesting attitude toward government, which is that the system ought to be protected virtually at all cost. Thus, if a lie must be told to defend the legitimacy and stability of the system, then it is, with Plato, a Noble Lie, and is justified. Confessing to the lesser truth of mismanagement can actually strengthen the system if it hides a greater truth that might tend to undermine that system. If the Reagan administration learned anything from President Nixon's tragedy, it is the virtue of planned ignorance.

The payoff for the new Cincinnati would have been success for the Reagan Doctrine in general, proof that a go-it-alone anticommunist foreign policy could accomplish more than a weak and confused approach through diplomacy, and, in the short run, it would help to maintain President Reagan's unprecedentedly high presidential approval ratings. The risks in life and sacred honor and, one has to add, mental health were worth taking.

The coup failed, and the Cincinnati was exposed, but no thanks to the alleged genius of American political institutions. The coup was actually foiled by the Iranians themselves with a leak to a Lebanese magazine. Irancon is a triumph of Iranian foreign policy. The Iranians sandbagged the Cincinnati and through that, America. Iranians apparently understand the American system much better than the Cincinnati understood the Iranians. Taking advantage of the pressure they know our president is under to produce palpable results for the American public, the Iranians drew the new Cincinnati into covert negotiations, holding out the three carrots of a China-type rapprochement, the release of hostages, and a flow of profit to divert to the Contras. Once the Cincinnati were in beyond the point of secret withdrawal and deniability (McFarlane apparently smelled a rat, but too late), the Iranians sprung the trap. Their success will be measured not only in Reagan's personal humiliation but in the significant reduction of American effectiveness as a peace force in the Middle East. And the Ayatollah deserves the Machiavelli award for the decade's most crafty diplomatic maneuver.

The silver lining is that the Iranian victory over America may have contributed to victory *for* America over the new Cincinnati society. But it will not be a lasting victory unless we recognize that the Iran–Contra affair and the new Cincinnati are reflections of a constitutional problem: What is there about the White House that makes its occupants do bad things? Pressure to produce results for the American people has made diplomacy and the presidency natural enemies. Each recent president has been pushed close to or over the brink of personal disgrace by one or more efforts to directly alter the history of a weak country that we have the military power to wipe out but lack the power to change. The evil here is not covert activity as such. There is ample constitutional justification for covert activity in foreign affairs, when that covert activity is duly constituted. But when it is duly constituted, it is called diplomacy!

As long as our system depends upon a presidency that requires a regular flow of international results, presidents will seek to short-circuit the slow-moving, bureaucratized diplomatic corps. That will require covert action by a rump group, and cooperation with such a group will leave the president vulnerable to true believers that are willing to put their own beliefs above the national and international procedures whose very purpose is to reduce the violence potential of intense ideologies. Procedures exist as protection against all mullahs, whether they are dressed in black or olive drab, speak Farsi or English, are bearded or clean shaven. Most of the fanatics who do not inhabit Teheran inhabit Washington. Orderly diplomacy is our protection against fanatics, wherever they are.

The Iran–Contra Hearings and Executive Policymaking

Francis E. Rourke

The Johns Hopkins University

Since World War II, much of what has happened in executive policymaking in the United States—especially in foreign affairs—has been shielded from public view by what organization theorists like to refer to with academic elegance as "information screens" but what the rest of the world more commonly thinks of as government secrecy. Events such as the Iran–Contra hearings in 1987 are thus very revealing episodes in American political life, and it is reasonable to expect that, in the years to come, the record of these hearings will greatly enrich our understanding of the way in which the American political system really functioned in the twilight of the twentieth century.

One point that these hearings made graphically clear is that executive officials may be as much the victims of the system of secrecy that they have created since World War II as are the members of Congress and the public from whom they are trying to withhold information. Poetic justice thus strikes again. The measures taken in the postwar era that expand the range of government secrecy—including the president's claim of executive privilege, the military's classification system, and the exemption provisions permitting secrecy that are enshrined in the Freedom of Information statutes—have been regarded in the past as devices by which executive officials enjoy privileged access to information denied to legislators and ordinary citizens. But as the hearings frequently demonstrated, the system of secrecy now in place can also keep executive officials in the dark about what the government is doing in their own area of central responsibility.

Or so at least the testimony at these hearings by Secretary of State George Shultz and Secretary of Defense Caspar Weinberger would suggest. In a set of hearings marked by bizarre disclosures, nothing was more startling than the revelation that the two cabinet members most directly concerned with making and carrying out national security policy in the United States were themselves deceived with respect to major innovations in American policy toward both

Iran and Central America by White House staff members. Equally striking was Secretary Weinberger's candid disclosure that his own knowledge of the sale of arms to Iran came from a report by an intelligence agency of a foreign country.

An optimist might conclude from this episode that as cabinet members begin to see that the practice of withholding information can be highly disadvantageous for them, they will become less sturdy in their defense of such secrecy. Conceivably, they might even become sympathetic to the more open style of government that the Freedom of Information acts were designed to achieve. But a more pessimistic scenario is also plausible. Cabinet officials may simply conclude that the lesson of the hearings is that they need to beef up their intelligence capability so as to gain access to covert information that is being concealed by other organizations within the executive apparatus.

The hearings could also be said to have contributed to open government by demonstrating to presidents that invoking executive privilege to protect their secrets is not nearly as essential to the White House as many chief executives have argued in the past, and that a presidential policy of *glastnost* may also have its advantages. Before the hearings began President Reagan waived the executive privilege he might otherwise have claimed on the basis of the Supreme Court's decision in *United States v. Nixon*.[1] This Court decision gave legitimate status to executive privilege, even as it disallowed Nixon's attempt to claim such a privilege by denying judicial access to his tapes. Instead, Reagan allowed his White House subordinates to testify freely about their role in the affair. Although much of their testimony was not very flattering to the president, his openness in this regard contrasted favorably with Nixon's vain effort to use executive privilege to conceal incriminating evidence in the Watergate scandal.

What the Iran–Contra hearings also demonstrated was the extent to which the growing power and prominence of the White House staff in executive policymaking has engendered a defensive alliance between the cabinet and congressional committees against a presidential entourage that they have both come to regard as a common enemy. Unfortunately, however, for the partners in this alliance, developments in the executive branch since the hearings were concluded also suggest that White House organizations can quickly bounce back from setbacks like the Iran–Contra affair.

Certainly, this affair brought great discredit to the NSC staff organization. The agency was tainted with the stigma of having been involved in flagrantly illegal activity. It had provided financial and other assistance to the Nicaraguan Contras in defiance of legislation enacted by Congress prohibiting such support. However, NSC staff members repeatedly lied to Congress about the extent of the agency's support for the Contras. They also participated in the delivery of missiles to Iran in clear contradiction to the Reagan administration's stated policy (which it had asked European powers to support) of not selling arms to a country it had labeled a terrorist nation. Worst of all perhaps, these covert activities by the NSC staff did not secure their ostensible objective—the release of the American hostages held by groups believed to be under Iranian influence if not control.

So in the wake of the Iran–Contra hearings in 1987, the National Security Council organization appeared to be in total disgrace "with fortune and men's eyes." And yet, only a few weeks after the conclusion of the hearings, the secretary of state and his aides were fretting in public and about the fact that members of the NSC staff were still playing an operational rather than their traditional coordinating role in the conduct of foreign affairs. This, in spite of the fact that the Tower Commission, appointed by President Reagan to investigate the Iran–Contra affair, had severely criticized the NSC organization for its direct involvement in national security operations.[2]

The chief target of this State Department criticism was Frank J. Carlucci, who had succeeded John M. Poindexter as head of the NSC staff after Poindexter resigned when the Iran–Contra affair first came into public view. State Department officials charged that Carlucci "usurped a traditional State Department mission when he carried out high-level consultations in West European capitals earlier this month" and that "the NSC staff has continued to overstep its bounds by meeting with ambassadors from foreign nations." Practices such as these, the State Department alleged, sow "confusion abroad about who is responsible for foreign policy."[3] So the relationship between the State Department and the NSC staff in the wake of the Iran–Contra affair bore a strong resemblance to the uneasy coexistence that had prevailed prior to that time.

Not only in the case of the State Department–NSC relationship but in a more general way, the Iran–Contra hearings showed how career bureaucrats can now be shunted aside in the framing of an administration's major policy decisions. During the hearings, career officials in both the CIA and the military establishment testified that they had either been ignored or their advice disregarded in the process through which the Administration reached its fateful policy decision. Indeed, the picture that emerged in the area of intelligence was that of bureaucrats being used merely to "cook" data to support the decisions that their political superiors were determined to make. For example, to justify its sale of arms to the Iranians, the White House solicited data that would show that Iran was currently losing its war with Iraq, in the face of an existing consensus within the professional intelligence community that it was Iraq that was in greater danger of defeat.

In this setting, the easiest way for a career official to acquire influence was to move from his or her bureaucratic niche to a position in the presidential entourage. This was the path to real power traveled by both Admiral John Poindexter and Lieutenant Colonel Oliver North, who on the record at least were the principal agents for the Iran–Contra strategy. As bureaucrats they would at best have played only a peripheral role in executive policymaking. As presidential aides, they ascended to positions where, according to their own testimony at least, they ran operations designed to achieve goals that were at the top of the president's agenda.

The Iran–Contra experience thus confirmed two trends that have become increasingly visible in executive operations in recent years: first, the dominance of the political over the bureaucratic sector in executive policymaking, and second, the tendency of presidents to rely on their White House staff rather than cabinet officials for the achievement of goals to which they are most deeply attached—what might be called the chief executive's personal as opposed to his official agenda.

Moreover, the fact that President Reagan relied primarily upon White House officials with a military background to carry out as risky an enterprise as the Iran–Contra initiative is not without a significance of its own. Both North and Poindexter remained steadfastly loyal to Reagan throughout an investigative process that must have been for them a very painful experience. Their fidelity was in stark contrast to the behavior of many of President Nixon's civilian aides during the Watergate episode, who sought to distance themselves from the president and his troubles, or even, as in John Dean's case, to give evidence against him. The lesson future chief executives may well read from the Iran–Contra affair may thus be the fact that the most unswerving loyalty they can expect from their White House staff will come from military aides who look upon the president as their commander-in-chief.

Finally, the Iran–Contra affair demonstrates once again, like Vietnam and Watergate before it, that, although the institution of the presidency has prospered and grown ever more powerful in modern American politics, presidents themselves continue to live a highly precarious existence. Prior to Reagan, this seemed to be true of all modern presidents, save perhaps for Dwight D. Eisenhower. As the powers of their office grew, their own fortunes seemed to decline. For much of his administration, Ronald Reagan seemed to have escaped this image of failure that plagued his predecessors. But as the Iran–Contra hearings progressed, it became clear that he too had fallen victim to the same fate. Reagan's term in office was widely perceived as having invigorated the presidency, but, as it neared its end, his own standing as president had come to rest on increasingly shaky ground. Thus, in Reagan's as in other cases, the apparent powers of the presidency create great expectations that individual presidents find it very hard to fulfill.

Notes

1. *United States v. Nixon*, 94 S. Ct. 3090 (1974).
2. See *The Tower Commission Report* (New York: Bantam Books and Times Books, 1987), p. 92.
3. See *New York Times*, August 26, 1987, p. 1.

Congress on the Defensive: An Hypothesis from the Iran–Contra Problem

Matthew Holden, Jr.

University of Virginia

D avid B. Truman said, some years ago, that "the 20th century has not been kind to legislatures." Congress is fundamentally on the defensive, in the face of a determined executive, when the claim of national security is presented. Nothing demonstrates this better than the travail of Congress in the face of the Iran–Contra problem.[1] In 1986, it became known that the United States had carried on discussions with officials of the Iranian government, a government the president had previously stigmatized as "terrorist." Those discussions entailed the transfer of certain weaponry, from American stores directly or from stores previously made available to Israel. In due course, it also became apparent that the operations involved efforts to supply the anti-government forces in Nicaragua, the Contras, using revenues from the sale of arms to the Iranians. Predictably, under the American constitutional system, a large and controversial action by the executive precipitated a congressional investigation.[2] Predictably, as well, the committees split in their report. The majority consisted of the Democrats, both Senate and House, and two Republican senators. The minority consisted of the House Republicans and the other two Republican senators.[3] At the end of the investigation, the Iran–Contra committees (from the Senate and from the House) either failed to see the essence or failed to declare it. The majority recommendations from the Iran–Contra investigations are extensive, and directed to a variety of procedural constraints upon presidential decision-making or decision-making in the name of the president. They deal primarily with findings, reports to Congress on a timely basis, "privatization," covert actions by other countries at the behest of an American agency, the organization of congressional oversight, and cognate matters.[4] The recommendations can, on their face, be evaluated fully only by those with detailed knowledge of the intelligence operation as it now exists. The majority report concludes that the affair "resulted from the failure of individuals to observe the law, not from deficiencies in existing law or in our system of governance.[5]

In one critical respect, it is precisely in the system of governance that the difficulty lies. Congress is potentially powerful but has found no means yet for a regular and responsible exercise of its power. *The American president, if willing to take the political risk, can exercise vast power to create, control, and restrict information, to commit forces, and to create conditions under which money will have to be spent.* The ease with which the members of the White House staff and their allies outside carried out their preferences makes it credible to believe that the *working* system tends to be closer to the Poindexter–North practice than the overt theory of political science or the conclusions of the committees might suggest. Congress is on the defensive. It is the victim of a structural weakening that long has been in process.

The Constitutional Structure

The logic of the constitutional structure requires joint action of president and Congress. Congress was given the power to declare war, which is to say to choose whether there would be war. Congress was given the power to raise armies and to provide and maintain a navy. Congress, moreover, was granted the power of appropriating funds, subject to the restriction that appropriations could not be made for longer than two years. Congress was also granted still other powers to define and punish piracies and offenses against laws of nations, grant letters of marque, make rules concerning captures, provide and maintain a navy, and make rules for the government of land and naval forces. Article II provides for the president in whom is vested "the executive power," who is made commander-in-chief of the army, and who is given power, by and with the advice and consent of the Senate, to make treaties and to receive ambassadors.

The rationale was to ensure that, in the fortunes of the United States, no one man should have the power to take the nation to war.[6] In contemporary terms, no president (or set of presidential subordinates) should have the ability purposefully to preempt or negate congressional consideration of the most important choices facing the country. Nor should a president (or set of presidential subordinates) have the effective ability to pursue a secret policy, financed outside the appropriations process.

The provisions of Article I and Article II exist today, not a syllable or punctuation mark altered from what they were to begin with. Admiral Poindexter and Colonel North, with many others, argue that the constitutional system assumes the "primacy" of the president. There should be little restraint on the president and, by extension, on those who act for the president. That argument's roots lie in Alexander Hamilton's "Pacificus" doctrine, a concept of "the executive power" substantially akin to what is "the royal prerogative" in English law.[7] The Supreme Court has given voice to the assertion that the president is the "sole organ" of the United States in foreign relations.[8] Even now, however, the Court has not imposed prerogative upon its interpretation of the president's powers. In the Iranian assets case, Chief Justice Rehnquist emphasized, quoting Justice Jackson, "the poverty of really useful and unambiguous authority applicable to concrete problems of executive power as they actually present themselves."[9]

The fact is that Admiral Poindexter and Colonel North did act *as if* "Pacificus" were American law. They did so with whatever degree of personal knowledge and assent from the president and with more knowledge and perception than cabinet-level officers at first admitted. The ease with which they did so makes it credible to believe the *working system* is closer to the Poindexter–North practice than might at first appear.

Alterations of the Real Constitution

Donald Robinson has perceptively discussed the manner in which the operating environment has substantially negated those constitutional provisions to which most attention normally has been paid.[10] The necessities of the time have, since the Korean War, been broadly agreed to require a large military establishment, long lead times for weapons development, and multiyear financial commitments.[11] Such changes lend some *practical* credence to the "primacy" argument. Moreover, the Iran–Contra problem is a struggle between different interests motivated more to dictate to each other than to bargain with each other in the hope of reaching a settlement. The people who favored the Contras had an absolute moral unwillingess to accept policy defeat. So also did those who opposed them. This sharp cleavage, found in the executive and on the Hill, was similar to the cleavages often been associated with American wars. In this case, the dispute merely extends to another country's war—and to the fear of some that the United States might ultimately be engaged in war.[12] There was one coalition that played *through* the president, his subordinates, and his agents and allies.

This was composed of the sponsors of the "private" aid to the Contras, or of private interest in Iran. Some, of course, were little more private than "The Equalizer." "Anticommunism," *as they understand* it, is as important as antislavery was to the Massachusetts backers of John Brown. They give signals of rejecting, as a legitimate idea for policy consideration, the positions taken by a large part of the population as embodied in the House Democratic caucus. In this struggle, the president himself appears to have become—predictably—a committed participant. Closed decision making was the natural result.

Closed decision making meant that the Congress was told what the president (or his subordinates) wanted known and when he (or they) wanted it known. Closed decision making was combined with greater control, by those who spoke for the president, over the details of administrative compliance within the executive branch. The course of action was possible because the real Constitution has been changed by technology. In each generation since the Civil War, presidents, and their immediate entourages, have had greater ability than their predecessors to exercise direct and immediate control on any particular policy or action item that they might choose to target. Abraham Lincoln could communicate his thoughts directly to his generals by the telegraph. He could not confirm that they had received his messages. Nor could he know, necessarily, why they did not respond immediately, or what they were doing in compliance. The telephone became available to President McKinley. Each administrative actor can know what the other has said, almost instantaneously. It did not follow that administrative compliance down the line was assured. Radio, teletype, and the computerized facilities of our own time allow greater and greater possibilities of what come formally to be called "command and control."

If this concept began with nuclear defense, it need not be so restricted now.[13] The president, or those who choose to act under claim of his authority, has the technological ability to follow up immediately on previous orders and to secure immediately a response indicating what has been done in compliance. The very existence of "PROF notes" is indicative of the hypothesis.[14] Without the technology, the activities of Colonel North would have been far less feasible because he would have been unable to act in real time, whereas the Congress was precluded from knowing in real time what he was doing. It is the physical technology of communication that gives such enormously greater possibilities of coordination within the executive, when someone is highly motivated to coordinate. The effectiveness of North depended precisely on his ability to coordinate those whom he needed and to preclude all knowledge on the part of those who did not have access to his message network. Without this enhanced technology, the activities of North would have been far less feasible.

Why Congress Is on the Defensive

Congress has found no means yet for a regular and responsible activation of its potential power. The constitutional language and the nineteenth-century history of Congress, jointly, provide a basis for reasoned claims far stronger than any the Congress now appears to make. Members of Congress are politicians. They know how to make claims. If they do not make claims, it is because they are reluctant or afraid to so or because they do not think it is right and proper to do so. Both factors are at work.

Three Pragmatic Factors

Congressional hesitation is grounded in at least three pragmatic or structural features.

Information is expensive in time and effort, as well as money. Effective Congressional intervention presupposes considerable information. Information requires intense effort, and effort is costly. Whenever substantial constituency demand is absent, the tendency of the Congress is to allow itself to be served, to an extraordinary degree, by trivial matters masquerading as "data," "studies," and "information." If there are no well-defined constituencies with good information and good support, as is likely to be the case on purely "political" matters, then the administrative "stonewalling" is much more likely to be effective. Congressional power centers generally are well-informed on weapons systems issues, though they are far more technical than the substance of foreign political issues. There are constituencies, outside the government and inside, with every interest in keeping members of Congress well informed. The very fact that the complex of activities examined in the hearings this summer could occur, over an extended period, without any substantial suspicion being generated and made the target of inquiry, indicates the problem. If the degree and character of oversight in defense, for example, were present in the national security political matters, the Iran–Contra Affair should never have occurred as it did. Members would have been given reason for much more than vague suspicion, simply in virtue of the intense, normal transactions between oversight committee members, their staffs, and the executive agencies.[15]

The appropriations power has proved, in recent times, substantially ineffectual. In the Federal Convention of 1787, there was an elaborate theory of the separation of the purse and the sword.[16] Edward Gibbon wrote, in 1776, that the"obvious definition of monarchy seems to be that of a state, in which a single person, by whatsoever name he may be distinguished, is entrusted with the execution of the laws, the management of the revenue, and the command of the army."[17] The "management of the revenue," in Gibbon's words, was separated from the immediate control of the army. So much of that has changed in the interim. Congress yielded over control of departmental estimates in the nineteenth century.[18] It turned over still more by the Budget and Accounting Act of 1921. Finally, the natural implication of multiyear commitments, for defense planning, reduces the range of congressional control still further. The appropriations tool is seldom available, in practice. Congress, even when a majority is opposed to the president, frequently cannot act against the president in military matters. If the president has sent ships somewhere and Congress generally believes they ought not to be there, withholding funds merely imposes pain upon the sons and daughters of its constituents, and even Congress's own sons and daughters.

The President always has agents in Congress, as the eighteenth century king always had agents in Parliament. Their mission, in their own political interest, is to see that Congress supports the president. Failing that, their mission is to shield the president. The minority report on the Iran–Contra hearings expressed the same purpose of shielding the president: "It is important at the outset . . . to note that the President himself has already taken the hard step of acknowledging his mistakes and reacting precisely to correct what went wrong. . . . The bottom line . . . is that the mistakes of the Iran–Contra Affair were just that—mistakes in judgment, and nothing more."[19] The tenor of the minority report is that the Iran–Contra Affair would not have occurred except for failures on the part of Congress that the president's subordinates had to act to compensate. Moreover, the minority report's five recommendations, with one exception, all are predicated upon increasing the discretion and control of the president.[20]

If Congress (meaning the dominant coalition therein) were to make stronger claims, self-evidently the president's agents and allies would resist. The issue would then become a major public opinion issue. The public debate would require the congressional coalition to challenge existing cultural and psychological predicates.

Two Cultural Psychological Factors

Congressional action is impeded by cultural values and psychological dispositions in the body politic. Congress disbelieves in itself and believes in presidential leadership. Within the last hundred years, higher education and political journalism have shaped a culture in which presidents automatically are respected and Congress is not. Every one who has gone to college since Woodrow Wilson's *Congressional Government* was popular has moved in an intellectual stream where presidential leadership *over* Congress was deemed the advanced and praiseworthy thing. Every one who has gone to college in that period has also learned that there was something bad about the strong position of the nineteenth-century Congress.

Congress *is* afraid to be accused of weakening the office of president. It stands intellectually naked and, apparently, psychologically naked. Congress itself is more or less representative and shares the underlying values of other Americans. "The president," abstractly taken, is a favorable symbol. "Congress," abstractly speaking, is an ambiguous symbol. Observe that there Mark Twain, Will Rogers, and the late-night comics had or have jokes about the ludicrousness of "Congress" and of *particular* presidents. There are no generic president jokes. Political scientists say that, in public opinion polls, people regularly give a low rating to Congress and a high rating to their member of Congress. I take this to be an indication of ambiguity. The public at large, I hazard, does not want Congress to have a capacity to override a determined president, unless convinced that that particular president has done something virtually criminal.

Everyone has also learned that "decision making by committee" is either inefficient or impossible. Moreover, one can observe the distaste for debate and discussion—"make up your mind!"—that is reflected in the television news language. A simple count of the number of times the word "bickering" appears when there is a serious issue, as if there were an obvious right answer to be gotten easily by any person of good morals and good intelligence. The legislative process, which must aggregate conflicting interests before a decision can be reached, is held in some disdain, and, by contrast, clarity is valued. Witness the dramatic response to the testimony of Colonel North.

There is, I suggest, a still deeper aspect. The presidential office benefits from politics as theater. Politics as theater relieves boredom and frustration, both practical and moral, and gives symbolic expression to people's deep *feelings*. That may be why crowds would shout, "Give 'em hell, Harry," even when the election results show that a good many of those shouting must have voted against him. The president's aspiration to do what is *right*, if the president makes clear that is what he wants, will be respected, even if not venerated. The presidential office benefits, as well, when the citizen turns from politics as theater to politics as serious business. Indeed, the Iran–Conra Affair ought to direct political psychologists from the surface "white caps" of momentary opinion to the deep currents of values and visceral "feelings." I suggest that the citizen has incorporated values closely akin to a profound distrust of self, if not indeed "self-hatred." The citizen knows that Congress, more or less, is representative of himself or herself. Congress is "a bunch of people" more or less like himself or herself. May there not be disenchantment in that very thought? He or she distrusts his or her own judgment or capacity. He or she wants an opinion and even wants to be gratified. But when judgment is called for, he or she looks for the statesman.

Conclusion

In summary, I propose as an hypothesis that interpretations of the Iran–Contra Affair, separate from the system of governance, are overoptimistic. The operating environment has substantially negated those constitutional provisions to which most attention normally has been paid. The constitutional language and the nineteenth-century history of Congress, jointly, permit far stronger claims than the Congress now appears to make. The natural implication is that "presidential responsibility" is a phrase with little, if any, external meaning. There were necessarily painful questions to ask about the performance of "this president," to use the phrase that so often emanates from executive subordinates. The ultimate conclusion, however, is that there is no mode of enforcing responsibility, short of the doubtful instrument of impeachment.

There is no reason, however, to think that the normal workings of the world will stop. We may expect intensely motivated presidents and even more intensely motivated entourages. We may expect political resistance in Congress. We should also ask, without that assumption, necessarily, how the country may approach other versions of the Iran–Contra problem that will present themselves again within the next ten or so years. We may expect highly controversial international problems in the near future—as in South Africa. Decision making in such matters may pose some of the more critical constitutional problems of the decade.

Notes

1. This paper is based upon notes for presentation at the Lawn Society, University of Virginia, November 14, 1987. I have advanced some of the argument in a preliminary format in "The Twenty Person Government," a discussion paper directed to the Board of Directors, Committee on the Constitutional System, December 1986; *Bargaining and Command in the Administrative Process*: I, Charlottesville: Institute of Government, University of Virginia, Working Papers in Public Administration, No. 3, September 1986; and "Iran–Contra Debacle No Fluke; Fault Is in the Constitutional Balances" (op-ed), *Newport News Daily Press*, Sunday, February 22, 1987, I3.

   I have not yet advanced this line of argument in full scholarly form, though part of its conceptual basis, so far as relations between chief executives and their own subordinates are concerned, will be presented in *The Mechanisms of Power* (in preparation for publication by the University of Pittsburgh Press).

   As these matters easily become both normative and emotional, I should be explicit. This note does not imply an invidious comparison with some other real-world, large-scale, nation-state. If necessary, I would state that the inquiry recently conducted yields a superior result to that likely in the Western democracies, where such inquiry would not be tolerated. (Consider, for example, the manner in which the British have avoided public inquiry into allegations that high ranking officers of the security and military services had conspired to displace the prime minister.) I would state, but cannot argue here, my disagreement with those of our colleagues, especially in international politics, who tend to impose a kind of "realpolitik" and advise us as to how Europeans are "mystified" and think the inquiry trivial. Europeans may think the question of how power is allocated in the

United States trivial, but then they have always done so—which may say something about various experiences in European politics. In *The Mechanisms of Power*, I shall have something further to say on why even the most respected European models may not be very convincing.

2. *Report of the Congressional Committees Investigating the Iran–Contra Affair: With Supplemental, Minority, and Additional Views. November 1987 (H. Report #100-433: S. Rept. #100-216).* Washington: Government Printing Office, 1987, p. 423.

3. There were, as well, a variety of individual and additional reports.

4. Ibid., pp. 423–28.

5. Ibid., pp. 428.

6. James D. Weaver, "The Commander in Chief: Constitutional Foundations," in Gordon R. Hoxie et al. (eds.), *The Presidency and National Security Policy*, New York: Center for the Study of the Presidency, 1984, especially at 249–52. Weaver's article is closely written and deserves close attention.

7. Hamilton defended President Washington's Neutrality Proclamation, which seemed to violate treaty obligations to France. Some thought the proclamation rather suspect because France was not only a treaty ally but had more or less paid the bills for the American Revolution. More critically, from a constitutional standpoint, the proclamation seemed to violate the rights of Congress to make that judgment. James Madison was solicited by Thomas Jefferson to take up the other side of the argument and cut Hamilton to pieces. Madison's arguments, much less well advertised among contemporary scholars, are in the "Helvidius" papers. They may be found together in *The Letters of Pacificus and Helvidius (1845) with the Letters of Americanus*, A Facsimile Reproduction with an Introduction by Richard Loss. Delmar, NY: Scholars' Facsimile & Reprints, 1976.

8. The two major cases are *Curtiss-Wright Export Corp. v. U. S.* (299 U.S. 304, 1935), with an opinion by Justice Sutherland; and *Dames & Moore v. Regan, Secretary of the Treasury* (453 U.S. 654, 1981), with an opinion by Chief Justice Rehnquist. Justice Sutherland apparently had spent many years forming his views on the question. Those views are criticized severely in an article that political scientists and current policymakers might well ponder. There is a sharp criticism of the Sutherland view in an article in the *Yale Law Journal*, some time in the later 1940s, but I cannot locate it at present. *Curtiss-Wright*, a delegation of powers issue, where the President was acting under a statute, and *Dames & Moore* involved a "taking of property" issue in connection with the Iranian assets problem.

9. 453 *U. S.* 660. Indeed, I am struck with the caution in Chief Justice Rehnquist's choice of language. These issues will, of course, be presented much more directly, if the Court takes up suits brought by members of Congress, against President Reagan, because of the president's refusal to use the War Powers Resolution. The Court could do a variety of things, including refusing to take the case. It might also decide the case on "legislative veto" grounds, following *INS v. Chadha*, or on "sole organ" grounds, following *Curtiss-Wright*. What theory the Court will adopt, I am not equipped to guess. However, as a value judgment, I should have preferred the Democratic members to stay out of the Court and to pursue a political strategy.

10. Donald Robinson made this argument with with great clarity at a conference on the Constitution, under the auspices of Project '87, at the National Center for State Courts, Williamsburg, Virginia, October 10, 1987. The conference was transcribed, and I presume the transcripts of that conference are in the custody of Project '87, 1527 New Hampshire Avenue, N.W., Washington, D.C. 20036.

11. James Canan, *War in Space*. (New York: Harper & Row, 1982).

12. "Politics stops at the water's edge" to the contrary notwithstanding, wars have generally been divisive in the United States. Some have been divisive before their initiation, and others have been divisive because of forces they set in motion. The roots of the party system lay, to a very large extent, in different approaches to the wars that rolled out of the French Revolution. The United States has been engaged in eight major wars since the Revolution. (By these, I refer to the War of 1812, the Mexican War, the Civil War, the Spanish-American War (1898), World War I (1917–18), World War II (1941–45), the Korean War (1950–53), and the Viet Nam War (1965–75). The years in parentheses show official American participation in wars that began, with the exception of the Korean War, well before the United States was officially involved.) Each has been divisive either in inception or in consequence.

This was so even in the nineteenth century when, according to Eliot Janeway, war was also an instrument of prosperity in the country, in contrast to recent war and mobilization that, he says, was a source of cost to the country. Eliot Janeway, *The Economics of Crisis: War, Politics, and the Dollar.* (New York: Weybright and Talley, 1968).

13. I am grateful to the anonymous reviewer who objected that Colonel North's activities had nothing to do with nuclear weaponry, etc., because the objection forces a clarification. Nothing in this paper suggests that he had. It is correct that the term arose in that connection. However, the principles entailed have far broader organizational ramifications and are so recognized by some. See Judith Merkle, *Command and Control: The Social Implications of Nuclear Defense.* (New York: General Learning Press, 1971). The "control" function "refers to a continual monitoring of the effects of command by overtly recognized and explicitly designed feedback mechanisms." If that concept is taken as stated, its ramifications clearly go beyond the big weapons scene. Moreover, I began to think about this when I circulated a series of papers relating to the triangular relationships of chief executives, executive entourage, and departmental leadership and found one of my colleagues with a military background referring to them as "your papers on command and control."

14. The report devotes a certain amount of space to its effort at computer analysis, and in its citations defines the PROF notes of which I, at any rate, had not heard before the inquiry began. "PROF Notes. Messages generated on a computer system used by the National Security Council staff. The exact time and date of the message are recorded." *Iran–Contra Affair,* p. xiv.

15. For one illustration of the close exchanges between members of the staffs and the agencies, see Canan, *War in Space,* on George Norris, Don Lynch, and Anthony Battista, three staff members who exercised a profound influence on naval programs and with whom people kept in day-to-day touch. For a second illustration see the discussion by Bob Woodward, *Veil* (New York: Simon and Shuster, 1987), on the role of the Senate Intelligence Committee leadership in choosing the number two person in the Central Intelligence Agency. Woodward describes at some length the demands of the Senate leadership for the choice of Admiral Bobby Ray Inman as deputy director. On my own responsibility, I assert that it is inconceivable that, when energy was a high-priority policy issue, such complicated transactions would have gone on without someone informing Congressman John Dingell. Why should the relationships involving the Iran–Contra problem have been different?

16. Weaver, "The Commander in Chief," has a helpful discussion.

17. Edward Gibbon, *The Decline and Fall of the Roman Empire.* (New York: Modern Library, n.d., 52).

18. Leonard D. White, *The Jacksonians: A Study of Administrative History, 1829–1961.* (New York: Macmillan, 1954).

19. *Iran–Contra Affair*, p. 437.

20. Ibid., p. 583. The sole exception is their recommendation that, in certain circumstances, the president should notify the speaker and the house minority leader and the senate majority leader and senate minority leader. It would drop any expectation of notifying the chairman and ranking minority member of the two intelligence committees.

The Iran–Contra Affair: Errant Globalism in Action

Ernest J. Wilson, III

University of Michigan–Ann Arbor

Metaphors of forests and trees come to mind when one considers the conduct of the Iran–Contra hearings and the public commentary on them. Much of the media coverage and the questions of the congressmen emphasized the details and technicalities of law and the administration of foreign policy. Far more disturbing, I will argue, are the profound defects in the fundamental conception of foreign policy by this administration that were so painfully revealed through these hearings. Although especially egregious under President Reagan, these flaws are not unique to him or his administration.

Analyses of what went wrong in U.S. foreign policy seem to fall into one of three categories: technical, managerial, or strategic/conceptual. The daily press and much of the commentary in the hearings themselves concentrated on what might be called technical failures. Policy analysts and managers failed to inform their boss, or get good information, or adequately weigh the implications of their many plans.

Other writers have stressed President Reagan's management style, which left plenty of leeway for his subordinates to run the day-to-day operations of U.S. foreign policy without the president's direct involvement. This excessively relaxed approach to managing foreign policy simply allowed too much autonomy to his eager staff to make policy on their own. There was too little direction and too much ambition doing too much damage to the president and the country. Management and technical explanations can complement one another, the latter nesting nicely inside the more inclusive argument about management styles.

Finally, some have insisted that these failures are not merely technical or managerial but all failures of conception and grand strategy. The President and his advisors failed to appreciate the local complexities of regions that have their own histories and political patterns. Our shortsighted and naive policies

110

in the Middle East were made worse by linking them to equally ill-considered (if not illegal) administration actions in another troubled region, Central America.

Thus, although technical and managerial factors did contribute to poor policy, it was the Reagan administration's basic conception of the enterprise of foreign policy that was fatally flawed. Most fundamentally, the Iran–Contra imbroglio is the logical outcome of the errant globalist policy perspective run aground on the regional realities of the Middle East and Central America.

Herein lies the major lesson of Irangate—Will our search for certainty in an ever more uncertain and unfamiliar world lead us to embrace, ever more tightly, archaic views of U.S. national interest? Or can we learn to adapt selectively to the world as it changes around us? Can we exert a positive influence on the direction of international change? The Iran–Contra hearings give us some room for optimism, as well as a warning, about the clash between regionalist realities and globalist ambitions.

Globalism encompasses three core beliefs about U.S. national interest and foreign policy. First, the Soviet Union poses the paramount threat to vital U.S. interests and should be vigorously opposed whenever possible. Second is a belief that the application of military solutions to international problems is an important, effective, and often underused component of our foreign policy. Finally, globalists assert that the United States can, under most circumstances, project its military and diplomatic power globally to achieve its goals.

Although globalists do attend to other political and economic matters that arise in the Third World or Europe, such developments are really secondary to checking the spread of Soviet influence. Indeed, to the degree that regional problems arise in Africa or Asia or Latin America, the most serious ones are typically the result of left-wing insurgents, often supplied and sustained, if not directed, from Moscow. In this perspective, U.S.–U.S.S.R. relations is high politics; the rest, low politics.

Regionalists, by contrast, have different beliefs about U.S. national interests. Regionalists stress intrinsic societal conditions that characterize particular regions and countries. Long-term political disputes, ethnicity, religious conflicts, and economic inequalities are the root causes of instability that may challenge U.S. interests. That there is war in Central America has more to do with land reform (or the lack of it) than Russian lackies. Nationalism, not communism, is the greater headache for U.S. policymakers. Just as the globalist will recognize the importance of local factors, the regionalist will admit that one should pay some attention to the U.S.S.R. But they place the Soviet threat more on a par with the threat of the politics of hunger and frustration in poor countries. Regionalists are also less sanguine about the capacity of the United States to influence international events, especially through military force.

But our concern here is really with the globalism practiced by the Reagan administration. The damage to U.S. national security interests was caused by an outdated and erroneous globalist view of the world that denigrates the importance of local political conditions. Yet ironically, it has not been the Soviet Union that has thwarted administration plans for the Persian Gulf or Central America; rather, it has been local social and political dynamics rooted in their own unique historical experience.

Ronald Reagan misread or ignored the history and politics of both regions and consistently promoted untenable options within both areas, and between them. In Central America, the antiregionalist policy was most evident. The president's single-minded desire to provide military aid to the Contras, while dismissing a series of regional diplomatic opportunities, is rampant globalism par excellence. For his administration, communism, not nationalism, drives Sandanista policies. Yet even in the gulf, it was arguably a globalist vision that led the advisors like Robert McFarlane. Globalists relegate complex internal dynamics, local history, and popular religion to secondary or tertiary factors that can all be "managed" by a strong-willed U.S. leadership. The policy committing our navy to a high-profile presence in the gulf is just a further extension of globalism in the gulf. Globalism has not advanced U.S. national interests in either Central America or the gulf.

A militant globalist foreign policy conception was the basis for these policy failures, not technical lapses or management miscues. Once the broad lines of the militant globalist policy were set out by the president, then whether implicitly or explicitly his subordinates got the message and their marching orders is a moot question. Perhaps the hands-off management style worsened a bad situation; but the fault lay in strategy and design, not in mistakes of implementation and technique. Indeed, I would argue that the decision to directly link U.S. policies in the Middle East and in Central America through an illicit financing scheme was itself driven in no small part by a globalist conception of the malleability of poor regions.

Still, it is a great if sad irony that the president, whose global vision of U.S. national security is so well articulated, should fall victim to a kind of personal sentimentality that led him to throw out perhaps the most important part of his own ideological vision—no negotiating and trading for hostages. Here personality plays its inevitable part in the conduct of foreign affairs. The president's concern over the fate of a dozen hostages led him to override his own policy aimed at protecting the millions of Americans who are not hostages. To technique, management, and conception therefore we must add Ronald Reagan's personality as the fourth element that explains this administration's policies in the gulf and in Central America.

One almost wishes that the failures were merely managerial or technical. They would be far easier to mend. The tendency of American foreign-policy makers to conceive of the world in black and white terms is not new. It has long roots in American diplomatic history. Restoring, or creating, a greater sense of proportion in a world where power is now distributed more proportionally will be a difficult task, requiring a broad political base and inspired leadership. One of the heartening facts that emerged from the hearings is that there is not a big constituency for a radically globalist foreign policy. The administration, knowing this, did its deed in secret. "Technical fixes" can help rein in a globalist presidency (i.e., reporting requirements, limits on arms sales, etc.), but technical fixes are not enough. The real solutions must go beyond the technical. They require, first, a much broader and more nuanced vision of the changing U.S. role in world affairs. Second, solutions require personal leadership to articulate this more realistic vision of the world as it is today. Third, long-lasting solutions require building a domestic political coalition in support of a more balanced foreign policy.

We no longer live in the kind of world that Ronald Reagan and other globalists like to describe. The world is becoming less globalist; it is becoming more regionalist. Radical globalist policies in a regionalist world will cripple U.S. foreign policy interests.

Therein lies the greatest challenge—to construct a new U.S. foreign policy that recognizes the realities of regional economic and political life, while taking serious cognizance of the real threats by the other major superpower that, more than any other nation, has the greatest power to destroy our country.

In a world where the U.S. administration achieves that greater sense of proportion, U.S. national security and world peace will both have a better chance to grow together.

Symposium II: Black Americans and the Constitution

Executive Authority, Constitutional Interpretation, and Civil Rights

Barbara Luck Graham

University of Missouri–St. Louis

Murphy, Fleming, and Harris' (1986:9-12) framework for explaining constitutional interpretation is structured around three interrelated interrogatives that are fundamental to all constitutional interpretation: (1) *What* is the Constitution that is to be interpreted? (2) *Who* are the Constitution's authoritative interpreters? and (3) *How* can/should/do these interpreters accomplish their task? This article addresses the second interrogative of who shall interpret the Constitution. At a first glance, the response to this question is deceptively simple—the Supreme Court is the most visible interpreter and has the final word on constitutional interpretation. Yet Murphy et al.'s framework demonstrates that Articles I and II place some interpretive authority in the executive and legislative branches of government as well.

Assertions of legislative or executive supremacy in constitutional interpretation have never gained substantial support. However, the significance of Murphy et al.'s (1986) analysis of who shall interpret, for the purposes of this paper, is that the question appropriately casts attention on the capacity of other branches of government to influence constitutional interpretation. The historical conflicts over who shall interpret have surfaced when the Court, Congress, and the presidency have strongly disagreed over major social and economic policy matters. Prominent examples of this lack of policy confluence among the three branches of government include the Reconstruction era, the New Deal era, and the civil rights movement of the 1950s and 1960s (see Goldman, 1987).

The elections of 1980 and 1984 have been considered by some observers as realigning elections. Thus, the Reagan victories offer yet another opportunity to observe the conflict over the question of who shall interpret. An examination of the 1980 and 1984 Republican party platforms indicates a range of issues on the Republican agenda: elimination of abortion, busing for desegregation, and affirmative action plans; a restriction of rights of criminal defendants; and calling for a return to school prayer (*Congressional Quarterly Weekly Report* [*CQWR*], 1980, 1984). Consequently, the purpose of this paper is to briefly examine how the Reagan administration attempted to implement its conservative social agenda through the federal judiciary. Special emphasis will be placed on (1) the Reagan commitment to appoint federal judges who share his vision on social and civil rights policy and (2) the aggressive nature of the Solicitor General's office in its attempt to persuade the Supreme Court to overturn important precedents in the civil rights area.

The surfacing of these policy conflicts is especially significant to the theme of this symposium because they come at a time when the nation is celebrating the bicentennial of the Constitution. The impact of the executive branch's attempts to influence constitutional interpretation will be examined from the perspective of excluded groups, primarily black Americans, and their assessment of the bicentennial celebration.

The Reagan Jurisprudence

The Reagan jurisprudence became more forcefully articulated when Edwin Meese, formerly counselor to President Reagan, was appointed to the position of attorney general in 1985. In a series of speeches in 1985, Attorney General Meese expounded the principal component of the Reagan jurisprudence—a jurisprudence of original intention. Original intent theory broadly suggests that the only legitimate way to interpret the Constitution is according to the intent of the framers. In a speech before the American Bar Association (ABA) in 1985 (in Witt, 1986:77), Attorney General Meese argued that original intent theory is "a deeply rooted commitment to the idea of democracy" and that "to allow the courts to govern simply by what it views at the time as fair and decent, is a scheme of government no longer popular; the idea of democracy has suffered." The essence of the Reagan jurisprudence was clearly stated by the attorney general:

> Those who framed the Constitution chose their words carefully, they debated at great length the most minute points. The language they chose meant something. It is incumbent upon the Court to determine what the meaning was. This is not a shocking new theory; nor is it arcane or archaic. (Ibid.)

The most controversial component of the jurisprudence of original intention was Attorney General Meese's disdain for incorporation theory. In the 1985 ABA speech, Meese intimated that the Bill of Rights was a curb *only* on national power as sustained by the Court in *Barron v. Baltimore* (7 Pet. 243 1883). Moreover, he criticized the Court's selective incorporation of the Bill of Rights (*Gitlow v. New York*, 268 U.S. 652 1925) as resting on an "intellectually shaky foundation" and thus contrary to the theory of original intent (Ibid.:176) (for critiques of the originalist technique to constitutional intepretation, see

Carter, 1985 and Barber, 1986). In the following sections, I shall elaborate on the manner in which the Reagan administration has aggressively pursued its jurisprudence of original intent by examining the nature of Reagan's judicial appointments to the federal bench and the policies pursued by the Solicitor General before the Court.

The Reagan Judicial Legacy

The Reagan administration has continued the legacy of court packing in making appointments to the federal bench. As part of his 1980 campaign, President Reagan promised that he would place conservatives on the federal courts who adhered to a philosophy of judicial self-restraint and to counteract the "activist" judges appointed by President Carter (CQWR 1980:38; Cohodas, 1981, 1983). Although not definitive at this point in time, research has revealed that President Reagan has indeed influenced the tenor of judicial appointments to the U.S. Supreme Court and to the lower federal courts, thus reshaping the federal judiciary.

Among the 367 judges appointed to the federal bench by Reagan over a seven-year period, only 1.6 percent (6) are black, 8.4 percent (31) are women, and 3.8 percent (14) are Hispanic. In contrast, Carter appointed 14.3 percent (37) blacks, 15.5 percent (40) women, and 6.2 percent (16) Hispanics to the federal bench out of 258 appointments during his single term in office (Greenhouse, 1988). Goldman's (1983, 1985) analysis of the Reagan judges revealed that they are predominantly white male, somewhat younger and wealthier, and include fewer nominees from the Democratic party. This lack of diversity among the Reagan judicial appointments represents a dramatic departure from the Carter administration and has been critically examined by the Senate Judiciary Committee (Greenhouse, 1988).

Data also show that the Reagan appointments to the lower federal bench are indeed implementing the Reagan conservative agenda. Stidham and Carp's (1987) empirical analysis of federal district court decisions from 1981 to 1985 revealed that Carter appointees were more likely to support the rights of disadvantaged minorities, civil liberties, and civil rights claims than Reagan appointees. Reagan's numerous appointments to the courts of appeals, especially to the Seventh and District of Columbia circuits, have prompted civil rights attorneys to "shop" for more hospitable circuits or state courts (Cohodas, 1987b). Affirmative action, rights of criminal defendants, and other race and sex discrimination claims are among the civil rights issues where the conservative appointments are having a broad impact.

Prior works on judicial selection have revealed at least three major factors that influence presidential choices for the Supreme Court: (1) merit (professional qualifications), (2) representational qualifications (factors such as geography, religion, race, ethnicity, and sex), and (3) political considerations (most notably political party affiliation and ideological compatibility) (Abraham, 1985; Goldman and Jahnige, 1985; Scigliano, 1971; Tribe, 1985). Clearly ideological and policy-position considerations emerge as the most significant factors in determining who sits on the Supreme Court under the Reagan administration. The first vacancy on the Court during the Reagan administration was filled by the appointment of Sandra Day O'Connor, a conservative judge on the Arizona Court of Appeals. O'Connor's notoriety as the first female justice to sit on the Supreme Court perhaps overshadowed her conservative judicial philosophy "in favor of state prerogatives, judicial restraint and deference to the political branches of government" (Witt, 1986:45). One measure of Justice O'Connor's conservatism is reflected in the voting agreements with Justice Rehnquist that occurred over 80 percent of the time between the 1981-1985 Supreme Court terms (see the November issues of the *Harvard Law Review*, various terms).

Ideology was again the most important factor in elevating Justice Rehnquist to the position of chief justice and the appointment of Antonin Scalia, formerly of the District of Columbia (D.C.) Court of Appeals, as associate justice to the Court in 1986. Justice Scalia's tenure on the Court, as one observer puts it, is "just what President Reagan wanted" (Witt, 1987). As a dependable conservative on the Court, Justice Scalia voted with Chief Justice Rehnquist 85 percent of the time during the 1986 term. Because Scalia filled the seat vacated by Justice Rehnquist, major ideological shifts on the Court were not expected to occur.

However, with Justice Powell's resignation in June 1987, President Reagan attempted to upset the delicate ideological balance on the Court by appointing an intellectually powerful conservative judge, Robert Bork of the D.C. Court of Appeals, to the U.S. Supreme Court. Bork's persistent disavowal of earlier controversial stances he had taken in extensive writings and speeches and the appearance of having moderated his views during questioning by the Senate Judiciary Committee prompted a charge of "confirmation conversion" by opponents. The perception of Bork's insensitivity to individual and civil rights facilitated interest group mobilization against his confirmation, perhaps unprecedented in the history of Supreme Court appointments. Bork's views on civil rights issues also contributed to the lack of support by key Southern senators who were elected by a large percentage of the black vote. These factors subsequently led to a rejection of the Bork nomination by the Senate. In February 1988, the Senate unanimously approved the less controversial appointment of judicial conservative Anthony Kennedy of the Ninth Circuit Court of Appeals to fill Powell's vacancy.

The Solicitor General before the Court

The Reagan jurisprudence has been aggressively pursued before the Supreme Court via the Solicitor General's office and is best exemplified by Attorney General Meese's statements:

> It has been and will continue to be the policy of this administration to press for a Jurisprudence of Original Intention. In the cases we file and those we join as *amicus*, we will endeavor to resurrect the original meaning of constitutional provisions and statutes as the only reliable guide for judgment (in Witt 1986:177).

Because of this unrelenting pursuit of the Reagan legal agenda through the Supreme Court, Caplan (1987a, 1987b) critically examined the politicization of the Solicitor General's office in a two-part article taken from his work *The Tenth Justice*. Caplan (1987a:40; 1987b:59) meticulously traced the transformation of the Solicitor General's office from one of having "the independence to exercise his craft as a lawyer on behalf of the institution of government without being a mouthpiece for the President" to one of becoming "a partisan advocate for the Administration" who viewed the law "as no more than the instrument of politics" because much of the Court's docket deals with the legal aspects of social policy.

Witt (1986d:616-18) found that the Solicitor General's office under the Reagan administration was engaged in unprecedented legal activism, having submitted more *amicus* briefs than previous administrations. The tone of the briefs, according to Witt, reflected a more restrictive interpretation of individual and civil rights while siding with property owners, businesses, or prosecutors as opposed to regulators, employees, or defendants. Table 1 illustrates the aggressiveness of the Solicitor General's office toward the pursuit of the Reagan legal agenda. A sample of the leading civil rights and criminal law cases argued before the Court during the Reagan administration indicates that the executive branch has not been supportive of civil rights claims. Whereas the Court's record on civil rights issues is mixed, the findings in Table 1 indicate that the Court, except in one instance, has agreed with the Solicitor General's position on restricting the rights of criminal defendants. These examples and others led Caplan (1987b:62) to conclude that "to understand how the Reagan Administration views the law, it is only necessary to know what it has done to the office of the Solicitor General."

Conclusion

This analysis has shown how the executive branch, in response to the questions of who shall interpret and how to interpret the Constitution, has attempted to influence constitutional interpretation by aggressively pursuing its social and civil rights agenda through the appointments of conservative federal judges. Moreover, this task was accomplished by politicizing the Solicitor General's office, advocating a jurisprudence of original intent and nominating an originalist judge, Robert Bork, to the Supreme Court. A brief examination of the Burger and Rehnquist Court decisions issued during the Reagan administration revealed that the Supreme Court was sympathetic to the Reagan legal agenda, although it did not directly overrule major precedents set by the Warren Court.

The large number of appointments to the lower federal judiciary and Reagan's four appointments to the Supreme Court suggest that it is indeed possible for the Reagan agenda to be realized through the federal judiciary. These events have generated much concern among black Americans for whom the federal courts were once viewed as safeguards for their civil rights. It is perhaps the Reagan civil rights record that prompted a rare, harsh criticism of a sitting president's civil rights policies when Associate Justice Thurgood Marshall rated Reagan's record as being "at the bottom" along with "Hoover and that group. Wilson. When we really didn't have a chance" (Taylor 1987). Ironically, this heightened advocacy of conservative civil rights policies comes

TABLE 1.
Reagan Administration's Position on Leading Civil Rights and Criminal Law Cases, 1981-1987

Cases	Amicus curiae Participation	Pro-civil rights	Anti-civil rights
Civil rights			
*Firefighters Local Union v. Stotts (1984) (A)	X		X
*Sheet Metal Workers v. EEOC (1986) (P)	X		X
*Firefighters v. Cleveland (1986) (P)	X		X
Wygant v. Jackson Bd. of Education (1986) (A)	X		X
United States v. Paradise (1987) (P)			X
Crawford v. Bd. of Education of City of Los Angeles (1982) (A)	X		X
City of Pleasant Grove v. U.S. (1987) (P)		X	
*Bob Jones University v. U.S. (1983) (P)			X
Criminal law			
U.S. v. Ross (1982) (A)			X
Illinois v. Gates (1983) (A)	X		X
U.S. v. Leon (1984) (A)			X
Nix v. Williams (1984) (A)	X		X
New York v. Quarles (1984) (A)	X		X
Oregon v. Elstad (1985) (A)	X		X
Batson v. Kentucky (1986) (P)	X		X
U.S. v. Salerno (1987) (A)			X

Note: Only nonunanimous cases are reported here. The Supreme Court's position on these cases is denoted by (P) if pro-civil rights (Justice Marshall voted in the majority) and (A) if anti-civil rights (Justice Marshall dissented).

*Statutory interpretation case.

at the same time the nation is celebrating the bicentennial of the Constitution. Among other things, the bicentennial celebration will mean that black Americans will have to exploit diverse political strategies in order to fully realize the goals of constitutional equality.

References

Abraham, Henry J. 1985. *Justices and Presidents: A Political History of Appointments to the Supreme Court,* 2nd ed. New York: Oxford University Press.

Barber, Sotirios A. 1986. "The New Right Assault on Moral Inquiry in Constitutional Law." *George Washington Law Review* 54:253-95.

Caplan, Lincoln. 1987a. "Annals of Law: The Tenth Justice—I." *The New Yorker*, August 10, pp. 29-58.

_____. 1987b. "Annals of Law: The Tenth Justice—II." *The New Yorker*, August 17, pp. 30-62.

Carter, Lief. 1985. *Contemporary Constitutional Lawmaking*. New York: Pergamon Press.

Cohodas, Nadine. 1981. "How Reagan Will Pick Judges Is Unclear, But Philosophy Will Play an Important Role." *Congressional Quarterly Weekly Report* 39:299.

_____. 1983. "Reagan's Judicial Selections Draw Differing Assessments." *Congressional Quarterly Weekly Report*, 41:83-83.

_____. 1987a. "Much at Stake as Senate Gets Ready for Bork." *Congressional Quarterly Weekly Report* 45:1429-31.

_____. 1987b. "322 of Reagan's Appointees Are Already Judges for Life." *St. Louis Post-Dispatch*, September 24.

Gailey, Phil. 1985. "Policy Role of Attorney General Raises Questions." *New York Times*, April 22, p. 15.

Goldman, Sheldon. 1983. "Reagan's Judicial Apointments at Mid-Term: Shaping the Bench in His Own Image." *Judicature* 66:335-47.

_____. 1985. "Reaganizing the Judiciary: The First Term Appointments." *Judicature* 68:313-29.

_____. 1987. *Constitutional Law*. New York: Harper & Row.

Greenhouse, Linda. 1988. "Policy on Black Judicial Nominees is Debated." *New York Times*, February 3, p. 11.

Murphy, Walter F., James E. Fleming, and William F. Harris, II. 1986. *American Constitutional Interpretation*. New York: Foundation Press, Inc.

O'Connor, Karen. 1983. "The Amicus Curiae Role of the U.S. Solicitor General in Supreme Court Litigation." *Judicature* 66:257-64.

Scigliano, Robert. 1971. *The Supreme Court and the Presidency*. New York: The Free Press.

Stidham, Ronald, and Robert Carp. "Judges, Presidents, and Policy Choices: Exploring the Linkage." *Social Science Quarterly* 68:395-404.

Taylor, Jr., Stuart. 1987. "Marshall Ranks Reagan as Last on Civil Rights." *New York Times*, September 9, p. 1.

Tribe, Laurence H. 1985. *God Save This Honorable Court: How the Choice of Supreme Court Justices Shapes Our History*. New York: Mentor Books.

Witt, Elder. 1983. "Reagan Pressing Court for Policy Changes." *Congressional Quarterly Weekly Report* 41:2439-42.

_____. 1985. "Court Takes Broad New Look at Affirmative Action Issue." *Congressional Quarterly Weekly Report* 43:2104-08.

_____. 1986a. *A Different Justice: Reagan and the Supreme Court*. Washington, D.C.: Congressional Quarterly, Inc.

_____. 1986b. "Reagan's Argument Rebuffed by High Court." *Congressional Quarterly Weekly Report* 44:1576-80.

_____. 1986c. "Reagan Crusade before Court Unprecedented in Intensity." *Congressional Quarterly Weekly Report* 44:616-18.

_____. 1986d. "The Supreme Court: A New Reagan Era Ahead?" *Congressional Quarterly Weekly Report* 44:2293-96.

Wermiel, Stephen. 1988. "Reagan Choices Alter the Makeup of Views of the Federal Courts." *Wall Street Journal*, February 1, p. 1.

Civil Rights and the Fragmentation of Government Power

Lawrence Baum

Ohio State University

O n the bicentennial of the Constitution, much thought has been given to its place in our national life. Appropriately, one issue that has received attention is the relationship between the Constitution and race. Supreme Court Justice Thurgood Marshall helped to create this attention by pointing to the acceptance of slavery in the original Constitution and the need for later action to bring the Constitution and the nation closer to racial equality.[1]

Unquestionably, the Constitution has influenced the status of black Americans powerfully through its provisions dealing with race. But it also affects civil rights, as it does all other issues, through the structure that it creates for political action and policymaking. In particular, the constitutional fragmentation of government power has helped to determine the direction and success of the twentieth-century movement for racial equality through the law. In this essay, I will consider the relationship between this fragmentation of power and the path of civil rights policy.

The division of power created by the constitutional system, both among levels of government and within the federal government, increases the number of significant policymaking institutions in government. In turn, this multiplicity of policy centers improves the opportunities for interest groups to gain meaningful access to government. But, what this fragmentation grants in access, it takes away from the capacity of groups that seek change to win effective victories. Policy change can be attacked and blocked at many points, giving an advantage to those who favor the status quo. These characteristics of the policy system have had complex and conflicting effects on the success of efforts to secure civil rights.

Early in the twentieth century, civil rights advocates faced a situation in which no level or institution of government had indicated much sympathy for racial equality. Certainly the Supreme Court had not been a friend of civil rights; it had weakened constitutional amendments and statutes intended to guarantee equality for black people, and it had promulgated the "separate-but-equal" doctrine that Southern states seized upon as a means to establish and maintain racial segregation. Yet the federal courts had some potential for favorable action that was lacking in the other branches. Federal judges enjoyed a degree of insulation from anti-civil rights sentiment in the larger society, and the duty of the courts to interpret constitutional guarantees of equality provided at least a basis for arguments against discriminatory practices. Furthermore, discrimination against black criminal defendants could be attacked directly only through the courts.

Accordingly, the NAACP for several decades focused a large part of its resources and collective energies on the courts.[2] This emphasis on litigation was reflected in its creation of the separate Legal Defense and Education Fund in 1939. For a considerable length of time, civil rights claims achieved only limited success in the courts. But as the societal climate became more favorable and the Supreme Court's membership more liberal, the Court increasingly became a strong supporter of black civil rights. The Warren Court of the 1950s and 1960s struck down school segregation and barriers to black voting and overturned actions by state governments to attack the civil rights movement. Its support for racial equality extended to decisions in areas ranging from libel to the rights of criminal defendants. The Court could have gone much further—it might, for instance, have demanded immediate school desegregation—but by past standards its civil rights positions were quite advanced.

Yet the fragmentation of government power that made the federal courts a meaningful point of access for civil rights organizations also weakened the impact of some of the victories that these groups won in the Supreme Court. A decade after *Brown v. Board of Education*, schools in the Deep South remained almost completely segregated. Despite several decades of court decisions attacking racial discrimination in voter registration, subterfuges were developed to keep black registration in the South at low levels as late as the early 1960s. And Southern state governments harassed civil rights organizations with considerable success. Even after the NAACP won a Supreme Court decision in 1958 that nullified Alabama's effort to prevent it from operating in the state, four more years of legal actions were necessary to secure a final victory, and in the meantime the organization had suffered massive losses in money and membership.[3]

Congress and the president could have used their own power to reinforce the legal rights proclaimed by the courts. But the presidents who served from the New Deal through the New Frontier varied in their attitudes toward civil rights, and the presidency was not a consistent source of support for racial equality. In Congress, the power of Southern Democrats prevented the adoption of civil rights legislation until 1957 and of strong legislation for several years after that.

As the limitations of litigation became more apparent and the other branches of the national government became more receptive, the energies of civil rights groups increasingly were focused on legislation. Two major statutes, whose adoption was achieved with great difficulty, finally fulfilled the promise of the Supreme Court's decisions on behalf of racial equality. The Civil Rights Act of 1964 and the Voting Rights Act of 1965 overcame the major barriers to school desegregation and the right to vote, in large part because they were enforced with some vigor by the Johnson administration. Financial incentives and other methods of control that were unavailable to the courts proved capable of breaking down resistance to equal rights among Southern state policymakers.

In the two decades since the late 1960s, the pattern of institutional support for racial equality has changed a good deal. The Burger and Rehnquist Courts have been less reliable supporters of civil rights claims than was the Warren Court, and groups with such claims increasingly question the value of going to the federal courts. The massive campaign against the nomination of Robert Bork to the Supreme Court reflected an awareness that the Court was moving away from its earlier commitment to equality and other civil liberties values. Presidential administrations have varied in their policies on civil rights, from the strong support of the Carter administration to the broad opposition of the Reagan administration. Meanwhile, changing political realities, especially the voting power of black citizens in the South, have helped to maintain support for civil rights in Congress.

These institutional changes are symbolized by two successful "appeals" from the Supreme Court to Congress. The first concerned standards for discrimination under the Voting Rights Act. In 1980, the Court ruled in *Mobile v. Bolden* that discriminatory intent was required to hold that an election rule violated the act[4]; two years later, a coalition of interest groups secured a provision in the act's extension to overturn that ruling. And in 1988, responding to the urgings of civil rights groups, Congress overturned a 1984 Supreme Court decision that narrowed federal laws denying financial aid to institutions in which discrimination occurs.[5] After the long period in which the Supreme Court was viewed as a friend of civil rights and Congress as resistant, these events indicate that a fundamental change has occurred.

These changes in institutional positions have created a more confused situation for civil rights groups than in any earlier period. No institution is a reliable ally or an implacable opponent of civil rights. Like most other interest groups, those that support civil rights must engage in a complex strategy, one in which they go to different institutions at different times on the basis of specific circumstances.

In this situation, the fragmentation of governmental power is not entirely a disadvantage. To a considerable extent, civil rights groups are now seeking to protect legal gains that they won earlier. Where this is the case, the difficulty of changing the status quo can work to their benefit. If the Supreme Court narrows the scope of civil rights laws, groups can turn to Congress to restore the earlier understanding. If a new administration opposes an existing policy of the Internal Revenue Service that prohibits tax exemptions to schools that discriminate by race, the courts can uphold the earlier policy—as the Supreme Court did in a 1983 decision.[6] The constitutional system may frustrate efforts to change policy, but in doing so, it now helps to preserve legal rules that favor racial equality.

Clearly, the constitutional fragmentation of power has affected the civil rights movement in several different ways. The existence of many independent power centers in government long frustrated efforts to secure effectively the rights that the Fourteenth and Fifteenth amendments guaranteed. Yet the policymaking power of the Supreme Court served as a vehicle in the twentieth-century drive for civil rights. And, at a time when many basic legal rights have been won, the fragmentation of power makes it more difficult for any single institution to weaken those rights.

The effect of the constitutional system in opening access to government has been especially important to civil rights groups. These groups traditionally lacked the economic resources and voting power that are the primary sources of political influence for most groups. Their own major source of influence was the weight of their moral claims. The ability to present those claims to any of several different institutions increased the likelihood of gaining serious attention for them. Especially important was the existence of a relatively powerful Supreme Court whose duty to interpret the Constitution and relative independence made it potentially receptive to the moral claims of the civil rights movement.

It can be argued that the courts were more a distraction than an aid in the early struggles for equality. Victories in the judicial branch were won at the cost of very considerable time and energy, yet these victories often were insufficient to secure fundamental rights in practice. Ultimately, mass political actions such as the Birmingham Bus Boycott of 1957 probably were far more important in strengthening the civil rights movement and spurring the legislation of the 1960s. Perhaps it would have been more effective to concentrate efforts on the other branches and on other political strategies at an earlier point in the development of the civil rights movement.

Yet the victories won through litigation were hardly meaningless. These victories led to some specific gains and may have helped to put civil rights on the broader national agenda. The *Brown* decision is an example; despite the resistance that it encountered, the decision at least brought about substantial desegregation of border-state schools, and it made the continuing segregation in the Deep South more difficult to ignore.

This issue underlines the impact of the constitutional structure of government on interest-group strategies. Faced with a government of relatively fragmented power, groups often are confronted with complex and difficult choices about where to focus their efforts. For the early civil rights movement, which confronted a largely unsympathetic government, the federal courts were the least unattractive locus for action. The current civil rights movement, confronting an ambiguous and changing pattern of sympathies in government, can choose among a larger number of potentially favorable institutions with less certainty about where to focus its efforts. Decisions about the allocation of energy and resources among levels and branches of government will continue to be a central concern for groups that seek equality for black Americans.

Notes

1. Thurgood Marshall, "Remarks at the Annual Seminar of the San Francisco Patent and Trademark Law Assocation," Maui, Hawaii, May 6, 1987.
2. See Richard Kluger, *Simple Justice: The History of Brown v. Board of Education and Black America's Struggle for Equality* (New York: Alfred A. Knopf, 1976).

3. See Stuart A. Scheingold, *The Politics of Rights: Lawyers, Public Policy, and Political Change* (New Haven: Yale University Press, 1974), p. 174.
4. *City of Mobile v. Bolden*, 446 U.S. 55 (1980).
5. *Grove City College v. Bell*, 465 U.S. 555 (1984).
6. *Bob Jones University v. United States*, 461 U.S. 574 (1983).

The Constitution, the Supreme Court, and Racism: Compromises on the Way to Democracy

William J. Daniels

Rochester Institute of Technology

The 200th birthday of the U.S. Constitution has been the occasion both for celebrating its long life and for criticizing some aspects of that long life. Professor Forrest McDonald of the University of Alabama, for example, concluded that the Constitution was the product of "America's Golden Age, the likes we shall not see again." Supreme Court Justice Thurgood Marshall was uncomfortable with the thought that bicentennial celebrations "invite a complacent belief" in the perfection of the work of the framers. Given Justice Marshall's skepticism as a point of departure, this essay uses this time of reflection to review the role of Supreme Court decisions in interpreting the Constitution on conflicts that involve race.

This republic began with support for the "peculiar institution" of slavery, and the Civil War ended that support. The matter of race, however, continues to be one of the most pressing issues on this nation's political agenda. Thurgood Marshall maintains that the Constitution was flawed and defective particularly because of the way in which slavery was handled in that document and the subsequent history of this country that flowed from this fact. However, one might argue that the framers made compromises about slavery and race that may not be apparent from a superficial reading of the Constitution.

Aristotle had written that slavery was part of a universal natural pattern:

> whether or not it is a just and better thing for one man to be a slave to another, or whether all slavery is contrary to nature ... Neither theoretical discussion nor empirical observation presents any difficulty. That one should command and another obey is both necessary and expedient.

Of the nearly 400,000 blacks in the colonies in 1765, all but a handful were slaves. Clinton Rossiter notes that there was no place for blacks in the American definition about the rights of man and that the mental climate was hostile to "the assumption that the Negro was a whole man."

Nonetheless, against this theoretical and practical background, the framers did not use the terms *Negro* or *slave* in the Constitution but refer always to the *person*. Consistent with natural law, "persons" are equal by nature or by God in a self-evident sense. This usage would have allowed justices of the Supreme Court in later years to interpret in favor of full equality had they not been acting within the social context of their time.

There can be no doubt, however, that slavery was condoned by passage of the Three-Fifths Compromise. Nonetheless, Herbert Storing suggests that the support for slavery that stems from this passage, when placed in the proper context, may be ambiguous. Briefly, he contends that the compromise did not signify that slaves possessed less humanity than whites, because it was the slave holders who argued most strenuously for the counting of slaves as whole persons. Rather, it was the leaders in the free states who maintained that slaves, because they were prevented from becoming citizens, should not be counted as full persons for the purpose of representation.

Of course, the question of citizenship for blacks did eventually surface in the celebrated case of *Dred Scott v. Sanford* in 1857. The Constitution had not defined the term *citizen* but had recognized a distinction between federal and state citizenship and, by implication, assumed that federal citizenship was derived from state citizenship. The Constitution specified that the president be a natural-born citizen and that the citizens of each state be entitled to the privileges and immunities of citizens of the several states.

The political issue at the time was that few states were willing to consider the extention of the benefits of the federal courts to blacks with comcomitant privileges and immunities of U.S. citizenship. Hence, the decision in *Dred Scott* did not build on the auspicious language nor grasp the natural law significance attached to the term *person* that the framers had placed in the Constitution.

Instead, Chief Justice Taney, writing for the majority of the Court, held that blacks were not and could not become citizens of the United States; they were not entitled to any privileges and immunities. Justice Taney had taken advantage of the fact that the federal government had not bestowed citizenship on free blacks when the Constitution was adopted (Dred Scott was not the descendant of a free black) and combined this fact with an acceptance of discriminatory legislation found in many states that blacks were not regarded as constitutient members of the body politic when the Union was formed. Therefore, no free blacks nor slaves were citizens of the United States. Justice Taney concluded his opinion and added remarks that indicated that the social context was perhaps more influential than his legal reasoning: blacks were "beings of an inferior order, and altogether unfit to associate with the white race, either in social or political relations; and so far inferior, that they had no rights which the white man was bound to respect."

All blacks had been debilitated by *Dred Scott*. Following the inevitable Civil War, three amendments were added to the U.S. Constitution to free the black slaves, grant the freed blacks citizenship, and protect their right to vote. In addition to these constitutional provisions, Congress provided support to the struggle for civil rights for blacks by passing seven civil rights acts during the

Reconstruction era. The first, passed in 1866 over the veto of President Andrew Johnson, overturned the *Dred Scott* decision by providing blacks the "full and equal benefit of all laws and proceedings . . . as is enjoyed by white citizens," especially the right to sue and be sued and to own property. The Fourteenth Amendment was intended to provide additional constitutional protection to these legislative provisions.

The next two acts, passed in 1866 and 1867, respectively made it a crime to "kidnap or carry away any other person, whether negro, mulatto, or otherwise, with the intent that such other person shall be sold or held in involuntary servitude, or held as a slave" and "to abolish and forever prohibit the System of Peonage in the Territory of New Mexico and other parts of the United States."

The fourth of the civil rights acts was known as the Enforcement Act of 1870. This act imposed criminal sanctions for those who interfered with the right of the franchise as granted in the Fifteenth Amendment. The Ku Klux Klan Act, the sixth passed by Congress in 1871, made it a crime to use "force, intimidation or threat" to deny any citizen the equal protection of the law. The final Reconstruction civil rights act was passed by Congress in 1875 and was known as the Public Accommodations Act. This act stipulated that

> all persons within the jurisdiction of the United States shall be entitled to the full and equal enjoyment of the accommodations, advantages, facilities, and privileges of inns, public conveyances on land or water, theatres, and other places of public amusement; subject only to the conditions and limitations established by law, and applicable alike to citizens of every race and color, regardless of any previous condition of servitude.

The justices of the U.S. Supreme Court began to interpret and dismantle this massive array of constitutional and statutory protections. The first interception of the Fourteenth Amendment, the *Slaughter House Cases* in 1873, produced an extemely narrow reading of one of its provisions, namely: "No state shall make or enforce any law which shall abridge the privileges or immunities of citizens of the United States."

On the surface, the case had nothing to do with the rights of blacks. The litigants were employees in several slaughterhouses who argued that they had been deprived of their privileges and immunities (jobs) because of a state contract with other slaughterhouses. The Court ruled that the amendment provision in question referred to citizenship in the United States, conferred no new privileges, immunities, or rights and merely served as a federal guarantee against state abridgement of existing rights. The Fourteenth Amendment, the Court argued, was designed to safeguard those privileges and immunities fixed by state law or those broadly articulated by the Constitution. The problem for blacks was that most of the racial burdens and disabilities they faced were under state law.

The civil rights legislation did not fare well under the review by the Supreme Court. In several cases, Sections 3, 4, 5, and 16 of the 1870 act were invalidated (*Reese*, 1876, *James*, 1903, and *Hodges*, 1906). Essentially, the Court held that: offenses created for interfering with voting rights were not limited to denial on the basis of race; the Fifteenth Amendment did not give anyone the right to vote but merely guaranteed the right to vote under state law; and also that Congress had exceeded its power when it provided penalties for state officials who denied blacks the right to vote.

The 1871 act was held to be unconstitutional in two cases (*Harris*, 1883 and *Baldwin*, 1887). The Court found that the penalties were "directed exclusively against the actions of private citizens, without reference to the laws of the state or their administration by her officials." Finally, in five cases announced as a single decision, the public accommodations section of the Civil Rights Act of 1875 was struck down by the Court. In a literal interpretation of its provisions the Court held that "individual invasion of individual rights is not the subject-matter of the amendment" and concluded that neither the Thirteenth nor the Fourteenth Amendments empowered Congress to enact legislation on private or social actions of citizens or to prohibit discrimination against blacks in privately owned public accommodations. In a review of the amendments respectively, the Court found that private discrimination did not violate the Thirteenth Amendment because an act of refusal has nothing to do with slavery or servitude. The provisions of the Fourteenth Amendment generally prohibited only state-sponsored discrimination and the "last section of the amendment invests Congress with the power to adopt appropriate legislation for correcting the effects of such prohibited state law." These findings of the Court notwithstanding, observes Lois Moreland, "it should be remembered that separation of the races in 1875 was achieved largely by voluntary, private action, not by law" (Moreland, 1970).

These rulings, which relied heavily upon the principle of federalism, had effectively prevented Congress from exercising its perceived authority to protect the rights of black persons. Interestingly, these rulings served to buttress the *Marbury* doctrine, namely that it is the province of the Court and duty of its judges to interpret the Constitution and say what the law is. Thus the decisions also served to increase the power of the Supreme Court. And, consequently, given the Court's role as interpreter of civil rights legislation, the Supreme Court became the most important institution for blacks in pursuit of civil rights in the next century.

The *Slaughter House* principle, effectively that state authorities are to recognize and protect the rights of blacks, was eroded beyond legal recognition by the time of the opinion by the Court in *Plessy v. Ferguson* in 1896. The status of black Americans was spelled out quite clearly when the equal protection clause was interpreted by the Supreme Court to mean substantial equality. The Court held that the Thirteenth Amendment was not intended to abolish distinctions based on color. Furthermore, laws that required or permitted separation of the races were valid and reasonable exercises of the police power of the state. This interpretation of the Fourteenth Amendment was also reasonable, according to the Court, because the amendment could not have, "in the nature of things," been intended to enforce "social" as distinct from "political" equality.

The actions of the Supreme Court between *Plessy* and the school desegregation cases in the area of race relations are highly visible. This is the period when organized black Americans and their associates worked to impress upon the Supreme Court the pernicious effects of the policies it had assisted in creating with its interpretations over the years. The opinion in *Brown* found the Court using "intangible factors" to strike down the tangible "separate-but-equal" doctrine and the tangible injurious effects that segregation had on public education.

Brown and related cases represented an effort by the Court to dismantle the legal framework that had supported separatism and racism. Congress again had joined the struggle by enacting several civil rights acts from 1957 through 1968. Consistent with the thrust of the earlier legislative measures, a major intent of Congress was the desire to protect and enforce the civil rights of black citizens and enhance social justice for the citizens who had suffered the ravages of racism and discrimination.

Again, the Court has been asked to interpret these measures as against the Equal Protection Clause. However, now the Court is weaving concepts of equal justice with requests based on compensatory justice. Whether litigation is based on claims of "reverse discrimination" or "benign discrimination," the key issue is whether racial neutrality will supplant racial affirmative action. The justices of the Supreme Court must sort through their social and legal philosophies and determine whether the remedial use of race is permitted by the Equal Protection Clause and, if so, whether the remedial use of race is allowable under civil rights legislation. The Supreme Court again is exercising its will regarding the Constitution and conflicts involving race.

The Constitution has not been color blind, the justices of the Supreme Court have not been color blind; and the people of the United States have not been color blind. There is a persisting legacy of racism. The disturbing historic role of the Supreme Court in this legacy warrants a special perspective when considering what might constitute acceptable and adequate remedies under the Equal Protection Clause. Under the color of law, the justices of the Court have not been disinterested, passive instruments of objective justice who have exercised judicial review to counteract the inequities that result from the political process. Clearly, the machinations of judicial interpretation that have mirrored fears and prejudices found in the social context have contributed significantly to the present residue of unclaimed opportunities for blacks.

The Constitution is, nonetheless, a remarkable document, for we yet debate its language, original meaning, and hermeneutics of constitutional interpretation. Justice Marshall again: "[T]he true miracle was not the birth of the Constitution, but its life." And perhaps words of Langston Hughes best describe the process of the first two centuries of its existence: "Those of us engaged in racial struggle in America are like knights on horseback—the Negroes on a white horse and the white folks on a black. Sometimes the race is terrific. But the feel of the wind in your hair as you ride toward democracy is really something."

Under the "color" of law, the Constitution, of course, was flawed. But it is perfectable. We must recognize that, historically, the Supreme Court was part of the racial problem. Now for political, legal, and practical reasons it must be part of the solution. We can admire its birth, praise its spirit, and celebrate its life, particularly when compared with the constitutions of other countries. But let us observe the anniversary of the U.S. Constitution, according to Justice

Marshall, with an awareness of the "hopes not realized and promises not fulfilled."

Note

The author wishes to thank his colleague John Christian Laursen for insights that were useful in framing the approach to this essay.

References

Books and Articles

Aristotle. 1981. *The Politics*, rev. ed. New York: Penguin.
Berns, Walter. 1987. "Do We Have a Living Constitution?." *National Forum*, pp. 29-33.
Brest, Paul. 1983. "Race Discrimination." In *The Burger Court*, Vincent Blasi, ed. New Haven: Yale University Press, pp. 113-31.
Cruse, Harold. 1987. *Plural but Equal*. New York: William Morrow and Company.
Daniels, William J. 1987. "Citizenship, Naturalization, and Citizenship," *Encyclopedia of the American Judicial System*. New York: Charles Scribners Sons.
Daniels, William J. "Mr. Thurgood Marshall." In *The Burger Court: Political and Judicial Profiles*. Charles Lamb and Stephen Halpern, eds. (forthcoming).
Hopkins, Vincent C. 1967. *Dred Scott's Case*. New York: Atheneum.
Hughes, Langston. (1958). "The Fun of Being Black." In *The Langston Hughes Reader*. New York: George Braziller.
Marshall, Thurgood. 1978. Concurring opinion in *University of California Regents v. Bakke*, 438 U.S. 265.
Miller, Loren. (1966). *The Petitioners*. New York: Pantheon Books.
Moreland, Lois B. 1970. *White Racism and the Law*. Columbus, OH: Charles E. Merrill, 1970.
Rossiter, Clinton. 1933. *The First American Revolution*. New York: Harcourt Brace Jovanovich.
Storing, Herbert J. 1985. *The Anti-Federalist*. Chicago: The University of Chicago Press.
Storing, Herbert. 1977. "Slavery and the Moral Foundations of the American Republic." In *The Moral Foundations of the American Republic*. Robert H. Horowitz, ed. Charlottesville, VA: University of Virginia Press.
Taylor, Stuart, Jr. 1987. "Marshall Sounds Critical Note on Bicentennial," *New York Times*, May 7, 1ff.
Tribe, Laurence H. 1985. Chapter 14, "Dismantling the House That Racism Built: Assessing Affirmative Action." In *Constitutional Choices*. Cambridge: Harvard University Press.
Woodward, C. Vann. 1957. *The Strange Career of Jim Crow*. New York: Oxford University Press.

Legal Decisions

Baldwin v. Franks, 120 U.S. 678 (1887).
Brown v. Board of Education I, 347 U.S. 483 (1954).
Brown v. Board of Education 11, 349 U.S. 294 (1955).

Civil Rights Cases, 109 U.S. 3 (1883).
De Funis v. Odegaard, 416 U.S. 312 (1973).
Dred Scott v. Sanford, 60 U.S. 393 (1857).
Firefighters v. Stotts, 81 L. Ed. 2 (1984).
Hodges v. United States, 203 U.S. 1 (1906).
James v. Bowman, 190 U.S. 127 (1903).
Marbury v. Madison, 5 U.S. 137 (1803).
Moose Lodge No. 7 v. Irvis, 407 U.S. 163 (1972).
Plessy v. Ferguson, 163 U.S. 537 (1896).
Regents of the University of California v. Bakke, 483 U.S. 265 (1978).
Slaughter House Cases, 83 U.S. 36 (1873).
Steelworkers of America v. Weber, 443 U.S. 193 (1979).
United States v. Harris, 106 U.S. 629 (1883).
United States v. Reese, 92 U.S. 214 (1876).

Review Essays:
Jesse Jackson and Presidential Politics

Black Presidential Strategies and Institutional Constraints

William E. Nelson, Jr.

The Ohio State University

Lucius J. Barker, 1988, **Our Time Has Come: A Delegate's "Diary" of Jesse Jackson's 1984 Presidential Campaign,** Urbana and Chicago, Illinois: University of Illinois Press, 233 pp., ISBN 0-252-01426-X.
C. Anthony Broh, 1987, **A Horse of A Different Color: Television's Treatment of Jesse Jackson's 1984 Presidential Campaign,** Washington, D.C.: Joint Center for Political Studies, 93 pp., ISBN 0-941410-54-4 (paper).
Adolph L. Reed Jr., 1986, **The Jesse Jackson Phenomenon,** New Haven, Ct.: Yale University Press, 170 pp., ISBN 0-300-03543-8 (paper).

Jesse Jackson's campaign for the presidency in 1984 symbolized the desire by many segments of the black community to halt the destructive tidal wave of Reaganism through the mass mobilization of black electoral strength (Jesse Jackson, 1984:2–9). The Jackson campaign also represented an effort by the black community to strike an independent position in the electoral process. This time, the key black strategy would not be working inside the camp of the most liberal Democratic candidate but fielding a progressive black candidate who would change the nature of political discourse and serve as a key power broker within top decision-making circles of the Democratic Party. Thus, the promise of the Jackson campaign was severalfold: (1) that Jackson would activate thousands of black citizens across the country who were unregistered to vote and alienated from the political process; (2) that Jackson would elevate the moral tone of the campaign and focus the attention of the nation on issues relating to blacks, the poor, voting rights, and liberation struggles in the third world; (3) that Jackson would renegotiate the position of the black community within the Democratic Party, compelling the party to adopt a progressive platform reflecting the fundamental needs and interests of the black community; and (4) that Jackson would be able to build a powerful "rainbow coalition," capable of helping to secure a Democratic victory against Ronald Reagan in the general election.

How realistic were these goals and expectations? The promise of the Jackson campaign was sharply muted by the realities of American presidential politics. These realities reflect the insulation of the black community from sectors of power and influence critical to the shaping of American public opinion and the mobilization of human and financial resources in presidential campaigns (Cross, 1984:529–35). Both the procedures and the outcomes of presidential elections are controlled by a complex network of institutional forces that reinforce the biases against the exercise of effective black political influence extant in the American political system. When Jesse Jackson announced his candidacy for the presidency, he was confronted with a host of institutional constraints on his ability to satisfy the pivotal objectives of his campaign. These constraints emerged in part out of the personal political history and style of Jesse Jackson; most crucially, they were endemic to the broader political environment in which Jackson, as a black presidential aspirant, was compelled to function. The books by Barker, Broh, and Reed address in various ways the problem of institutional constraints in the Jackson campaign. These volumes raise questions concerning the impact of institutional constraints on black presidential strategies that are worthy of serious analysis. This essay will illuminate and critically examine several of the most important political dilemmas created by institutional constraints identified by these works.

Managing the News: The Problem of Image Projection

Contemporary presidential campaigns are a media phenomenon. To be credible, a candidate must have strong media support. The reason for this is quite simple: The media represent crucial intervening mechanisms in the political system, interpreting for the public at large the meaning and significance of campaigns (Lineberry, 1983:258). The media's ability to control the flow of information and images to the public virtually establishes the character and the content of presidential campaign politics. Strategies for presidential success must include methods for obtaining the kind of media attention best calculated to project and sustain a candidate's image as a serious contender for the White House.

The critical role played by the media in presidential politics constituted a formidable institutional constraint on the political effectiveness of the Jesse Jackson campaign. Jackson was destined by race and ideology to be badly served by the conservative, white-dominated media that directs the flow of images and information in presidential campaigns. At no point in the presidential contest was Jackson able to rise above his designation by the media as a black presidential candidate. This designation had important political implications. It meant that although Jackson would be acknowledged by the media as a serious presidential candidate, he would not be viewed as a candidate that had a reasonable chance of capturing the Democratic nomination. According to C. Anthony Broh, who conducted an extensive examination of television's treatment of the Jackson campaign, Jackson was viewed not just as a dark horse but a black horse—a horse of a different color (Broh, 1987). The media's dismissal of Jackson as a possible Democratic nominee had enormous ramifications for Jackson's campaign. In the frequent horse-race assessments by the media of winners and losers in key state primaries, Jackson's standing as a candidate was usually ignored. Broh observes in this regard that television assessed Jackson's chances of winning in only 13 percent of his campaign roles. This percentage placed him at the bottom of the ranking of television's treatment of the horse-race roles of the five Democratic candidates (Broh, 1987:13–14).

The failure by television to report on Jackson's standing compared to the other Democratic candidates was no accident; rather, it was a natural outgrowth of the universal assumption that Jackson could not win the Democratic nomination. Given this assumption, it made no sense to focus on the Jackson campaign as a serious competitor in the primary game. Hence, stories about the strategy and tactics of the Jackson campaign were not considered newsworthy and were routinely dismissed. The Jackson campaign could generate substantial media attention only as an interesting campaign aberration or as a source of instant hot news during periods of campaign controversy.

Broh raises the possibility that if Jackson had been given the same kind of comprehensive treatment by the media given to John Anderson, a "long-shot candidate" in the 1980 campaign, Jackson may have had a greater impact on the party platform at the 1984 Democratic convention or even have been considered as a vice-presidential candidate. This kind of speculation is illogical because Jesse Jackson could not maintain his political identity and generate the coverage given to typical white candidates. The Jackson campaign was slighted by the white press because it was viewed as a race campaign directed exclusively to black America. Jackson was viewed as a monochromatic leader whose role in the struggle for pluralist democracy was confined to activating black voters and articulating their grievances. Evidence to support this proposition is quite extensive. Many white reporters went to great lengths to underscore the fact that Jackson's primary vote did not reflect the rainbow orientation emphasized by Jackson in his campaign statements: "Jesse Jackson did extremely well with blacks, getting better than three-fourths of the black vote. But the rest of the rainbow coalition didn't show up."[1] Some media spokespersons even criticized Jackson for appealing to black votes, arguing that Jackson was raising false hopes in the black community because it was clear the mobilization of "hitherto unmobilized masses" would not put "one of their own" in the Oval Office.[2]

Beyond the issue of race, Jackson did not fit the acceptable ideological mode of the media establishment. Embracing a radical platform that challenged the continued dominance of the corporate structure over the American economy, Jackson would have had a difficult time generating effective media support regardless of his color.

Black radical candidates like Jesse Jackson find themselves caught in a double bind. Their efforts to articulate a new national agenda are not only thwarted because of race but because they are found to be objectionable on ideological grounds as well. At the same time, they are expected by their black constituents to forcefully and aggressively give voice to their needs in the political arena. This dilemma raises the issue of new strategies for black presidential aspirants. The absence of a plan for overcoming the constraints on black electoral efforts by the media represents the greatest shortcoming of Broh's excellent book. Clearly, the centerpiece of such a plan must be fund raising. Black presidential candidates cannot afford to rely upon regular media sources to filter their message down to the mass public. The name of the present game is professional public relations. Since Nixon's victory in 1968, major presidential candidates have invested heavily in media consultants to promote their presidential ambitions. The direct purchase of television advertisements has become an essential ingredient of successful presidential campaign efforts. In view of the weak financial base of the campaign and the extraordinary media assault against the campaign in the wake of the "Hymie" controversy, Jesse Jackson's accomplishments in 1984 were truly remarkable. Black people cannot expect to move substantially beyond the 1984 accomplishments if extensive sources of independent finance for national campaigns are not mobilized on a permanent basis.

An effective plan of action to combat media bias against a black radical candidate must also include the construction of a well-organized campaign organization to carry the candidate's message directly to the voters. It is conceivable that the Rainbow Coalition can be sufficiently developed to play this role. We know from the experiences of local campaigns that effective grassroots organizations provide an important substitute for money in elections; they can provide the vital link between the central campaign and community required to vastly increase registration and turnout in low income communities. In a presidential campaign, these organizations must be established nationwide and coordinated through a task force operating out of the national headquarters.

The impact of media bias may be significantly diluted by an emphasis on the protest aspect of the black presidential campaign. Leaders of the political campaign in the black community must attempt to distill the essence of the policy objectives of the campaign. The central message to the black electorate must be that the black presidential candidate is not involved in a horse race but a quest to change the fundamental relations of the black community to the broader social, economic, and political order. Thus, the question of winning the White House must be subordinated to the deeper issue of mobilizing sufficient *systemwide* black political strength to alter the black community's position at all levels of the political system. In this sense, the campaign for the White House does not become an all-consuming point of reference but a convenient field of operation for the realization of more primordial objectives. If black voters clearly understand the larger political purposes of the campaign, depiction of the candidate by the media as a loser and an "exotic choice" will not substantially affect the campaign by the black presidential organization to capture the hearts, souls, and unswerving loyalty of the black electorate through the skillful utilization of grass-roots mobilization techniques.

Overcoming Democratic Party Resistance

Jackson found in 1984 that the Democratic Party constituted a powerful constraint in the realization of his political objectives for the black community.

He had hoped that by running in the primaries and winning a substantial number of delegates he could avoid the political catastrophy of 1980 when Jimmy Carter received strong black support in the primaries and virtually ignored the requests of black leaders at the Democratic convention. When he arrived in San Francisco, Jackson found that, despite his clout at the ballot box (having won some 394 delegates), it would be enormously difficult to translate this clout into internal party influence.

Jackson had received a glimpse of things to come during the primaries when party officials refused to abandon the 20-percent threshold rule that cost him nearly half the delegates to which he would have been entitled if his delegate allotment had equaled his voting strength in the state campaigns. In San Francisco, Jackson discovered that the Mondale forces were exercising tight control over major convention committees and were refusing to yield to requests by Jackson for substantive input and strategic compromises. In the final analysis, the Mondale forces made almost no concessions to the Jackson camp, orchestrating a negative vote on three of the four changes the Jackson camp proposed for the platform. Jackson's dream of playing the role of political broker for the black community shattered on the rocks of racism and intransigence. Party leaders made the strategic decision to give Jackson his day in the sun on national television and exile him to the outer reaches of political obscurity.

One Jackson delegate, Professor Lucius Barker of Washington University, kept a detailed diary of his experiences at the 1984 Democratic convention. His book, *Our Time Has Come*, based in large part on his diary notes, captures the agony and disappointment of the Jackson contingent in the wake of the shabby treatment Jackson delegates experienced at the hands of top party officials (Barker, 1987). In retrospect, the depth of their pain is surprising. In refusing to compromise with the Jackson forces, the party was merely living up to its history as an instrument for the promotion of the interest of dominant elites in American society. The electoral potency of the Reagan revolution made it extremely unlikely the party would make radical changes in the platform that might alienate important sectors of the white population. Mondale was under enormous pressure from Southern officials to reject efforts by Jackson to change the party platform; Mondale's analysis suggested that his candidacy would be stillborn if he did not have the support of a white Southern electorate that had provided strong support for a number of victorious Republican candidates in recent years.[3] On the other hand, he believed he could count on overwhelming black support because blacks had nowhere else to go. The prospects for black influence on the policymaking process of the party have not improved since the 1984 convention. To the contrary, party officials appear to be moving further to the Right to win back the millions of Democrats who defected to the Republicans in the last two elections.

Appropriate strategies for overcoming party resistance are open to wide debate. In 1984, there were many in the Jackson camp who were in favor of walking out of the convention to teach party officials a lesson. This idea was dropped because Jackson was opposed to a walkout and because the delegates did not want to do anything to embarrass Mr. Jackson or prevent him from obtaining the respect he so richly deserved. The history of the Mississippi

Freedom Democratic Party clearly shows that a walkout can produce meaningful results. This avenue should remain an option for individuals who attend the convention as Jackson delegates in 1988.

Barker has suggested that Jackson might wish to consider a toning down of
his policy objectives in order to build an effective electoral coalition (Barker,
1987:198). Similarly, Monte Piliawsky has called upon blacks to eschew exclusionary racial solidarity appeals in favor of more moderate appeals that would
attract whites into an effective coalition (Piliawsky, 1985:22–23). The strategy
of toning down runs the risk of turning off black voters previously mobilized.
Black voters should not be asked to sacrifice their interest for the sake of
accommodating the interest of others. Jackson must do everything possible to
hold on to his black base. This is not an easy task; after the glamour of a "first"
campaign has worn off, black voters must often be remobilized in order to
produce a repetition of their political involvement in future campaigns.

As a substitute for toning down, black candidates should consider broadening their appeal to other groups by adding select non-black issues to their
campaign repertoire. White farmers and blue-collar workers often face economic problems similar to those faced by unskilled urban black workers. An
appeal to the pocketbook interests of these new groups could yield extraordinary results. Early reports suggest that Jesse Jackson has had phenomenal
success with the broadening strategy in the 1988 campaign.

In terms of national party politics, blacks must pursue both an internal and
external party strategy. Barker has correctly argued that the strong support for
Jesse Jackson by black voters establishes the essential precondition for the
pursuit of aggressive policy positions within the Democratic Party. The fact
must be stressed by black leaders that the Democratic Party cannot win a
national election without strong black support. It must be made clear that
blacks are no longer prepared to give up their votes without an adequate quid
pro quo. Blacks must enter into the realm of political reciprocity. If party
officials are unwilling to make concessions, massive nonvoting by blacks as a
protest response may be the most appropriate option to pursue.

In the final analysis, black political interests may well lie beyond the arena
of traditional two-party politics. Blacks must again return to the idea of a third
party strategy. Such a party need not be electoral in nature. There exists a
burning need for an instrument to execute the responsibility of political education. A third party option may also place enormous pressure on the two
regular parties to expand their racial and ethnic policy agendas. It is critically
important that black people not confuse their interests with those of the
Democratic party; the two are not synonymous. Blacks should also avoid the
danger of becoming so caught up in party politics that they overlook the
importance of other arenas of political activity in the development and implementation of public policy, including the enormous influence wielded by
labor unions and private corporations.

Intracommunity Conflict and Social Change

Matthew Holden has called attention to the existence of a black quasi-
government functioning through a variety of institutions and held together by

the reciprocal relations existing between interdependent elites (Holden, 1973:3–4). Conflict often emerges in the black community when the interests of the leaders of politically active black institutions clash. Jesse Jackson's decision to run for the presidency generated considerable conflict among important leadership elements in the black community. Members of the Atlanta leadership corps close to the Carter administration were quite vocal in their opposition to Jackson's bid for the presidency. Andrew Young, Julian Bond, and Coretta Scott King were all sharply critical of Jackson's decision to run. Their principal argument against his running was that Jesse could not win and that his campaign would therefore be self-defeating. Behind this argument lay the poignant reality that these individuals had previously committed themselves to support Mondale and were not free to endorse a competing black candidate. Jackson's candidacy was also opposed by the heads of leading civil rights organizations, including Benjamin Hooks of the NAACP and John Jacob of the National Urban League. These individuals expressed the belief that the time was not right for a black presidential bid; they expressed fears that Jackson's candidacy would lead to the nomination of an unacceptable white conservative as the standard bearer of the Democratic Party.

Additional opposition to Jackson's candidacy was expressed by black elected officials, including Mayor Richard Arrington of Birmingham, Mayor Wilson Goode of Philadelphia, and Mayor Coleman Young of Detroit. The active public opposition of this array of prominent black leaders created enormous problems for the Jackson campaign. Barker contends that it was the blatant display of disunity by black leaders in the 1984 campaign that most strongly inspired Democratic party officials to reject Jackson's proposals at the national convention (Barker, 1987:177).

Adolph Reed, Jr., in *The Jesse Jackson Phenomenon* (1986) places the blame for the internal black conflict surfacing during the campaign squarely on the shoulders of Jesse Jackson. Reed describes Jackson as a self-appointed protest leader without legitimate links to a grass-roots constituency in the black community. Jackson as a presidential candidate, he argues, has been a product of an uninformed media unable to distinguish between a social movement and feverish church meetings. Jackson, he argues, has emerged out of the undemocratic, authoritarian structure of the black church that practices governance from the top down rather than the bottom up. During the campaign, Jackson claimed to have a monopoly on the racial voice; his pretensions of speaking for the entire black community were accepted unchallenged by a racist media that believed that black America could and should be represented by one individual. Black leaders opposed Jackson's presidential bid not because they were afraid of being overshadowed or dethroned as brokers for the black community, but because the Jackson campaign projected the false image of Jackson as not merely the premier black leader but the only legitimate leader with an authentic popular following (Reed, 1986:107–8).

According to Reed, relations between Jackson and black elected officials began to deteriorate substantially when the Jackson forces—in their zeal to demonstrate their candidate's political clout—began to run candidates against entrenched incumbent black politicians and to tinker in other ways with the balance of power in local black communities. Reed argues that black elected

officials who obtain their positions through the democratic process are preferable as leaders to protest leaders who are self-appointed and do not represent in an organic way any identifiable community constituency. In the post-
voting-rights era, black elected officials have come to view themselves as the
authentic spokesmen for the people. They naturally resent the intrusion of
noncommunity forces into their jurisdictional areas. Over the years, they have
labored hard to build organizations that relate to human needs on a daily
basis. Jackson's efforts to superimpose his political organization on existing
organizational and leadership structures were deeply resented by local black
political leaders and were major sources of conflict and disunity throughout
the campaign. Reed contends that much of the increase in voter registration
and turnout attributed to the Jackson organization was actually the work of
local organizations unaffiliated with the Jackson campaign. Indeed, he asserts
that much of the growth in these areas evident during the 1984 campaign was
the by-product of trends that began in the 1970s and continued into the early
years of the 1980s. In sum, Reed contends that descriptions of the impact of
the Jackson campaign on black mobilizations have given an exaggerated and
distorted view of reality. The mobilization that occurred was the product of a
complex of factors, of which the Jackson effort was just one.

Although Reed's book is an interesting study, it does not accurately capture
the basis for internal institutional disunity in the black community during the
1984 campaign. The notion of Jesse Jackson as a self-appointed leader without
a valid constituency in the national black community has no basis in fact.
Jackson is a long-time civil rights leader whose credentials as a major black
spokesman have been established for over a decade. Long before he announced his candidacy, he had elevated his stature from that of a local leader
to that of a major national black leader. His posture as a national leader was
cemented both by his work with Operation PUSH and his involvement in a
multiplicity of protest campaigns at the local level. Obviously, Jackson was not
sharply criticized by the Atlanta leadership forces and leaders of prominent
civil rights organizations because of his status as a protest leader. They also
were members of this same leadership class; to criticize Jackson on this basis
would have been to turn the critical eye on themselves. Their principal concern
with Jackson's candidacy was that it threatened to upset their clientage relations with external white patrons. This was probably also the motivation for
the criticisms from prominent black politicians who had forged major commitments to the Mondale campaign.

Reed's major mistake is his failure to view the Jackson campaign as an
authentic political movement. At its apex, the Jackson campaign became a
political crusade reminiscent of grass-roots movements mounted in cities to
elect black mayors to public office. Jackson did not superimpose his campaign
on local organizations. The constituents of these organizations became caught
up in the Jesse Jackson phenomenon. Jackson symbolized for them another
episode in the civil rights revolution launched by Dr. King. The impact of the
Jackson campaign was twofold. First, Jackson activated thousands of citizens
who had remained unmotivated by local organizing activity. It is estimated
that the Jackson campaign increased black registration by 2 million. It is
interesting that Reed notes that, in primary states with large black popula-

tions, black turnout rates were considerably larger in 1984 than in 1980, with increases of up to 87 percent in Alabama and 27 percent in New York (Reed, 1986:20). Second, the Jackson campaign created dual loyalties among blacks firmly tied to local organizations. Far from disrupting and undermining local organizations, the Jackson campaign complemented and strengthened local mobilization efforts. Many local organizations used Jackson's coattails to reactivate waning memberships and expand their electoral appeal through the recruitment of new members activated by the Jackson crusade.

Conclusion

The term *institutional racism* frequently conjures up images of processes and procedures that covertly undermine free access by blacks to economic markets and educational resources and deprive blacks of equal protection and due process of law in the legal system. In truth, institutional racism in America takes many forms. During the 1984 presidential campaign, Jesse Jackson exposed elements of the electoral process that served as barriers to the full expression of black political power in local and state elections. The studies examined in this essay call attention to the institutional forces at work in the electoral process that operate as formidable obstacles to the success of a black presidential candidate. There is simply no way a black candidate can circumvent the politically delimiting power of key institutions such as the media and major parties. Strategies for dealing with the central racial tendencies of these institutions must be factored into any agenda for black progress developed in the context of a black presidential campaign.

A pivotal starting point for this kind of strategic planning must be the recognition that successful black movements are typically constructed from the bottom up rather than the top down. It is, in fact, politically naive to assume that a black presidential campaign can be built from within the internal organizational structure of the Democratic Party. An effective black candidate must first attempt to concretize bases of strength within black communities, utilizing every diplomatic and administrative skill possible to minimize fragmentation and conflict between key institutional forces in the black community. Once an operational base in the black community has been built, the candidate will be in a position to enter into policy negotiations with party politicians and reach out to other constituencies beyond the institutional environment of the party.

Black presidential campaigns must be unidirectional, encompassing a medley of organizational approaches simultaneously. Internal party negotiations, for example, must be buttressed with pressure from below, emanating from continuing protest campaigns around specific issues. Effective use must be made of the veto power that can be exercised by the black electorate in a number of Congressional districts. Substantive policy agreements made between the candidate and Congressional incumbents would possibly avoid the deterioration of the black programmatic agenda at the national convention to an empty plea for "respect."

Finally, black presidential politics must seek to establish viable and productive linkages with progressive forces in the international community. The interdependence of Afro-American and African policy objectives virtually demands that the mobilization of domestic black political strength be executed within a broad and creative international context.

Notes

1. This was the way CBS news reported Jackson's exit polling results on the day of the New York primary (see Broh, 1987, p. 36).
2. This position was taken by *The New Republic* in a sharply worded editorial criticizing Jackson's decision to run (see Walton, 1985, pp. 39–41).
3. On the ascendancy of the Republican Party with Democratic support (see Piliawsky, 1985, pp. 19–20).

References

Barker, Lucius J. 1987. *Our Time Has Come: A Delegate's "Diary" of the Jesse Jackson 1984 Presidential Campaign.* Urbana and Chicago: University of Illinois Press.

Broh, C. Anthony. 1987. *A Horse of a Different Color: Television's Treatment of Jesse Jackson's 1984 Presidential Campaign.* Washington, D.C.: Joint Center for Political Studies.

Cross, Theodore. 1984. *The Black Power Imperative: Racial Inequality and the Politics of Nonviolence.* New York: Faulkner Books.

Holden, Jr., Matthew. 1973. *The Politics of the Black "Nation."* New York and London: Chandler Publishing Company.

Jackson, Jesse. "The Keys to a Democratic Victory in 1984." Speech before the 13th Annual Convention of Operation Push, Inc., published in *The Black Scholar* (September/October 1984).

Lineberry, Robert L. 1983. *Government in America: People, Politics and Policy.* Boston and Toronto: Little, Brown.

Piliawsky, Monte. "The 1984 Election's Message to Black Americans: Challenges, Choices and Prospects." *Freedomways* (First Quarter, 1985).

Reed, Jr., Adolph. 1986. *The Jesse Jackson Phenomenon: The Crisis of Purpose in Afro-American Politics.* New Haven: Yale University Press.

Walton, Jr., Hanes. 1985. *Invisible Politics: Black Political Behavior.* Albany: State University of New York Press.

Jacksonian Democracy—Black Style: Differing Perspectives

William Crotty

Northwestern University

Lucius J. Barker, 1988, **Our Time Has Come: A Delegate's "Diary" of Jesse Jackson's 1984 Presidential Campaign,** Urbana, IL: University of Illinois Press, 288 pp., ISBN 0-252-01426-X.

C. Anthony Broh, 1987, **A Horse of a Different Color: Television's Treatment of Jesse Jackson's 1984 Presidential Campaign,** Washington, D.C.: Joint Center for Political Studies, 93 pp., ISBN 0-941410-54-4 (paper).

Adolph L. Reed, Jr., 1986, **The Jesse Jackson Phenomenon,** New Haven, Ct.: Yale University Press, 170 pp., ISBN 0-300-03543-8. (paper).

For many, Jesse Jackson's campaign for president was the most noteworthy occurrence of the 1984 election year.[1] Jackson's being black and an outsider to conventional politics challenged the system's ability to adapt and accommodate itself to a less-than-mainstream voice for those left behind by the Reagan era's boosterism and good times. It was an uncomfortable proposition for the nation's political parties and especially the Democrats, its nominating systems, the media, and, equally unaccustomed to such a challenge, its citizenry.

In the age of Reagan and the "I've-got-mine" mentality it fostered, Jackson was an intruder, a proponent of unwelcome ideas and a visible symbol of much that many people would like to ignore. He was a threat to the centrist-middle-class image the Democratic frontrunner, Walter Mondale, and his party hoped to project. In one sense, it was all good theater, a fight over substance and for a stubborn reality that was overwhelmed by the dominant imagery of good cheer, "a renewed pride in America," the harnessing of an impressive communications technology in the service of the reigning political ideology, and a stubbornly issueless political year not open to effective challenge (witness the Reagan–Mondale debates).

What did Jackson have to offer in such a political climate? No one quite knew how to treat him: articulate, outspoken, a representative of, in his words, "the hurt, . . . the rejected, the despised," hardly the target groups for a win-

ning candidacy in 1984; a preacher who often broke into the rhythmic ca-
dences of the Black Baptist Church and quoted from the Bible in an age
suspicious of both; and a man who had never run for, much less held, political
office. From beginning to end, the reaction was negative. The emphasis was
on the difficulties for others that the Jackson campaign created and the
motives of its candidate. Why was he running? What problems did this represent for the Democrats and for the front-runner Walter Mondale? How would
the Democrats respond? How could a man who had never held public office
run for the presidency? Where was Jackson's organization? His financial resources? Why had he entered the race so late? Why did many of the most
prominent black leaders refuse to back him? Where would his support come
from? Did Jackson have the "stature" to seek the presidency? Would he embarrass himself and hurt the black "cause" through a weak or foolish effort?

Jackson, his critics claimed, had too many enemies, even in the black community, to be effective; he was too flashy and unpredictable; he had little
perseverance and was noted for his failure to stick with projects; he courted
publicity and media attention but left the hard day-to-day work to others. And
he scared whites. Again, why was he running?

This was the dominant question. In many respects, it is a question that the
media and many politicians never could satisfactorily answer. At the end of
the campaign, the perceptions of many were much as they had been at the
beginning. The media seemed as perplexed by the campaign as ever.

The eventual Democratic party's presidential nominee, Walter Mondale,
seemed equally perplexed and a little resentful. Assessing his campaign bid in
the wake of the Reagan reelection landslide, Mondale accused Jackson of
making "life quite difficult for me." Mondale continued: "I tried to treat the
first black candidate for president of the United States with dignity and to
accept the seriousness of that candidacy. . . . I don't believe that Jesse treated
me in an equivalent manner."[2] Mondale referred to his support during the
1960s for civil rights ("I earned my spurs in the civil rights movement") and his
expectation of black backing based on his record. He went on to refer to
another aspect of the Jackson candidacy that clearly rankled: a white backlash
to Jackson that Mondale believed hurt his chances. "There was some residual
feeling in this country that Rev. Jackson would have more influence than he
would have had [in a Mondale Administration] and I think it hurt."[3]

Others shared many of the same sentiments. Mayor Coleman A. Young of
Detroit: "Jesse first of all has no experience. And he has no platform. And he
has no chance. As a politician, he is out of his head."[4]

Richard Scammon, the NBC voting analyst and an election expert, took an
even dimmer view of the Jackson effort. Jackson, he said, "had no real program and he doesn't know what he is doing." Jackson, according to Scammon,
was "a black George Wallace—a Rodney Dangerfield. He wants respect."[5]

And writing after the election in one of the first of the academic-based
reviews of the campaign, Henry A. Plotkin, although crediting Jackson with
calling for "a revitalization of the [Democratic] party's left," at the same time
accused him of running a campaign "haunted" by "black separatism, anti-
semitism, [and] prototalitarianism."[6] According to Plotkin, there "was the implicit threat in Jackson's campaign of a separatist black politics, which not only

endangered any possible Democratic electoral victory but menaced the pluralistic basis of American politics."[7]

All of this may be more of a comment on American politics and its pundits than it is on Jesse Jackson. Nonetheless, it is fair to ask what, if anything, Jackson added to the politics of 1984. What did he and his campaign represent? What did they accomplish?

Three arguments can be made. First, Jackson spoke for a distinctive constituency, one predominately black whose concerns were either unvoiced (Reagan) or underemphasized (Mondale) in the political climate of the 1980s. Second, he mobilized a substantial black constituency that resulted in a surprisingly durable challenge to his party's frontrunners. And finally, he helped pave the way for a more issue-oriented, liberal campaign four years later and one in which he could run with less notice as to his skin color and have more acceptance by the media and Democratic party voters as a legitimate spokesperson for a particular point of view.

First, Jackson, as claimed, spoke for a fundamentally different constituency than that represented by the major candidates. In truth, it consisted predominately of blacks, the poor, the unemployed, the less educated, those who felt left out of government and who had the least confidence in it. The Jackson constituency ranked as the most alienated, angry, and economically and politically disadvantaged.

It was also a constituency with markedly different issue priorities than white mainstream America. A survey commissioned by the Joint Center for Political Studies and carried out by the Gallup Organization makes the point. Blacks (unlike whites) strongly disapproved of the Reagan administration and its economic, social, and foreign policies. They were significantly more liberal on questions such as government spending and programs for the poor, civil rights, nuclear disarmament, and sensitivity to Third World concerns. They favored decreased defense allocations. In a basic contrast to whites, blacks saw Reagan as prejudiced, unfair, ineffective, insensitive, and lacking in compassion. Most blacks saw Jackson as a forceful proponent for their views and supported him in the Democratic race. Four percent of the whites did. In 1984, blacks and whites lived in two different political worlds, and Jackson spoke for one of these.[8]

Second, Jackson contributed to what was a surprisingly effective job in mobilizing this politically least influential of constituencies. Black registration increased in eleven southern states between 11,000 and 132,000 between 1980 and 1984. Over 695,000 new black voters were added to the rolls, an average of 63,000 per state. At the same time, white registration decreased by a total of one-quarter of a million voters in the same eleven states. Recognizing that blacks constitute an average of 22 percent of the population for these states, it could mean a relative increase in the political strength and influence of the black electorate, if the registration and corresponding increases in turnout can be sustained (a big if).

The 1984 voter turnout in some state primaries (Alabama, Georgia) and the District of Columbia jumped by 60 to 80 percentage points over 1980. In the large industrial states of New York and Illinois, the Democratic primary turnout was up between 38 and 40 percent. Overall, in the seventeen primary states in which Jackson received 10 percent or better of the vote, turnout increased over 1980 by an average of 22 percentage points. In "black areas" (precincts in which blacks comprise 80 percent or more of the population) of the twelve states studied by the Joint Center for Political Studies and for which data were available (the CBS/*New York Times* exit polls), turnout was up an average of 50 percentage points. In three primary states (California, Maryland, and North Carolina), first-time black voters constituted 11 percent of the total vote. By any gauge, these are impressive results. They are made even more politically significant when one realizes that, at the most, only between one-fourth to one-fifth of the voting age population participates in the primaries (the average in 1984 for the thirty Democratic primaries was 14 percent).

Jackson's campaign was to claim credit for much of this. Certainly, the Jackson campaign helped dramatize black concerns, giving them a focal point for their political energies and drawing many into the political arena who otherwise would have had little to motivate them. As he said he would, Jackson made a difference here.

Despite speaking for and mobilizing a definable segment of the electorate, Jackson's influence on the nominating process was minimized by the rules in effect in 1984. Jackson claimed that the Democratic Party's nominating procedures worked against his campaign, diluting his support and weakening his, and his constituency's, impact on party decision-making. He had a point. During the 1976–1984 period, nominating structures had been specifically redesigned to favor front-runners, presumably mainstream, centrist Democrats supported by party regulars (such as was the case with Walter Mondale). In the name of the elusive goal of party consensus, third, fourth, fifth, and other minicandidacies would be discouraged. Suffice it to say that under the rules applied in 1984, Mondale gained a sufficient edge in the allocation of national convention delegates' votes to allow him to claim the nomination.[9] Jackson was penalized, commanding fewer national convention votes than his state primary and caucus support would have indicated. Under different allocation formulas, ones closer to one person, one vote or a proportional distribution of convention votes based on state outcomes, rather than the bonus votes, superdelegates, and approximations of winner-take-all formulas in effect, Jackson could have played a significantly more influential role at the national convention.[10]

From start to finish, Jackson ran an unusual campaign and presented an unwelcome problem to mainstream American politics. It could be argued that his was the first substantial black candidacy to contest for the presidency; that his campaign made a significant impact on the prenomination politics of 1984 and the nature of the 1988 race; and, what is more important, on the manner in which politicians, the public, and the press might well perceive and deal with future minority candidacies.

The press and the political parties, however, were not the only ones unsure as to how to handle the Jackson phenomenon. The academic works that have appeared since the campaign have been ambivalent, stressing often competing interpretations of the value of the effort. The three books reviewed here are indicative of different perspectives on the campaign.

I read Lucius J. Barker's *Our Time Has Come: A Delegate's "Diary" of Jesse Jackson's 1984 Presidential Campaign* both in manuscript and present postpublication form. Then, as now, I believe it the best single interpretive account available on the Jackson campaign.

Barker, Edna F. Gellhorn Professor of Public Affairs and professor of political science at Washington University in St. Louis, served as a Jackson delegate to the Democratic national convention. He is able to blend his personal and practical experience as a delegate with his political science background to produce a most unusual "diary." On one level, this book recounts Barker's experiences and his reactions to these. In this regard, it is a highly readable and insightful addition to the literature. Barker also critiques the Jackson campaign, its strengths and failings and its, and the Democratic Party's, likely future prospects.

On another level, Barker grounds the Jackson candidacy in the civil rights movements of the 1960s and in the visions of Martin Luther King, Jr. He envisions the Jackson movement as a second-level step, the channeling of a generation of protest movements into the explicitly political arena of elective policies. It is a significant point. "At best a campaign like Jackson's illuminates the nature and vagaries of our political system," Barker writes. "Given the kind of strong supports needed to surmount various structural and ideological barriers, electoral politics is unlikely to process definitive, non-negotiable demands but may be able to process the kind of broad parameters in which such demands can be more favorably negotiated" (p. 201).

If Jackson has accomplished anything approaching such a condition—and the argument can be made, as Barker has made it, that he has directly contributed to such a development—then the value and contribution of the Jackson candidacy is clear.

Adolph L. Reed, Jr. in his *The Jesse Jackson Phenomenon: The Crisis of Purpose in Afro-American Politics* takes a quite different tack. He makes an argument—basically that the Jackson campaign hurt the development and maturation of black politics—frequently advanced during the election year by both white and, in more pointed form, black intellectuals and academicians. Reed's argument is probably the best reasoned and most clearly stated presentation of this point of view available. It is a subtle argument that examines both the evolution of black advocacy from the days of the civil rights protests to the present and the competing political leadership, economic, and social strains among blacks. Reed writes:

> . . . the Jackson phenomenon became [in the book] simultaneously a topic for examination in its own right and a window onto the larger dynamics that have structured post-civil rights era black political activity in general. Most prominent among these are: (1) the development of competing criteria for legitimation of claims to black political leadership; (2) the sharpening of lines of socioeconomic stratification within the Afro-American population; and (3) the growth of centrifugal pressures within and external attacks on the national policy consensus represented in the Democratic coalition, which has been the main context for articulation of black political agendas for at least a generation. (p. x)

Reed continues:

> The central thesis of this book is that the 1984 Jesse Jackson phenomenon must be understood not only in relation to these dynamics; the Jackson phenomenon also is emblematic of the inadequacy of conventional patterns of discourse concerning black political activity, which originate in a pre-civil rights context of racial protest, for generating either critical interpretations or appropriate strategic responses in the present situation. (p. x)

It is a provocative argument and a valuable opening of the Jackson campaign onto a canvass that allows an examination of the complexities of current black political demands and the adequacy of the system in responding to them, particularly in terms of their channeling through the Democratic Party as historically they have been.

Reed is clearly critical of the Jackson effort, both on a tactical level and as an effective vehicle for black interests. Any number of significant issues are raised, each worthy of notice and debate, and all done within the pages of what is a slim volume. As examples, Reed claims that "Jackson's leadership status lies outside the realm of palpable constituencies of discrete individuals" (p. 29) and specifically disputes his base in and centrality to the South; he believes that the "discussion of Afro-American affairs is so often dominated by a patronizing, exceptionalist bias that suspends norms of critical reflection and judgment" and is engaged in "without constraint by requirements of validation." Reed goes on to question the political viability and impact of the black church and ascribes to it a Marx-like narcotic effect on the populace (p. 59); contends that "Jackson himself and his presidential initiative were situated within the black political elite structure from the first . . . [and] Jackson's attentive public was drawn from upper income, upwardly mobile strata in the black community" (p. 69, Chapter 2); sees the fear of white countermobilization to a black candidacy such as Jackson's as quite real (p. 25); feels that the "black elite's commitment to its narrowly instrumental orientation" within, for example, the Democratic Party and the bounds of conventional political patterns hurts black aspirations more broadly defined (p. 83); and says that "the cathartic frenzy that Jackson cultivated" eliminated debate among Afro-Americans, specifically in relation to the "Hymie" incident and, as Reed sees it, negated Jackson's one great opportunity to provide a balanced perspective in the Middle East.

Clearly, Reed's book—provocative, argumentative, speculative—has little in common with Barker's more personal, hands-on approach and his positive depiction of the Jackson campaign. Yet it raises significant questions as to the nature of black political interests and the best means of their implementation. Taken together, one could see the makings of an interesting intellectual debate with significant political consequences or the beginnings of a good course treating such topics.

C. Anthony Broh's book, *A Horse of a Different Color: Television's Treatment of Jesse Jackson's 1984 Presidential Campaign*, is quite different from either Barker's or Reed's. Complex, yet clear, both quantitative and interpretative, creatively conceptualized and painstakingly analyzed, brief but full, Broh's work will serve as the definitive treatment of the media's response to the Jackson candidacy, and it can serve, conceptually and methodologically, as a guide to further media analyses of candidates in the future. Broh reviewed the videotapes of 2,189 television news stories presented on ABC's, NBC's and CBS's evening news between November 1, 1983, when the first of the Democratic candidates announced for the presidency, and July 15, 1984, when Walter Mondale received the Democratic nomination. He coded each story in relation to the manner or role in which reporters cast the candidates. The four roles were: "horse-race roles," a favorite of reporters that essentially includes projections of who would win, descriptions of a race's strategy and tactics, and the consequences of individual victories and losses; "democracy roles," depicting the extent to which candidates play by the rules of the game, raise issues, represent constituency opinion, or draw groups into the electoral process; "personality roles," which focus on the candidates' character, relations with others, personal qualities and background; and "outsider roles," or the degree to which candidates are presented as being outside the limits of traditional mainstream approaches and the bounds of conventional politics.

The presumption underlying the analysis is that "the roles in which television presents candidates affect the expectations of the members of the public who watch the programs" and that "reporters' preconceived categories of electoral politics, as expressed in the roles in which reporters cast candidates, are transformed into the public's perception of the campaign" (p. 4).

Broh devotes a chapter to each role perception, developing the conceptual and historical dimensions of the role and then applying it to the data collected on the 1984 campaign. Each role is subdivided and analyzed in terms of its component parts (for example, personality roles were subclassified as "worker," "opportunist," "entertainer," and "negative role model"). Particular attention, of course, is given to the representation of the Jackson campaign. Broh concludes the monograph with chapters summarizing his findings and projecting these into the future.

The results are intriguing. How did the media treat Jesse Jackson? There were pluses and minuses. Jackson stories dominated in the categories of personality and outsider roles. He received the least attention in the Democratic field (which also included Alan Cranston, John Glenn, Gary Hart, and Walter Mondale) in relation to the horse-race roles.

The ambivalence and difficulty inherent in television's reporting of the Jackson candidacy can be seen in its depiction of him in relation to "democracy" roles. As Broh notes, "in Democracy Roles the way television news cast Jackson implied both that he was a legitimate candidate for the presidency and that he was somehow different from the other candidates who were also in the race" (p. 49). Reporters clearly reinforced Jackson's right to be in the race, which was helpful but not an issue with the other candidates. They also publicized his efforts to bring apolitical and disadvantaged groups into the electorate, a plus, again in terms of image perhaps, but one that emphasized, correctly, the uniqueness of his constituency. And television concentrated a significant proportion of its stories on the problems Jackson had both in broadening his constituency and in relating to other more traditional Democratic groups. These emphases, in addition to those relating to his outsider role and distinctive background, plus the implicit issue of race, served to reinforce the idea that, although a legitimate contender, he had little chance for the nomination. Perception is reality in politics, and questions then arose in a continuing debate as to why Jackson ran, a theme that may be understated in the analysis.

Broh concludes:

> By showing Jackson as fully a Democrat, television helped legitimate his candidacy. Even though many blacks had doubts about the viability of a black presidential candidate and many whites had doubts about the desirability of a black presidential candidate, television news was definitive about Jesse Jackson's right to be in the race. He was to receive fair treatment like any other presidential candidate because he was using established electoral procedures in an attempt to gain public office. More important than the fact that he won some primaries and lost some was the fact that he was shown as fully participating in the entire process. . . . The image of a supporter of the constitutional framework, an adherent of the democratic regime, a believer in the structure of government itself, is an image the media bestow on all political leaders who follow the democratic rules of the game. In short, Jesse Jackson was a significant presidential candidate because he shared and acted on the values that most Americans see as underlying the nation's electoral and governmental system. (p. 79)

Yet in all of this, Jackson was presented as an outsider with little real chance at the nomination. The depictions of Jackson in outsider and personality roles was heavily negative.

> Why did the media not include Jackson in the horse race? Why was he not viewed as being in contention for the nomination? The answers to these questions are multifaceted and complex, but one factor is paramount: In 1984 the United States was not ready to elect a black man as president. Television news reporters recognized this, and their reports became a self-fulfilling prophecy guaranteeing that the United States was not ready to elect a black man as president in 1984. (p. 82)

Broh is right on the mark here as he is when he argues that "television is as formidable an obstacle as are the party's rules and procedures" to winning a presidential nomination (pp. 84–85).

The Jackson candidacy was unique. It was entertaining; it represented a largely ignored and politically underdeveloped constituency; it raised significant issues; and it tested the bounds and institutions of American politics. Each of these books, and each in its own distinctive way, has something of importance to say on the Jackson campaign and its implications for American politics.

Notes

1. Parts of this essay are based on William Crotty, "The Presidential Nomination Process and Minority Candidates: The Lessons of the Jackson Campaign," prepared for the Conference on the 1984 Presidential Election sponsored by the Joint Center for Political Studies, Washington, D.C., April 30, 1985.

2. "Mondale Raps Jesse, Admits Campaign Flops," *Chicago Sun-Times*, April 8, 1985, p. 20.
3. Ibid.
4. *Congressional Quarterly*, January 7, 1984, p. 9.
5. Quoted in Henry A. Plotkin, "Issues in the Campaign," in Gerald A. Pomper, ed., *The Election of 1984* (Chatham, N.J.: Chatham House Publishers, 1985), p. 48.
6. Ibid, p. 47.
7. Ibid.
8. These points are developed further in William Crotty, "Jesse Jackson's Campaign: Constituency Attitudes and Political Outcomes," in Lucius J. Barker and Ronald Walters, eds., *Jesse Jackson's Presidential Campaign: Challenge and Change in American Politics*, Urbana, Illinois: University of Illinois Press, forthcoming.
9. For a more in-depth discussion, see Crotty, "The Presidential Nominating Process and Minority Candidates. . . ."
10. Ibid, pp. 17–18.

Bibliographic Essays

The Current Literature on Black Politics

Hanes Walton, Jr.

Savannah State College

The American political process since the 1965 Voting Rights Act and its subsequent renewals has witnessed innumerable black political innovations and much political creativity at the local, state, and national levels. In the main, these efforts were attempts to overcome remaining obstacles and problems and to try to maximize black political influence and clout to solve enormous and debilitating social and economic problems. And many of these acts of political creativity and innovation have captured the attention, interest, and concerns of academicians, scholars, laypersons, and media observers. For instance, the first effort by the Reverend Jesse Jackson to capture the Democratic party's nomination for president has produced nearly a dozen books—with more in the offing—and countless published and unpublished articles, to say nothing of commentaries—print and electonic. Yet this was just one of many acts of black political innovation. Therefore, out of this new attention and interest has arisen a stream of books and studies, some of which are greatly enhancing and enriching the new fledgling subfield of black politics. These current and recent works are extending and enlarging the scope and parameters of the area.

The current books (1985–1987) on black politics fall readily into some fifteen categories (see Table 1).[1] Although seven of these categories[2] are continued from an earlier appraisal of the literature that revealed nine categories (one category on black mayoral studies and another on current events had no books in this time frame), some seven new categories of study did appear, and it raised the present total to some sixteen different areas of concentration within the field of black politics. Indeed, there was growth and enhancement.

Textbooks

Perhaps the expansion in the number of textbooks suggests something of the popularity and acceptance of this new field in political science. At any rate, the growth in this area signals some very rich possibilities. Three of the works

Table 1. The Categories of the Current Literature on Black Politics, 1985–87*

Category	Authors	Percentage of Whole
Textbooks**	Marable; Elliot; Preston; Henderson, and Puryear; Jones Adair, Anderson, and Tollerson; Smith, Jones, and Rice	9.5
Methodology**	Pinderhughes; Walton	3.7
Ideology**	King; Hatch and Watkins; Tryman; Cross	7.5
Political opinion	Schuman, Steeh, and Bobo	1.9
Pressure and protest politics	Eagles; Cruse; Norrell; Pride and Woodward; Reed; Fairclough; King; Bumiller; Edds	17.0
Coalition politics	Browning, Marshall, and Tabb	1.9
Electoral studies**	Foster; Lawson; Cavanagh	5.7
Judicial studies	Smith; Wright; Ware	5.7
Political leadership	White; Horne; Marable; Garrow; Garrow	9.4
Presidential politics	Landess and Quinn; Walker; Reed; Faw and Skelton; Collins; Burk; Lisio; Beatty; Walters	17.0
Urban politics	King; King and Jennings; Schultze; Eisinger	7.5
Rural politics	Morrison; Hanks	3.7
Policy studies**	Perry; Whalen; Jones and Rice; Thernstrom	7.6
African politics**	Tryman and Mwamba	1.9

*A few of the books in the table appeared before 1985.
**The old categories.

are edited collections, and two are fully written narratives. But this does not tell the full story. First, the Marable (1985) volume offers the reader a class analysis of recent black politics and social movements. The Elliott edited volume (1986) pioneers in another way. It permits twenty-four black politicians and activists—national, state, and local—to speak for themselves and their efforts in a period of Reaganomics. The Preston, Henderson, Lenneal, and Puryear (1987) edited text is a second edition. The editors update this popular textbook by including articles on the 1984 Jackson candidacy, the struggle for black political power in a congressional district in Mississippi, and an analysis of Mayor Tom Bradley's 1982 gubernatorial loss in California. The volume also looks in detail at black mayors in Chicago, Cleveland, Detroit, New Orleans, and Philadelphia. And there are two overview articles by Henderson and Williams.

Another pioneering text—by Jones, Adams, Anderson, and Tollerson (1987)—is not only designed for the standard course in black politics but will work well as a supplementary text in American government, the political process, and other areas. It is a breakthrough volume in that those individuals who want to enhance the limited data on ethnic and minority groups in the standard textbook will find balanced and comprehensive coverage in this volume.

Finally, the text of Smith, Rice, and Jones (1987) takes a bold new direction. It looks at black politics from the standpoint of public policy. Where many of the older and current textbooks and works on black politics devote most of their coverage and time to the *political process* and black political participation in it, this new text emphasizes policy formulation, adoption, implementation, and evaluation. In short, this volume provides a policy analysis of black politics with the emphasis shifting from the process to legislation and its impact. This is a unique step in creating a textbook, and it provides those that are policy oriented with a means to get beyond the concern with political participation.

Overall, each textbook has a uniqueness and different focus and perspective. Hence, for those who are teaching black politics—they now have a very rich literature to choose from.[3]

Methodology

Beginning in the 1960s, political scientists developed a series of theoretical and methodological perspectives that would refocus and dominate the discipline for decades to come. Pluralism and behavioralism were two such theoretical perspectives to emerge and dominate the discipline. But shortly after their emergence, several critical remarks about their appropriateness for blacks and black politics arose quickly.[4] Soon, however, the accolades for these models were quickly buried by insights into the inherent weaknesses and limitations of the models. Maybe the lack of impact was due to the critiques themselves, that is, their article and essay form. But that has now been rectified.

The Pinderhughes (1987) volume takes the pluralist theory to task for its crucial weaknesses and shortcoming in explaining, evaluating, and predicting the black political experience in Chicago. Her analysis reveals that black politics does not fit the pluralist analytical framework. The larger implication of Pinderhughes's findings are profound; and, in the future, when one mentions the contributions of Dahl, Pinderhughes must be recognized in the same breath. The book is a signal achievement.

Walton surveyed behaviorism and the enormous literature that it has generated on black politics under sustained scrutiny, evaluation, and reflection (Walton, 1985). He found that an individualistic methodology fails badly when it seeks to appraise group politics on issues that develop around race. Second, his analysis reveals that much of this so-called black political behavior literature is little more than the comparing of differences in political responses of blacks and whites. Walton has demonstrated that the simple tasks of comparing blacks and whites and describing their differences in individual-level explanations have nothing to do with the nature, scope, and significance of black politics but more to do with a conscious or unconscious ideological perspective and public policy designs. Finally, black political behavior is more than individual actions: It also includes systemic realities. Like the Pinderhughes study, the implications in terms of the weaknesses and limitations of the behaviorial perspectives for black politics transcends the area itself.

Ideology

Two of the four books on black political ideology are selected volumes of speeches, sermons, interviews, eulogies, and essays, both focusing upon two major civil rights leaders, the Reverend Martin Luther King, Jr., and his disciple, the Reverend Jesse L. Jackson. The King volume (1987) is edited by his wife Coretta and includes excerpts from 120 of his speeches, sermons, and papers as well as a copy of Public Law 98-144 that made King's birthday a legal holiday and the proclamation by Ronald Reagan declaring the holiday. Only the last two items in the book are given in their entirety; all of the King material consists of excerpts. This is its weakness.

The Jackson volume, which he fully endorses in the preface, comes from some thirty-six of his public speeches. The editors of the volume, Hatch and Watkins (1987), provide solid headnotes for each speech, as well as a cogent and useful introduction. The book provides some very useful insights into the political social and economic beliefs of the Reverend Jackson, and many of the speeches are included in their entirety. This is indeed a major strength of the book.

The other two works take a look at not the ideology of black political leaders but at ideologies inherent in the social and political system. Tryman's (1985) edited book explores institutional racism in a variety of forms, ranging from health policy, family structures, the criminal justice system, political primaries, civil rights policy, to new forms and facets; and finally, it includes statements about a technological society rushing toward the future. This work is a solid updating of an ideological reality brought to academia in the late 1960s.

Cross's book (1987) combines two black ideologies—nonviolence and black power—and seeks to describe how the two must and should be used to empower blacks in America today. Essentially this is a how-to book, a road map and a strategic plan. Beyond all of the verbalism and tabular and statistical data, Cross offers this rather large volume as the *answer*, or the most viable answer, as he sees it, to black people and their problems in modern America. Before he finishes the book, he arrives at some questionable ideas: "The powerlessness of blacks," he writes, "is also closely connected to group attitudes and habits that have emerged as rational adaptations to historical forces applied against them. Many blacks still bear the imprint of their traditional schooling in subservience and deference to others" (p. 530). His solution to all the black problems in America is based in black unity. Without this unity, Cross argues, blacks' problems will persist.

Public Opinion

In an era of endless surveys, opinion polls, elite and mass interviews, and organizations that archive and save public opinion data, it was quite likely that such information would give rise to studies of black public opinion. Schuman, Steeh, and Bobo (1985) offer a trend analysis of racial attitudes using data from the National Opinion Research Center, Gallup, and the Institute for Social Research. Besides the introduction and methodological chapters, there are two chapters (one on whites and one on blacks) devoted to trends, and one (on whites) on interpreting the trends. Herein lies the problems and the weaknesses of the work. The chapter on blacks is not only the smallest one in the book, but it includes both a trend analysis and an interpretation under one roof. This is not so with whites. The paucity of survey data on black opinions is obvious. Besides saying that blacks wanted changes, which was and is obvious, the book is merely a comparison of blacks and whites and a discussion of the differences. Hence, the book leaves black public opinion where it found it—in the dark.

Pressure and Protest Politics

Although the Schuman et al. volume reveals next to nothing about black public opinion, black pressure groups have continuously sought to impact, shape, and change black attitudes. This decade is witnessing a major scholarly effort to reexamine the civil rights movement and its leadership. The Eagles-edited book (1986), using five historians and one political scientist, offers *six* different explanations for that movement in 150 pages. And in several of the six essays, blacks become the sole cause for the movement's failure. Many of the reasons given are nonsensical and unconvincing.

Cruse (1987) advances a similar but different argument. The civil rights movement is over, he asserts, because black leaders and their organizations and the black middle class never developed a coherent economic and cultural theory for the black masses. He seeks to show why, by looking at the role played by Jews who excluded or relegated blacks to specific positions in the civil rights movement, the black middle class has been unable to overcome this and harness the black potential.

Norrell (1986) looks at the civil rights movement in Tuskegee, centering on the leader, a black academic, Charles C. Gomillon,[5] and concludes that his concept, "civic democracy," meant shades of black reconstruction with little role for whites. Pride and Woodward's volume (1985) looks at Nashville and the black struggle to get school desegregation and ends up arguing that busing is a redistributive policy that takes rights from whites to give them to blacks.

The edited Reed (1986) work moves away from specific cities to look at black protest politics and participation in the 1960s in general and critiques the ideology of the leaders, strategies, and achievements. Fairclough (1987), on the other hand, seeks to analyze the Southern Christian Leadership Conference and its leader, Martin Luther King, Jr. He, in effect, looks at one of the major civil rights organizations, its strengths, weaknesses, leadership, and accomplishments. It is a massive, detailed study that covers much ground. The King (1987) book looks at a single white female and her role in the civil rights movements. It describes the trials, tribulations, and impact of that participation on the subsequent life fortunes of the participators. It is the civil rights movement as seen from a white participant–observer.

If the King work probes the role of white individuals in the movement, the Bumiller (1988) volume looks at the end of the movement and the antidiscrimination laws that it eventually produced. She shows that these anti-discrimination laws actually victimize the people who were discriminated against, and it increases their powerlessness. That, however, is not quite the problem—simply because many people have filed complaints does not mean that the civil rights regulatory agencies have not failed to investigate and enforce the law. Hence, it is not the laws, but the lack of governmental enforcement that make them victims.

Finally, Edds's (1987) journalistic account of what happened when the civil rights movement installed black elected officials in the previous all-white governmental bodies throughout the South argues that black moralism gave way to black pragmatism, but that is not quite the entire story. Like most journalistic accounts,[6] it is excellent in descriptive flow, colorful interviews, and anecdotal materials but short on perspective, analysis, evolution, and intellectual understanding. It does provide one major cogent point. She found that corporations and big business enterprises will not locate factories and businesses in counties with a population over 35 percent black.

Singularly or together, these works on black protest politics and participation in the recent civil rights movements leave much to be desired. They are filled with questionable and unsupportable theories, vast ascriptions, and most of all, limited perspectives on both the movement and black politics.

Coalition Politics

One book, by Browning, Marshall, and Tabb (1984), explores black and Hispanic efforts in ten California cities to empower themselves. Based on their findings, these authors develop a theory of the incorporation of racial minorities as they move from protest to electoral politics. The book is unique in that it looks not at the typical black–white coalitions that received much discussion before and after the black power book but at two racial minorities that are currently trying to enter the political arena and process. This gives the book its richness and pioneering quality. But its theory of incorporation is its essential weakness. By not exploring the question of black–white coalitions and putting the black–Hispanic coalition into perspective, the work, like those on pluralism and its theoretical framework, leaves much to be desired. Thus, the reader leaves the volume knowing nothing about coalitions vis-à-vis ethnicity and regions. Subsequent efforts to extend the theory and flesh it out have run precisely into part of this problem but without fully comprehending and realizing it. Hence, the authors conclude that protest is not enough—in regard to what? This book, in the final analysis, is a resurrection of the "appropriate" black–white coalition argument without acknowledging the existence of a problem with such a resurrection.

Electoral Studies

Studies of black electoral realities continue, and the three books on the subject take two different approaches to assessing black electoral efforts. Two of the three books center on the Voting Rights Act. The book edited by Foster (1985) offers nine scholarly articles in five categories (overview, judicial im-

pact, legislative enrichment, administration enforcement, and electoral response). Lawson's (1985) book on the Voting Rights Act of 1964 looks at the
federal government's efforts to broaden and enhance that act via its renewals
in 1970, 1975, and 1982 as well as the legal and bureaucratic efforts at enforcement and implementation. Relying on presidential papers, the papers and oral
histories of civil rights leaders, and public documents, Lawson ends by saying
that "on balance, the Second Reconstruction has been most successful in
preserving black ballots" (p. 302). The last work in this category is an edited
work by Cavanagh (1987). This book addresses the problem of how to mobilize black voters who have just achieved the right to vote because of the 1965
act. Using data from four case studies—Chicago, Philadelphia, Birmingham,
and the second congressional district in North Carolina, Cavanagh sets forth a
how-to strategy.

Collectively, these works reveal that the task of improving the act and its
enforcement is only part of the problem facing black political leaders; they
must then work to overcome the systemic consequences of the preact environment and get out the vote. Thus, the job or task is twofold.

Judicial Studies

Three works analyze black judicial behavior and politics. Two of the books
look at a single black judge—one on the New York bench and another on the
federal bench. The third book is a survey of state and federal black judges'
attitudes and perceptions and how those attitudes and perceptions are shaped
by background, recruitment, training and so forth.

Taking the last book first, Smith (1983) mailed out a "nine-page" thirty-
eight-question instrument to 288 black judges. Using role theory and correlat-
ing background factors (SES, family, law school, political recruitment, civil
rights activity, and judicial attitudes) with role perceptions, Smith found only
one major factor that reached a level of statistical significance and association—*racial consciousness*. Smith concludes by noting that even those judges
who wanted to engage in judicial activism for members of the black community usually tempered such efforts because of "expectation of disapproval
from [white] colleagues."

New York Judge Bruce Wright's (1987) commentary on his seventeen years
on the state bench reveals in great detail what happens when a black judge
actively seeks to help the poor and racial minorities. First, the media nick-
named him "Turn 'em loose Bruce." After media criticism, job opportunities
dried up, and mobility within the judicial system was stymied. Once the media
attacks started, then law enforcement associations began their harangues and
political pressures. Black and white colleagues on the bench started to engage
in negative behavior, and eventually the black jurist was transferred out and
sent to youth court. It took a federal lawsuit against the administrative judges
and four years to get him transferred back to the bench. Therefore, it is little
wonder what Smith found in his attitudinal and role study. Here systemic
factors shaped judicial behavior more so than individual-level ones.

Ware's (1984) work constructs a well-written and comprehensive political
biography of Judge William Hastie. Ware follows Judge Hastie from his early

years at Amherst and Harvard through his federal judgeship in the Virgin Islands that later led him to his gubernatorial post in the same place. Perhaps the most fascinating part of the biography is that Ware analyzed the "critical" role that Hastie played in getting Harry Truman elected president, relinquishing his gubernatorial post, coming to the states, and campaigning throughout the country for Truman. In short, Hastie did for Truman what Andrew Young did for Carter. This is an informative work. As Smith indicates in his conclusion, black judicial biographies and autobiographies might prove much more fruitful than the behavioral survey studies.

Political Leadership

Black political leaders continue to attract attention, and some five new works have emerged recently. White (1985) tries, in a single volume, to assess black leadership in America from Booker T. Washington to Martin Luther King, Jr. Therefore, he devotes chapters to Washington, DuBois, Garvey, Malcolm X, and King. The book has an excellent bibliography and does a very creditable job in summarizing the careers of black leaders. It is a very good place to start.

If White's work is an overview, Horne (1986) looks at the leadership role of W. E. B. DuBois in the Cold War era. Using the recently opened DuBois papers, Horne develops a portrait of DuBois that had not emerged from other studies. Thus the book is rich in detail and information. Perhaps one limitation is that Horne becomes too involved with his subject. Hence, nothing DuBois did in the last days of his life was wrong or in error (except in Horne's view, his support of the creation of the State of Israel). Nearly everyone and everything went awry except DuBois. Such a position is not wholly defensible.

Following the Horne book is one by Marable (1986) on DuBois. Instead of taking a specific period, the Marable volume is a political biography focusing on the main theories of DuBois's social thought. Marable argues that DuBois was a radical democrat but never defines the concept. In this vein, he offers a revisionist interpretation of DuBois's life. However, Marable is not afraid to criticize DuBois and offers a balanced interpretation of him in regard to other black scholars and intellectuals. Such works on DuBois are few.

Garrow (1986) has written a monumental volume on Martin Luther King, Jr. It is to date the most comprehensive effort attempted on him. Therefore, it is suffuse with dates, names, places, and explanations heretofore unseen and unknown. It covers the period from 1955 to 1968. Although no conceptual framework is formally structured and stated in the book, the epilogue suggests an implicit one. By emphasizing the weaknesses, shortcomings, and limitations of King and his efforts, one will not see King as a hero and therefore not idolize him. Hence, his achievement and efforts can be attempted to be duplicated by any ordinary citizen and black individual.

But this emphasis on King's qualities, that is personal, organizational, leadership, doctrinal, and tactical, have led to a barrage of criticisms that the work unfairly disparages King and his work. Although this is an acceptable line of reasoning and logic, it tends to foreshadow the problem inherent in con-

ceptualizing and intepreting black leadership behavior in a democratic society
where race is a dominant factor in the social and political life of the country.

Garrow (1987) has also edited a work on a black woman leader—Jo Ann
Gibson Robinson—who made the Montgomery Bus Boycott succeed. In his
search for King, he uncovered this unpublished work. He is to be commended,
and Robinson is to be praised for giving the academic and folk community this
work. It offers an insight not only into the profound role that black women
have played in every stage of the black freedom struggle but also an in-depth
look at the role they played in Montgomery that elevated King to the forefront
of black leadership. This book is *must reading*.

Taken together, the leadership books reveal an overview, two perspectives
on DuBois, one on King, and one on a black woman that are poignant and
incredibly insightful. The Robinson memoir, edited by Garrow, provides balance to works that only reflect on black men.

Presidential Politics

The 1984 presidential campaign of the Reverend Jackson produced a score
of books. Five works specifically look at this campaign. The first book to
appear was by Landress and Quinn (1985) and seeks to thoroughly and completely demonstrate that Jackson is a flawed individual unworthy of support
and admiration. Not only does the book point out every flaw, personal weakness, and shortcoming, it suggests that Jackson is similar to the white populist
racial demagogues such as Tom Watson, Cotton Ed Smith, Eugene Talmadge,
Theodore Bilbo, and James Vardaman. He is, in effect, a black racist. The book
has a foreword by the Reverend Ralph David Abernathy.

Following this book, one of Jackson's civil rights associates and participant
in the trip to free Lt. Robert Goodman, Wyatt Tee Walker (1985), offers a
participant–observer's view of that trip and its success. It offers the best detail
presently available on the realities of the mission and its outcome. There are
rare photos, key documents, and verbatim discussions. The documents make
it worth having.

In 1986, three new works emerged. Reed's (1986a) book not only continued
the flawed-character approach but uses the existence of the Jackson candidacy
as a point of departure to criticize black politics from a liberal-left perspective.
The work has generated much heated controversy, debate, and reviews.
Hence, a further detailing here would avail little. Next, two CBS journalists
that were assigned to cover the 1984 Jackson campaign, Faw and Skelton
(1986), offer their assessment of this effort. Like Landress and Quinn and
Reed, they continue the flawed-character model and end up with a devastating portrait of Jackson. In fact, the Landress and Quinn, Reed, and Faw and
Skelton books all compete with each other in terms of their negative assessment of the candidate. All three books offer perhaps the most devastating
critiques of a presidential candidate ever.

Finally, a Jackson staff and campaign worker, Collins (1986), tries her hand
at assessing the campaign. Although she offers a liberal/left perspective like
Reed, it is the best organized and the most comprehensive in terms of
coverage. She touches nearly every facet of the campaign that the other books

missed. Although the book offers data from a participant–observer position, giving it a view and coverage that the others miss, it is critical of Jackson's black political managers and leaders and less of Jackson himself. Thus, the Jackson campaign failed because blacks were politically selfish and did not know or desire to tap the other parts of the Rainbow Coalition. Although both Reed and Collins started with a class analysis approach, they ended up with varying views about the campaign.

If these works on black presidential politics center on one individual, the next group of books looks at black presidential politics in several presidential administrations. Had Landress and Quinn, Reed, Faw and Skelton, and Collins had a decent working knowledge of these books and earlier ones, the numerous conceptual, methodological, and interpretative flaws in their works would not have been so detrimental.

Burk (1984) looks at blacks, civil rights, and the Eisenhower administration. What was the Eisenhower legacy to civil rights? Burk puts it as follows: "Much of the blame for the administration's excessive caution [in civil rights] lay squarely with the president himself" (p. 263). This is a very useful work. Lisio's (1985) book looks at blacks and civil rights in the Hoover administration. The traditional scholarly view is that Hoover used black leaders, black newspapers, black delegates and votes to secure the nomination and get elected, and then capitulated to lily-white Republicanism in the South. He simply betrayed blacks politically. Because the facts are so incontrovertible on this point, Lisio offers a revisionist account of this political betrayal by arguing that it was not intentional. This new argument is not convincing, nor are the data he offers sufficient to successfully refute the well-known reality. How can a man like Hoover grow up in America, hold a host of public offices including the presidency, and not understand racism? Maybe Lisio's next book will tell us. This one did not.

Beatty's work (1987) covers all of the presidential campaigns from 1876 through 1896. She detailed, in great specificity, black participation in, support for, and opposition to each campaign, covering Hayes, Garfield, Arthur, Cleveland, Harrison, and McKinley. Did these six presidents reward and assist black loyalty, partisanship, and voter support? Like most historical studies, the book makes its case from presidential papers, correspondence, newspaper accounts, editorials, and other official sources. What is absent is the election return data. This greatly hampers the work as a useful resource.

Walters's book (1987) brings all of this together in one volume through the 1984 presidential campaign. Looking at black presidential politics, he shows that much of it had rested on *dependent leverage*, that is, behind-the-scenes bargaining. The recent efforts of Chisholm and Jackson in the primaries and at the national convention were an attempt by blacks to exercise *independent leverage*. Walters forthrightly addresses the question of an appropriate black strategy in Presidential politics and what the limitations and successes of that strategy are. This is both a landmark and breakthrough work. It shows clearly that the debate should center on *dependent* and *independent leverages* as strategies and not simply on a candidate's flaws. It will inform several generations on presidential politics in political science. Currently, none of the scholars, academicians, or journalists have ever viewed the problem for black people in presidential politics in such crystal-clear terms.

Urban Politics

In this area, books on black mayoral candidacies dominate. Recently, however, individuals have decided to speak to and search out the broader realities in the black urban centers of America. In King's (1984) book, he develops and articulates three stages that are necessary for the recapture and massive development of urban black ghettos. This how-to book is based on the author's own experience in Boston as a grass-roots organizer and elected state representative. The book has many thoughtful ideas.

Additional insights are provided on the Boston area by Jennings and his co-author, King (1987). This edited volume examines King's two unsuccessful attempts to become mayor of Boston and his efforts to mobilize the black community to take control of their destiny. The detailed insights it offers are quite useful to scholars probing the black urban reality.

Schutze (1986) provides one of the most unique books yet to emerge on black urban politics. Instead of focusing on blacks, he looks at whites and how a white business elite controlled the city. From 1955 to 1978, the white business elite organized as the Citizen's Charter Association, and maneuvered other whites and blacks, though the Dallas Negro Chamber of Commerce, to put individuals in office who helped economic growth. The author shows that this arrangement permitted massive racial violence to occur against middle-class blacks as well as permitting the taking of blacks' land for white resale. Hence, he shows that Dallas did not become democratic until 1978, and black political efforts in the city made little progress until then.[7] Schutze, a white journalist, has expanded the scope of black urban politics by centering on white players in the game. This is a path-breaking work because it makes students aware of another dimension—the other players in the urban game. More than any other book, it presents an in-depth look at the white power structure—an area that is still closed to many black academics and scholars.

Eisinger's (1983) monograph delineates black employment in forty major cities from 1973 through 1980. In his regression analysis of the data, he finds "that growth in black city jobs is certainly in part a function of black executive power and very likely a response, in addition, to black voting strength. In the absence of black political power, black employment opportunities are greater in cities with healthy economies" (p. 47). However, in regard to federal aid to the cities and black public sector employment, Eisinger is on both sides of the issue. On the one hand, he argues that federal aid is negatively related to growth of black employment. Yet on the other hand, he argues that the Great Society has helped minorities by creating public sector jobs. This is a natural outgrowth of massive aggregate data, statistical techniques, and low, or modest, correlation. They are, in the final analysis, imprecise. But this impression in an era of neoconservatism can be read as support for the contention that federal aid does not help but hurts black social and economic advances.

Rural Politics

Two new works have now brought black politics full circle. These works provide some excellent insights into black rural politics. These new, pioneering books offer new vistas and add a component that has been little addressed before. Morrison's (1987) book probes black rural politics in all of its dimensions and manifestations in three Mississippi towns—Bolton, Mayersville, and Tchula, Mississippi—with populations under 2,000. What kind of politics do poor rural blacks practice in one of the most repressive states in the country? It is truly an unseen reality. In his analysis, he reveals that all of the behavioral studies of the 1960s and 1970s explain little about black political mobilization under conditions of a low-socioeconomic level. The book offers a chapter on the political economies in these townships and how the federal government is needed to rescue the people from dirt-poor circumstances. If urban black mayors need federal assistance, Morrison has shown how these rural black mayors need similar help. This singular revelation puts the book in a class by itself.

If Morrison brought rural Mississippi townships to the forefront, Hanks (1987) brings three rural and poor Georgia counties into focus. Hanks looks at Hancock, Peach, and Clay counties, all predominantly black. Yet only one is under black political control, and Hanks shows in great detail why and what factors lead to black political empowerment in this rural black-belt county. It is fascinating reading. Moreover, Hanks reveals what role Jimmy Carter played in the empowerment process in Hancock county when he was governor. Yet he did nothing for the county after he became president. In fact, neither President Carter nor any of his numerous black political appointees—many of whom were from Georgia—did anything for the county. Why? Hanks offers some excellent insights. Both books provide additional evidence for Edds's 35-percent finding.

These two books have set the standard for forthcoming works on black rural politics, and they open a sector of black politics that surely needs more illumination. This promises to be a very exciting area.

Policy Studies

The Perry (1985) volume looks at a little-known but crucial policy area: energy policy during the Carter administration. He asks the important question of whether blacks had any impact on Carter's national energy policy. He found there was considerable minority input from black organizations but none in the upper levels of the Department of Energy. The absence of a black presence retarded the input from black organizations. Hence, this type of finding is what makes Perry's slim volume so important in terms of implications.

The Whalens volume (1985) vividly reveals the lack of black input in their discussions of the legislative history of the 1964 Civil Rights Act. This former congressman and his wife clearly reveal that as *he reads* the legislative realities of this historic legislation, blacks had little input in the formulation and policy-

enactment stages. That process was literally dominated by key white politicians and a little-known conservative Republican from Piqua, Ohio—William
McCulloch. It was McCulloch more than anyone who saw the bill through.
Civil rights groups' input was that of lobbying the public and mobilizing the
religious community. King, who led the key marches and demonstrations that
moved the nation, was basically only kept informed.

Jones and Rice's (1986) edited volume on black health care and how Title VI
civil rights regulatory agencies enforce the delivery of such services on a
nondiscriminatory[8] basis is quite illuminating. It also reveals the lack of input
and poor response to black political pressures to improve and enhance these
specific policy areas in terms of the need in the black community.

The continuing debate around the question of affirmative action has finally
now come to the matter of voting rights. Thernstrom (1987) tries, in her book,
to develop the argument that minority voting rights is no longer a simple
constitutional right but that due to the extension of the 1965 Voting Rights Act
and the insertion of Sections 2 and 5, voting rights now are a form of affirmative action. She argues that a shift has occurred. Through court interpretations, bureaucratic enforcement, and administrative decision making, blacks
are now entitled to proportionate officeholding (pp. 144–43). She writes this
treatise alleging sympathy for past black history but, in effect, argues that the
cure is worse than the disease. Changing the black right to vote to "fair-share"
officeholding is a violation of the constitutional intent of the founding fathers
and moves the constitution from its original intent. For, as she sees it, minority
votes count more than the majority. Hence, this is a form of reverse discrimination, and it is unconstitutional.

Basically speaking, this is the neoconservative argument and the thesis of
Robert Nozick about entitlement, extended to voting rights. To arrive at and to
support her contentions, she sweeps aside volumes of studies and insights. In
fact, she argues that the civil rights commission report, the "Voting Rights Act
Ten Years Later," is little more than a brief in favor of minority voters as offered
by the Democrats (p. 89). Instead, she feels that it should have been objective.
To sustain such an argument requires tortured logic, enormous references to
dissenting federal judges and opposing law school professors, and other neoconservative critics. To hold this melange of discarded thought together, numerous repetitions and circular arguments and reasoning and dissuasive
findings are simply thrown together and tossed about. Thus, the work becomes a polemic and advocacy scholarship. It is surely not a balanced treatment, nor could it be.

Finally, she shows no knowledge of the regulatory process and the nation's
use of it to solve social and economic and cultural problems, nor how that
process permits both sides, the two opposing camps, to influence the outcome.
There is a similar misunderstanding about the legislative process and the way
political majorities and coalitions are fashioned. In both areas, her ideological
groups lost, and now she is crying over spilled milk. More important, laws,
rules, and regulations do evolve. That is the very nature of the system, and
these evolutions are natural outgrowths of the lack of enforcement and protection. The continual violation of human rights had led to stronger efforts to
protect them. Thernstrom, and those of her persuasion, never advocate pro-

grams, policies, and regulatory devices to restrain the violations so that stronger measures will not be needed. Because the national government only responds in a crisis when tougher measures are needed, then those of this persuasion are forced to decry in stilted scholarship that these stronger measures are unconstitutional. Then they blame the victims for these newer and tougher measures. Overall, these beginnings in the policy area are noteworthy for the direction in which they point and the potential that they suggest exists in this category. They are indeed promising.

African Politics

A recent volume of papers edited by Tryman and Mwamba (1986) explores the relationship of American foreign policy toward the racist South African region. The essays offer a fresh perspective that is critical to the U.S. foreign policy toward this racist regime.

Conclusion

Overall, the literature in this time period has not only advanced and broadened the field, it has created new insights into old problems and realities. The new works on black rural politics establish a major beachhead and illuminate a slowly evolving sector in the field. The works in methodology alert both the old and new as well as the coming generation of scholars of black politics that there is much to be reexamined, redefined, and refocused in the discipline when attempts are made to use some of the major models and theoretical perspectives in black politics.

The diversity of the textbooks offers new and better ways to bring younger individuals into the field. And the works on urban politics that move beyond the continued gaze on the black mayor are quite promising. Public policy works, particularly the works of Walters and Burk, are quite suggestive and profound. The great surprise is the negative works on the Jackson candidacy and the limited use of the interest and protest volumes. At best, these works signal that a major effort has to be made in those areas. Despite the quantity and quality of these works, the rich suggestions they make, and the leads they offer, the best is yet to come. Numerous areas and categories are yet to be explored, analyzed, evaluated, and written. The task is before us, and these current works are beacons and signposts on a rich journey to the future.

Notes

1. See the reference list, at the end, for full bibliographic information about each of these books. For an earlier appraisal of the literature (1980–1985) see Hanes Walton, Jr., "The Recent Literature on Black Politics," *PS* (Fall, 1985), vol. XVIII, pp. 769–780.
2. See the asterisks in Table 1 for the eight old categories.
3. This count does not include a monograph by Thomas E. Cavanagh and Lorn S. Foster, *Jesse Jackson's Campaign: The Primaries and Caucuses* (Washington, D.C.: Joint Center for Political Studies, 1984). For some of the books in progress, see

    Lucius Barker and Ronald Walters, eds., *Jesse Jackson and the 1984 Presidential Campaign* (Urbana: Illinois Press, 1988) and Lorenzo Morris, Charles Jarman, and Arnold Taylor, eds., *The Social and Political Implications of the Jesse Jackson Candidacy* (New York: Praeger Publishers, forthcoming).

4. The critiques dealt essentially with pluralism and elitism and not behavioralism. In the critique of pluralism see Michael Parenti, "Power and Pluralism: A View From the Bottom," *Journal of Politics* (August, 1970), pp. 501–30 and for elitism, Samuel D. Cook, Hacker's "Liberal Democracy and Social Control: A Critique," *American Political Science Review* (December, 1957), pp. 1029–39. See also Hanes Walton, Jr., "Black Political Behavior and the Elite and Pluralist Models: An Analysis," *Political Science Review* (January–June, 1984), pp. 143–148.

5. Gomillion brought the landmark Supreme Court Case that abolished racial gerrymandering in Tuskegee. See Bernard Taper, *Gomillion versus Lightfoot: The Tuskegee Gerrymandering Case* (New York: McGraw Hill, 1962).

6. For a similar journalistic account of Black politics, see L. H. Whitmore, *Together: A Reporter's Journey into the New Black Politics* (New York: William Morrow, 1971).

7. For a similar work, but one that addresses only the questions of annexation, see John V. Moeser and Ruthledge Dennis, *The Politics of Annexation: Oligarchic Power in a Southern City* (Massachusetts: Schenkman, 1982).

8. For a discussion of affirmative action as a policy direction and orientation, see Michael Combs and John Gruhl, eds., *Affirmative Action Theory, Analysis and Prospects* (North Carolina: McFarland, 1986).

Bibliography

Beatty, Bess. 1987. *A Revolution Gone Backward: The Black Response to National Politics, 1876–1896.* Westport, CT: Greenwood Press.

Browning, Rufus P., Dale Rogers Marshall, and David H. Tabb, 1984. *Protest Is Not Enough: The Struggle of Blacks and Hispanics for Equality in Urban Politics.* Berkeley: University of California Press.

Bumiller, Kristin. 1988. *The Civil Rights Society: The Social Construction of Victims.* Baltimore: John Hopkins Press.

Burk, Robert Frederick. 1984. *The Eisenhower Administration and Black Civil Rights.* Knoxville: University of Tennessee Press.

Cavanagh, Thomas E. 1987. *Strategies for Mobilizing Black Voters: Four Case Studies.* Washington, D.C.: Joint Center for Political Studies.

Collins, Sheila D. 1986. *The Rainbow Challenge: The Jackson Campaign and the Future of U.S. Politics.* New York: Monthly Review Press.

Cross, Theodore. 1986. *The Black Power Imperative.* New York: Faulkner Books.

Cruse, Harold. 1987. *Plural But Equal.* New York: William Morrow.

Eagles, Charles W., ed. 1986. *The Civil Rights Movement in America.* Mississippi: University Press of Mississippi.

Edds, Margaret. 1987. *Free At Last: What Really Happened When Civil Rights Came to Southern Politics.* Maryland: Adler and Adler.

Eisinger, Peter. 1983. *Black Employment in City Government: 1973–1980.* Washington, D.C.: Joint Center for Political Studies.

Elliot, Jeffrey M., ed. 1986. *Black Voices in American Politics.* New York: Harcourt Brace Jovanovich.

Fairclough, Adam. 1987. *To Redeem the Soul of America: The Southern Christian Leadership Conference and Martin Luther King, Jr.* Athens: University of Georgia Press.

Faw, Bob, and Nancy Skelton. 1986. *Thunder in America: The Improbable Presidential Campaign of Jesse Jackson.* Texas: Monthly Press.

Foster, Lorn S., ed. 1985. *The Voting Rights Act: Consequences and Implications.* New York: Praeger.

Garrow, David J. 1986. *Bearing the Cross: Martin Luther King, Jr. and the Southern Christian Leadership Conference: A Personal Portrait.* New York: William Morrow.

Garrow, David J., ed. 1987. *The Montgomery Bus Boycott and the Women Who Started It: The Memoir of Jo Ann Gibson Robinson.* Knoxville: University of Tennessee Press.

Hanks, Lawrence J. 1987. *The Struggle for Black Political Empowerment in Three Georgia Counties.* Knoxville: University of Tennessee Press.

Hatch, Roger D., and Watkins, Frank E., eds. 1987. *Reverend Jesse L. Jackson: Straight From the Heart.* Philadelphia: Fortress Press.

Horne, Gerald. 1986. *Black and Red: W. E. B. DuBois and the Afro-American Response to the Cold War—1944–1963.* New York: State University of New York Press.

Jennings, James, and Mel King, eds. 1986. *From Access to Power: Black Politics in Boston.* Massachusetts: Schenkman Books.

Jones, Franklin D., Michael O. Adams, with Sanders Anderson, Jr., and Tandy Tolleson, eds. 1987. *Readings in American Political Issues.* Iowa: Kendall/Hunt.

Jones, Woodrow, and Mitchell R. Rice, eds. 1986. *Health Care Issues in Black America: Policies, Problems and Prospects.* Westport, CT: Greenwood Press.

King, Coretta Scott (selected). 1987. *The Works of Martin Luther King, Jr.* New York: Newmarket Press.

King, Mary. 1987. *Freedom Song: A Personal Story of the 1960's Civil Rights Movement.* New York: William Morrow.

King, Mel. 1981. *Chain of Change: Struggles for Black Community Development.* Boston: South End Press.

Landress, Thomas H., and Richard M. Quinn. 1985. *Jesse Jackson and the Politics of Race.* Ottman, Illinois: Jamerson Books.

Lawson, Steven. 1985. *In Pursuit of Power: Southern Blacks and Electoral Politics, 1965–1982.* New York: Columbia University Press.

Lisio, Donald J. 1985. *Hoover, Blacks, and Lily-white: A Study of Southern Strategies.* Chapel Hill: University of North Carolina Press.

Marable, Manning. 1985. *Black American Politics: From the Washington Marches to Jesse Jackson.* London: Verso.

Marable, Manning. 1986. *W.E.B. DuBois: Black Radical Democrat.* Boston: Twayne Publishers.

Morrison, Minion K.D. 1987. *Black Political Mobilization: Leadership, Power and Mass Behavior.* New York: State University of New York Press.

Norrell, Robert. 1985. *Reaping the Whirlwind: The Civil Rights Movement in Tuskegee.* New York: Knopf.

Perry, Huey L. 1985. *Democracy and Public Policy: Minority Input into the National Energy Policy of the Carter Administration*. Indiana: Wyndham Hall Press.

Pride, Richard. 1985. *The Burden of Busing: The Politics of Desegregation in Nashville, Tennessee*. Knoxville: University of Tennessee Press.

Pinderhughes, Diane M. 1987. *Race and Ethnicity in Chicago Politics: Reexamination of Pluralist Theory*. Urbana: University of Illinois Press.

Preston, Michael B., Lenneal J. Henderson, Jr., and Paul Puryear, eds. 1987. *The New Black Politics: The Search for Political Power*. New York: Longman.

Reed, Jr., Adolph L. 1986a. *The Jesse Jackson Phenomenon*. New Haven: Yale University Press.

Reed, Jr., Adolph. 1986b. *Race, Politics, and Culture: Critical Essays on the Radicalism of the 1960s*. Connecticut: Greenwood Press.

Smith, J. Owen, Mitchell Rice, and Woodrow Jones, Jr. 1987. *Blacks and American Government: Politics, Policy and Social Change*. Iowa: Kendall/Hunt.

Smith, Michael David. 1983. *Race Versus Robe: The Dilemma of Black Judges*. Port Washington, New York: Associated Faculty.

Schuman, Howard, Charlotte Steeh, and Lawrence Bobo. 1985. *Racial Attitudes in American Trends and Interpretations*. Cambridge: Harvard University Press.

Schutze, Jim. 1986. *The Accommodation: The Politics of Race in An American City*. New Jersey: Citadel Press.

Thernstrom, Abigail M. 1987. *Whose Votes Count? Affirmative Action and Minority Voting Rights*. Cambridge: Harvard University Press.

Trymana, Mfanya Donald, and Mwamba. 1987. *Apartheid South African and American Foreign Policy*. Iowa: Kendall/Hunt.

Tryman, Mfanya Donald, ed. 1985. *Institutional Racism and Black American: Challenges, Choices, Change*. Massachusetts: Ginn Press.

Walker, Wyatt T. 1985. *Road To Damascus: A Journey of Faith: The Untold Story of the Release of Lt. Robert O. Goodman*. New York: Martin Luther King Fellows Press.

Walters, Ronald. 1987. *Black Presidential Politics in America: A Strategic Approach*. New York: State University of New York Press.

Walton, Jr., Hanes. 1985. *Invisible Politics: Black Political Behavior*. New York: State University of New York Press.

Ware, Gilbert. 1984. *William Hastie: Grace Under Pressure*. New York: Oxford University Press.

Whalen, Charles and Barbara. 1985. *The Longest Debate: A Legislative History of the 1964 Civil Rights Act*. Washington, D.C.: Seven Books Press.

White, John. 1985. *Black Leadership in America 1895-1968*. New York: Longman.

Wright, Bruce. 1987. *Black Robes, White Justice*. New Jersey: Lyle Stuart.

Similarities and Differences: Reflections on Political Science Research on Women and Politics

Liane C. Kosaki

Washington University–St. Louis

R ecently, Congresswoman Patricia Schroeder announced that she would not run for the presidency. During the course of her announcement, the would-be candidate was overcome by the highly emotional atmosphere and broke down in tears. Press and public response to this behavior was largely negative. Indeed, when another potential woman presidential candidate, Jeane Kirkpatrick, also announced her decision not to run, she was asked for her reaction to Schroeder's tears. Kirkpatrick replied that she personally saw nothing wrong with Schroeder's crying. She note, however, that, "for better or worse, women have to be prepared to play by the same criteria as men are judged by."

The incident reflects an important theme in the study of women and politics—the theme is equality and the various paradoxes that result from its consideration. Much of the political science research has dealt with the question of the differences between men's and women's political participation. If women do not participate at the same rates or in the same ways as men, ought we to be concerned? If we are concerned, then what should we do about it? Should we try to make men and women identical? Or should we try instead to retain the differences, on the theory that women's greatest contributions lie in the different perspectives and values they bring to political life?

In this essay, I will look at three areas of research on American women and politics: electoral behavior, political candidates, and finally, public policies regarding women. Obviously, given the plethora of research that has taken place on this topic, this will not be an exhaustive examination. I will discuss some of this research from the perspective of equality and difference, that is, the extent to which women are similar to, or different from, men and the political consequences of these similarities and differences.

Women's Political Participation on the Mass and Elite Levels

As noted by Carroll, political scientists in the past have considered women and men to be motivated by the same passions and interests (Carroll, 1985:3). Women were perceived to vote in much the same way as men, and so the scholarly concern about women was not very great. This perception is interesting in light of the controversy that surrounded women's suffrage. Both opponents and proponents of suffrage argued that women would have distinctly different viewpoints from men and would exercise their votes accordingly. Those who feared suffrage argued that women would be too moral, enacting temperance laws or even worse, preventing involvement in war. Those who favored suffrage argued that women's moral qualities would bring a reform influence to politics that would reduce corruption and increase compassion. Thus both sides believed that an expected difference between women and men would have important political consequences (Carroll, 1985:3–4; also Stucker, 1977).

The result of the passage of the Nineteenth Amendment to the Constitution was a disappointment to proponents on both sides. Not only did a "woman's vote" fail to emerge on issues, but it also failed to emerge at all (Stucker, 1977). Women did not vote in great numbers after the amendment passed. Indeed, women voted at lower rates than men until the 1980s. Sapiro notes that between 1948 and 1972, women's turnout rates were lower than men's by an average of about 10 percent (Sapiro, 1984:22–23; see also Stucker, 1977). This difference in voting rates, however, failed to cause much alarm among political scientists. Indeed, as Bourque and Grossholtz point out in their critique of voting research, the prospect of greater women's political participation was chimerical to researchers because it would lead to the destruction of traditional family life (Bourque and Grossholtz, 1974).

The emergence of the women's movement changed the thinking in political science. Political scientists, mostly women, began to investigate women's political opinions and voting behavior. Contrary to the accepted wisdom, women did have some markedly different political views than men. The distinctiveness of women's attitudes has been noted (see, for example, Lansing, 1974; Sapiro, 1984:143–167). Moreover, as Klein has noted in her research on gender politics, this difference was evident as early as 1972 (Klein, 1984:143–51).

These differences in the attitudes of women are explained in two ways by political scientists. The first explanation is socialization. It is argued that women are likely to be taught from early childhood that politics is a "male activity" and that it is unseemly for women to engage in political activity. Sapiro argues that women are more likely to hold attitudes that reflect their socialization to private roles. Thus women are more likely to hold a moralistic view of politics (Sapiro, 1984:166).

The second explanation focuses on situational factors. In this theory, it is argued that women participate less than men because they are in situations that make it difficult to become involved in politics. In an interesting study of children from grade school to high school, Orum et al. find that boys and girls at all levels show virtually identical levels of political knowledge, political affect, and political partisanship (Orum et al. 1977). It is interesting that given the lower level of political activity reported by girls at the high-school level, this finding leads them to consider the effects of situational factors. A similar finding is raised by Flora and Lynn (1974). In their study of new mothers in Kansas, they found that new mothers reported having a difficult time maintaining any interest in politics after the baby was born. Both these explanations suggested that women's voting rates would increase when the effects of the women's movement resulted in changes in sex roles. As a result of changing conceptions of gender, women would no longer feel that politics was "unfeminine," nor would they continue to be primarily responsible for child care and other domestic chores. This was an argument that said that women would act like men when they began to take roles in society that were equal to men's roles.

However, research by Jennings (1979) suggests that the old picture of women as apolitical was a distortion. Jennings was interested in examining the effects of the life cycle on political participation. Although women did participate less and showed less interest in national politics, they were more knowlegeable and interested than men in school board elections. Jennings notes that, although women confirm the apolitical stereotype with regard to national politics, they have the "definite advantage" with regard to school politics (1979:766). Thus, shifting from treating women in identical ways as men casts women's participation in a more favorable light.

As women have begun to vote in greater numbers (women cast more votes than men for the first time in the 1984 election), the impact of their vote becomes more important. The much-discussed "gender gap" has become a factor when politicians map out campaign strategy. This is especially true in marginal or close races, where winning the women's vote can mean victory or defeat. Although it is true that women are not a "bloc" vote, there are significant and substantial differences between women's and men's opinions on issues. This is especially true in the case of working women. Klein (1984:89–93) and Poole and Zeigler (1985:18–19) find that working increases a woman's feminist consciousness. For these researchers, the increase in women's labor-force participation led to questioning and rejection of "traditional" female roles and a growing awareness of the barriers women face in the workplace. This suggests that, as more and more women enter the labor force, the ideological differences between men and women will continue to grow. Coupled with the increasing numbers of women voters, this finding suggests that the "gender gap" will become even more important. Far from being "identical" or equal to men in their preferences, the "gender gap" is evidence that women have different interests and attitudes from men, and these differences are beginning to be felt at the polls.

The problem of equality arises again in research on women elites. This research focuses on women who become active in politics by working for their communities or political parties, or running for office. The questions here show a concern for differences between women and men: for example, given that women are socialized to find politics to be "unfeminine," why do they enter politics? How are women candidates different from men candidates? Finally, if women candidates are elected, what difference does it make?

The question of women's entrance into politics is generally attributed to psychological differences. Kirkpatrick's classic *Political Woman* (1974) argues that women who enter politics must be able to overcome their socialization in order to operate successfully in a "man's world." Work by Fowlkes (1984) proposes that ambitious women who enter politics are examples of "counter-socialization," a pattern of socialization that defies the prevailing sex-role socialization. Regardless, the argument here is that women who are political elites are different from women generally and that they are also different from male elites. In a study of California party activists, Constantini and Craik (1977) found that women activists exhibited higher levels of psychological anxiety than did men. Sapiro and Farah (1982), using data from the 1972 delegate study, found that women party activists were less likely to entertain ambitions for public office than men. It has also been observed that women candidates tend to be older and from different occupational backgrounds than men candidates.

There is also evidence that women candidates experience different problems. Mandel found, in her study of women candidates, that these women perceive that voters have different expectations of them (Mandel, 1981:Chapter 2). This finding is echoed in other research (see, e.g., Lee, 1977; Flora and Lynn, 1977). Thus Mandel reported that women candidates and officeholders said that their constituents expected them to be more compassionate and more sympathetic (1981:58–9). Interestingly enough, the "womanly image" can be an asset for women candidates. As Mandel points out, voters may see women candidates as "fresh, untainted by 'politics as usual.'" (1981:60) Ironically, this image is based on the stereotype of the "virtuous woman." On the other hand, women felt more pressure to prove their competence, feeling that the voters would be skeptical of women's expertise on the issues. Mandel quotes one candidate: "I have to be three times as competent as my opponent . . . You need all kinds of little gimmicks to establish credibility, because the basic assumption is that as a women, you are frivolous and not competent" (1981:53).

Given that women candidates perceive reluctance in the electorate to accept them as legitimate candidates for office, it would not be surprising to find that women are less likely to run for office than men. But there are other obstacles to success for women candidates. According to Carroll: "[T]he lack of greater involvement in recruitment by party officials is not the only significant aspect of the relationship between women candidates and party leaders. For even when party leaders were active in recruiting women, they often were doing little to facilitate the movement of women into elective positions." (Carroll, 1985:41) She reports that women are less likely to be recruited by the party leadership to run and when they are, they are more likely to be "sacrificial lambs," that is, candidates who have little chance of winning (Carroll 1985:36). Women candidates are also likely to experience more problems in raising funds (Carroll, 1985:49–51; Mandel, 1981:181–90; but cf. Darcy et al., 1987:91).

Women must not only work against disadvantages set for them by political party leadership; they often have personal barriers to overcome as well. Women are more likely to continue to be primarily responsible for the household chores. Contrary to men, who can expect that their spouses will keep the homefires burning, women get relatively little help. Women are also still primarily responsible for child care; the fact that women are more likely to enter politics at an older age than men is attributed to the presence of young children. Women will delay their political careers to take care of their children (Lee, 1977; Stoper, 1977). Finally, Sapiro reports women are much more likely than men to forego political careers if their spouses object (Sapiro, 1982). Carroll finds that women candidates report that their families' support is important to their decision to run for office; the absence of this finding in research on male candidates leads her to conclude that family support "may be of greater importance to female than to male candidates" (Carroll, 1985:30).

Once in office, women officeholders are at once different from and equal to men. Both Githens's (1977) and Diamond's (1977) research show that women officeholders will hold distinctively different roles from men. In both, the roles run the gamut from the passive spectator to the feminist advocate. Githens suggests that these roles are all roles that result from women's weakness as outsiders in the legislative setting (1977:208). Moreover, the research suggests that women officeholders are not very likely to have strongly feminist views or be particularly supportive of women's issues (Mezey, 1978; Mueller, 1982). This view has been mitigated by research conducted by Carroll, who finds that women candidates are more favorable toward feminism (1985:152–56). However, she still finds considerable reluctance on the part of women candidates to discuss so-called "women's issues" during the campaign or to join feminist organizations.

It is also important to note that the reluctance on the part of women officeholders to advocate a so-called "women's agenda" may be the result of structural factors. As Antolini (1984) points out in her discussion of women officeholders on the local level, lack of attention to "women's issues" on the part of women officeholders results from the impact of "realpolitik, tokenism, and institutional sexism" (1984:34). As she points out, women officeholders may put women's issues lower on the agenda because of a widespread consensus that other issues are more pressing. Women also operate within a predominantly male domain. The fact that women are "tokens" in the legislative environment greatly increases the pressures on them to perform within the constraints of the mainstream definition of the political role. Finally, the fact that politics is a male-dominated field excludes women from the "corridors of power" or "old boys' network" that is so important in exercising influence (Antolini, 1984:35–36; see also Githens, 1977:208).

These results suggest that, as women officeholders become more common, their reluctance to advocate women's issues will decrease. It also suggests that women will become more powerful as their numbers grow and as they have a chance to establish their own networks. Thus, the current low level of support that women officeholders exhibit toward a feminist agenda is certainly not expected to be a permanent phenomenon. The prospects for change, however, are dependent on more women achieving political office.

The Impact of Difference: Women and Policy

The emergence of the women's movement has had some major effects on policy. The first major push of the women's movement in this century has been to secure economic equality for women. Other areas of feminist concern, such as reproductive rights, including birth control and access to abortion, and violence against women, including rape and women-battering, reflect a deep concern for equality. Important policies have been created and implemented in the face of these demands.

The problem is that equality becomes problematic when trying to define and implement effective policy. Consider, for example, the problem of economic inequality. The first set of policies to address the problem focused on expanding opportunities for women by legally mandating an end to discrimination against women in hiring, pay, and education. Almost two decades later, women still experience a "wage gap" relative to men. It was thought that guaranteeing identical treatment for women would go far in reducing that gap. And yet, Trieman and Hartmann's summary of economic studies conducted on the wage gap shows that trying to account for the gap using differences in education, absences from work, job training, and any other conceivable differences in job skills do not account for the difference between men's and women's wages (1981:Chapter 2).

The problem has turned out to be more complicated than was recognized in those early days. It was not enough to provide equal opportunity; women, after all, are not treated equally by society. Thus, it is not that women are necessarily less skilled or otherwise desirable as workers, but rather, that women find themselves in different kinds of jobs than men. A women with a high-school or college education might take a job as a secretary. Her male counterpart might take a job as a janitor or a truck driver. The man will make significantly more money, even though his educational attainment might be lower. This fact reflects what economists call labor market segregation—in this case, it reflects that women are more likely to be found in "women's jobs," for example, secretarial help, nurse, elementary-school teacher, and those jobs are paid less than comparable jobs held by men. (For a discussion of these phenomena, see Trieman and Hartmann, 1981:Chapter 3; Feldberg, 1984:313-18.)

Even if women decide to enter traditionally male jobs, labor market segregation is accompanied by labor market segmentation. That is, economists postulate that the labor market is characterized by two "segments". The first segment consists of those industries that have developed a highly developed internal labor market. The industries in the primary segment are likely to use advanced technology, to exhibit high levels of capital investment, to use unionized and highly trained and educated labor—in short, these industries are the large corporations that we find in the American economy. What is significant about this primary segment is that labor competition is relatively low. The secondary segment of the labor market is one that is characterized by high levels of competition for labor because the work is generally of low skill. As such, the jobs in the secondary segment exhibit high turnover, and workers in the secondary segment are not paid well nor are they given much in the way of fringe benefits. Women are more likely to be employed in the secondary, rather than the primary, segment (Trieman and Hartmann, 1981:Chapter 3).

This discovery has led to the current policy proposal that women's wages reflect their "comparable worth." Under such a policy, women's wages would increase. Thus the policy would require that women's wages be determined by evaluating the value of women's jobs and skills to see if they are equal to male jobs and skills and to set pay rates accordingly. However, there has been widespread resistance—even among women—against such policies. The Reagan administration's EEOC chair, Clarence Pendleton, has called comparable worth "the looniest idea since Looney Tunes." The problem here is that comparable worth policies are perceived as treating women unequally. By intervening in the labor market on women's behalf, the public sector would be wreaking havoc on the market, all because women's wages are perceived as too low.

The perception of comparable worth programs as unfair is due to more than sexism. In fundamental ways, these programs require that different values be considered in employment policy. They are what public policy analysts call "redistributive" policies. Redistributive policies, because they require a redistribution of values or resources in society, are apt to be greeted with resentment. Thus, opponents to both programs will complain that the programs treat women and minorities differently—that is, unfairly—because they get an unfair advantage in the market. However, given the causes of women's economic inequality, it would be difficult to secure economic equality for women by simply treating them as if they were identical with men.

This conceptualization parallels the discussion of public policies affecting women by Gelb and Palley (1987). In their discussion, they distinguish policies that are concerned with "role equity" as opposed to "role change." As they define it:

> Role equity issues are those policies which extend rights now enjoyed by other groups . . . to women and . . . appear to be relatively delineated or narrow in their implications. In contrast, role change issues appear to produce change in the dependent female role of wife, mother, and homemaker, holding out the potential of greater sexual freedom and independence in a variety of contexts (Gelb and Palley, 1987:6).

Role-equity issues are not likely to generate much opposition, whereas role-change issues do generate opposition and controversy. I think that most policies that seek to achieve equality for women will generate opposition because at base, these policies seek to implement changes in fundamental values and perceptions regarding sex roles. Moreover, these policies often require a recognition of the different situations that women face. As a result, policies that seek to enhance the status of women must treat them differently.

This problem of "different treatment" as a basis for policy can also be seen if one considers the impact of family arrangements on women's economic situation. Female-headed households comprise a large proportion of poor families in the United States. A major study of shifts in family income by Corcoran et al. found that an important cause of poverty for women is divorce (1984:241). Not surprisingly, a common way for women to escape poverty is to remarry. Small wonder, then, that reforms of the existing divorce laws, often encompassed under the rubric of "no-fault divorce," that were proposed by feminists had unexpected consequences.

In a much discussed study of divorce reform in California, Weitzman (1985) discovered that divorce reform was an economic disaster for women. Although it has never been true that alimony in modern times was an automatic award, divorce reform substantially reduced or even eliminated it in many cases. This was devastating for those women who had been housewives or who had no job skills. In the absence of the husband's income, household income could be expected to drop sharply. Because women are much more likely to retain custody of children, this means a sharply reduced standard of living for women (see also Corcoran et al., 1984).

What had gone wrong with California's divorce reform was that it was predicated on an assumption of equality. The laws reflected an assumption that women in divorce would no longer be homemakers and that they would hold jobs that would allow them to be economically equal to their spouses. The reality for many women—including those who work—is much different. As Fineman notes in her critique of Weitzman's work, the fact that women are economically dependent on men, and thus not equal to them, mandates solutions that reflect that fact (Fineman, 1986:785).

The inequality between women and men is also believed to be a cause of violence against women. Brownmiller explains rape not as a sexual crime, but rather as a violent crime that is a part of the means men use to control women's behavior (Brownmiller, 1975:5; see also Griffin, 1977). Likewise, research on women battering links it to a need for the battering male to control the battered woman (LaRossa, 1980; Schechter, 1982:219-24). In the case of battered women, their economic and psychological dependence on men coupled with a lack of services to support battered women who want to leave makes it difficult for the woman to break away (Schechter, 1982:224-8).

Yet in both cases the legal system tends to ignore the problem of inequality and to treat women victims of these crimes as if they were capable of tapping the same resources as men. For example, women who are rape victims may be blamed for not resisting their attackers, as if they had equal strength with their assailants. Women who are battered are heavily criticized for staying in the abusive relationship, as if they had equal ability to support themselves. Even more interesting is the assumption that both men and women respond in the same way to crime victimization. That is, it is assumed that women, like men, will be outraged at the victimization and will press for "justice." This ignores the fact that women who are battered or raped are likely to have been assaulted by people known to them. Thus, when women victims express misgivings about prosecuting their attackers, the criminal justice system can only respond with bewilderment or worse (Kosaki, 1984). In fact, it is not surprising that women would have misgivings about prosecution of family members or friends. However, in refusing to recognize the differences that characterize these crimes, the criminal courts serve to discourage the effective prosecution of those crimes.

Conclusion

In considering these issues that involve women and politics, the extent to which women's participation in politics can facilitate the achievement of equality is unclear. Women's greater turnout at the polls will certainly have only marginal effect on policy if the candidates who are running continue to present the same issues. Thus women's greater turnout must be accompanied by greater awareness of the problems that women face in our society and concomitant demands that candidates, both male and female, respond to those concerns. Likewise, women officeholders might be expected to advocate "women's issues" and policies to deal with women's inequality more often if their numbers increase and they are no longer "tokens" in political life.

However, the concept of equality, crucial to the discussion of women and politics, is hardly a neutral concept here. If equality is defined as identity, then treating women in a way that is identical to the way we treat men may well lead to failure. This is because such equal treatment assumes that women have already achieved equality in some fundamental fashion. Giving women equal opportunity in employment, for example, assumes that women's lives, and the choices they make, are subject to the same constraints as men. They are not.

The current unequal status of women means that achieving equality for women will require that we treat women unequally. This implies that policies that will really help women achieve equal status are likely to face great opposition because they require a shift in our way of thinking about equality. As in the case of affirmative action and comparable worth, policies that seek to achieve equality through unequal treatment of women will probably be perceived as unfair and will be met with resistance. The achievement of these goals, however, cannot be achieved independently, nor can they be achieved overnight. We may have come a long way, but there's a long way left to go.

References

Antolini, Denise. 1984. "Women in Local Government: An Overview." In Janet Flammang, ed., *Political Women: Current Roles in State and Local Government*. Beverly Hills, Calif.: Sage.

Bourque, Susan C., and Jean Grossholtz. 1974. "Politics an Unnatural Practice: Political Science Looks at Female Participation." *Politics and Society*, 4:255–266.

Brownmiller, Susan. 1975. *Against Our Will: Men, Women and Rape*. New York: Bantam.

Carroll, Susan J. 1985. *Women as Candidates in American Politics*. Bloomington: Indiana University Press.

Constantini, Edmond, and Kenneth H. Craik. 1977. "Women as Politicians: The Social Background, Personality, and Political Careers of Female Party Leaders." In Marianne Githens and Jewell L. Prestage, eds., *Portrait of Marginality: The Political Behavior of the American Woman*. New York: David McKay.

Corcoran, Mary, Greg J. Duncan, and Martha S. Hill. 1984. "The Economic Fortunes of Women and Children: Lessons from the Panel Study of Income Dynamics." *Signs* 10:232–248.

Darcy, R., Susan Welch, and Janet Clark. 1987. *Women, Elections, and Representation*. New York: Longman.

Diamond, Irene. 1977. *Sex Roles in the State House*. New Haven: Yale University Press.

Feldberg, Roslyn L. 1984. "Comparable Worth: Toward Theory and Practice in the United States." *Signs* 10:311–328.

Fineman, Martha L. 1986. "Illusive Equality: On Weitzman's *Divorce Revolution*." *American Bar Foundation Research Journal*, 1986:781–790.

Flora, Cornelia B. and Naomi B. Lynn. 1974. "Women and Political Socialization: Considerations of the Impact of Motherhood." In Jane S. Jaquette, ed., *Women in Politics*. New York: John Wiley.

Fowlkes, Diane L. 1984. "Ambitious Political Woman: Countersocialization and Political Party Context." *Women and Politics* 4:5-31.

Gelb, Joyce, and Marian Lief Palley. 1987. *Women and Public Policies.* Princeton: Princeton University Press.

Githens, Marianne. 1977. "Spectators, Agitators, or Lawmakers: Women in State Legislatures." In Marianne Githens and Jewel L. Prestage, eds., *Portrait of Marginality.* New York: David McKay.

Griffin, Susan. 1977. "Rape: The All-American Crime." In Duncan Chappell et al., eds., *Forcible Rape: The Crime, the Victim, and the Offender.* New York: Columbia University Press.

Jennings, M. Kent. 1979. "Another Look at the Life and Political Participation." *American Journal of Political Science* 23:755–71.

Kirkpatrick, Jeane J. 1974. *Political Woman.* New York: Basic Books.

Klein, Ethel. 1984. *Gender Politics: From Consciousness to Mass Politics.* Cambridge: Harvard University Press.

Kosaki, Liane C. 1984. *The "Known" Criminal: Non-Stranger Violence and the Criminal Courts.* Ph.D. dissertation, The University of Michigan.

Lansing, Marjorie. 1974. "The American Woman: Voter and Activist." In Jane S. Jaquette, ed., *Women in Politics.* New York: John Wiley.

LaRossa, Ralph. 1980. "'And We Haven't Had Any Problems Since': Conjugal Violence and the Politics of Marriage." In Murray A. Straus and Gerald T. Hotaling, eds., *The Social Causes of Husband-Wife Violence.* Minneapolis: University of Minnesota Press.

Lee, Marcia M. 1977. "Toward Understanding Why Few Women Hold Public Office: Factors Affecting the Participation of Women in Local Politics." In Marianne Githens and Jewel L. Prestage, eds., *Portrait of Marginality.* New York: David McKay.

Mandel, Ruth. 1981. *In the Running: The New Woman Candidate.* Boston: Beacon Press.

Mezey, Susan Gluck. 1978. "Women and Representation: The Case of Hawaii." *Journal of Politics* 40:369–85.

Mueller, Carol. 1982. "Feminism and the New Women in Public Office." *Women and Politics* 2:7–20.

Orum, Anthony, et al. 1977. "Sex, Socialization, and Politics." In Marianne Githens and Jewel L. Prestage, eds., *Portrait of Marginality.* New York: David McKay.

Poole, Keith T. and L. Harmon Zeigler. 1985. *Women, Public Opinion, and Politics.* New York: Longman.

Sapiro, Virginia. 1982. "Private Costs of Public Commitments or Public Costs of Private Commitments? Family Roles Versus Political Ambition." *American Journal of Political Science* 26:265–279.

Sapiro, Virginia. 1983. *The Political Integration of Women: Roles, Socialization, and Politics.* Urbana: University of Illinois Press.

Sapiro, Virginia, and Barbara G. Farah. 1980. "New Pride and Old Prejudice: Political Ambition and Role Orientations among Female Partisan Elites." *Women and Politics* 1:13–36.

Schechter, Susan. 1982. *Women and Male Violence: The Visions and Struggles of the Battered Women's Movement.* Boston: South End Press.

Stoper, Emily. 1977. "Wife and Politician: Role Strain among Women in Public Office." In Marianne Githens and Jewel L. Prestage, eds., *Portrait of Marginality.* New York: David McKay.

Stucker, John J. 1977. "Women as Voters: Their Maturation as Political Persons in American Society." In Marianne Githens and Jewel L. Prestage, eds., *Portrait of Marginality.* New York: David McKay.

Trieman, Donald J., and Heidi I. Hartmann. 1981. *Women, Work and Wages: Equal Pay for Jobs of Equal Value*. Washington, D.C.: Academy Press.

Weitzman, Lenore J. 1985. *The Divorce Revolution: The Unexpected Social and Economic Consequences for Women and Children in America*. New York: Free Press.

Chicano Politics in the 1980s and Beyond: A Review of the Literature in the Decade of the Hispanics

John A. Garcia

University of Arizona

R esearch on the politics of the Chicano community, prior to the decade of the 1980s, portrayed a divided community that was either passive, isolated, and marginally associated with mainstream politics or one that has become assertive, challenging the conventional political norms and values and exerting its growing political muscle (Barrera, 1979). In many respects, contemporary research on Chicanos has dealt with these "tendencies" in relation to the political system. This review essay will be an attempt to examine the results and discussions of political participation among persons of Mexican origin in the United States. The specific areas of discussion will include modes and levels of political participation, electoral activities and representation, political organizations and leadership, and the nationalization of Latino populations.

Political Participation

Over twenty-five years ago, the descriptions "sleeping giant" and "an awakening minority" were used to describe the political potential of Mexican-origin persons. The rise of Brown Power and direct action in the 1960s further enhanced the transformation from its potential to more concrete manifestations of political power (Antunes and Gaitz, 1975). With the advent of a new decade, the 1980s, the demographic forces of significant population increases from both higher birth rates and international migration promised more of the same. Social scientists and journalists projected that the significant growth would produce two major results—Latinos becoming the nation's largest minority group within the next twenty-five to thirty-five years as well as becoming a major participant in the formation and passage of an evolving political agenda (Estrada et al., 1981).

Certainly, the pain and promise of a better future for Chicanos and other Latinos were projected into this decade and beyond. Yet, what have been the results of an impressive "demographic imperative" in the political life of this community? Studies conducted in the 1980s suggest raised expectations have not been met. For example, Chicanos still lag in voter registration and turnout levels in comparison to blacks and whites, and they still have a lower percentage of persons belonging to organizations—any type of organization (Garcia and de la Garza, 1985).

The manifestations of political involvement by Chicanos have surfaced in many forms and at various levels of the political arena. Within the electoral arena, efforts to broaden the base have taken the form of intensive voter registration and education campaigns throughout the Southwest. Organizations like the Southwest Voter Registration and Education Project and the Midwest Voter Registration and Education Project have served as coordinating and catalytic organizations. As a result of such campaign efforts, the door-to-door canvassing has served as an informal method to tap the political views of Chicanos (de la Garza and Brioschetto, 1982). Such views include a sense of distance from the polity, its institutions, and its actors.

Studies examining the political opinions of Chicanos indicate significant levels of cynicism and apprehension about the responsiveness of government (Gutierez and Hirsch, 1973). In addition, studies of levels of efficacy produce a mixed picture of a greater sense of collective personal efficacy while, at the same time, a view of the political arena as too complicated and less than fully accessible. Some studies examining levels of political information suggest that Chicanos are still playing "catch-up" in terms of formal knowledge about the political system and its institutions (Davis, 1983). At the same time, historical accounts, both past and contemporary, strongly conclude that Chicano community efforts have been in response to inequitable and differential treatment by the government and its agents (Barrera, 1979).

This latter point illustrates the key ingredient of structural factors and conditions that influence the modes and level of political participation among Chicanos. The inclusion of the "rules of the game," the structure and nature of political institutions, and judicial interpretation serve to affect how Chicanos participate and where (de la Garza and Vaughn, 1984). For example, in the electoral arena, practices of literacy tests, poll taxes, annual registration systems, limiting registration to take place in certain offices, and so forth were dealt with by the Voting Rights Act of 1965 and subsequent extensions (Garcia, 1986).

Yet in the 1980s, the critical structural factors have been election structures, particularly at-large elections, and purge laws. That is, litigation and political pressures at the local and state levels have tried to change the basis for representation on local decision-making bodies from an at-large system to a district system. Given the residential concentration of Chicanos, and, in many communities, the significant but less than a clear majority voting bloc they comprise, it has been very difficult for Chicanos to be elected to public office. The factor of voter polarization has also been a contributing factor in lessening the opportunity for electoral successes. Attempts to change electoral structures have been through the provisions of the Voting Rights Act, emphasizing the negative effect of limited access to elective office.

Another area of concern with structural factors is voter purge requirements. Some states (e.g., Arizona) have tried to facilitate greater numbers of individuals to register by allowing a person to register to vote when renewing his or her driver's license. Voters registered in this manner would not be subject to purge due to failure to vote in the last general election, whereas other nonvoting registered voters would be purged and required to reregister. Although it is not clear if significant numbers of Chicanos and other minorities will be negatively impacted, previous experiences with voter registration campaigns would suggest that many Chicanos are being reregistered due to previous purges.

One significant development of the decade of the 1980s lies with the requirement of political jurisdictions to redraw districts in accordance with the decennial census. As a result, new congressional districts were "awarded" to several Sunbelt states (especially the five southwestern states). Also, legislative districts and city wards were redesigned with Chicano majorities in some instances (Cain and Kiewert, 1984). The redistricting plans, although partisan efforts, afforded Chicano leaders and organizations the opportunity to utilize political leverage and litigation to influence the outcomes of redistricting plans. Some of the more immediate consequences included gains in elected officials (particularly at the federal level), more Chicanos contesting for public offices, and greater political awareness among the citizenry of political opportunities within the Chicano community.

Electorally, the latter point is evidenced by some significant gains in voter registration and turnout levels among Chicanos and other Hispanics. Examining voting registration from 1980–1984, Hispanics increased from 2,984,000 registered voters to 3,794,000 (a 27 percent increase). During the same period, gains in black and white voter registration were 24 and 9 percents respectively. Clearly, organizations like the Southwest and Midwest Voter Registration and Education projects contributed to the rise of more Chicano voters. At the same time, political opportunities such as redistricting were salient issues that helped to provide the motivation to expand involvement in the electoral arena. A similar pattern exists for voting levels during the 1980–1984 period; that is, the number of Chicanos and other Hispanics voting increased from 2,453,000 to 3,092,000, which represented a 26 percent gain. Again, for the same period, black and white voters increased 24 and 8 percents respectively.

Despite the significant absolute gains of Chicano voters since the beginning of this decade, a game of "catch-up" still exists. There is still a gap between Hispanics and black and white voters. In 1984, 59 percent of Hispanics were registered, compared to 69 and 71 percent for black and white registrants. Similarly, only 48 percent of the voting-age Hispanics voted in 1984 compared to 58 percent and 64 percent for black and white voters. Clearly, the electoral gap has been closing during this decade, but the convergence of comparable registration and voting levels may still be 5 to 10 years away.

Two demographic factors that will influence this pattern in the future are the age structure in the Chicano community and the foreign-born segment. On the average, Chicanos are 10 years younger than the general population, and slightly less than one-half are under the age of 18. During the rest of this decade and into the 1990s, a greater proportion of Chicanos will enter the voting-age category so that greater increases in numbers of registrants and voters will occur naturally. This increase coupled with sustained efforts by Chicano leaders and organizations should contribute in closing the gap.

The other demographic factor is more unpredictable. A major segment of the Chicano community was born in Mexico. For example, in California 37.9 percent of Spanish-origin individuals are foreign-born, whereas in Texas, they constitute 17.7 percent (Garcia, 1981). Overall, slightly over one-fourth of the Mexican-origin population is foreign-born. The electoral significance of this segment has had two different interpretations. That is, the social distance and lack of political integration of Mexican immigrants makes political mobilization costly (de la Garza and Flores, 1983). The costs to be incurred include organizational resources, insightful strategies, and leadership attention to permanent resident aliens in whom activism is still not understood. On the other hand, the size of this segment of the Chicano community warrants immediate attention in order to capitalize on the growing Chicano political base. Conversion of this segment may entail redirecting experiences in the United States toward the consequences and payoffs of political involvement (Garcia, 1987; Portes and Mozo, 1985). In this light, greater political information, knowledge, and awareness among immigrants can serve to expand a "latent" segment of the Chicano community.

A concomitant aspect of the foreign-born segment is the issue of naturalization among Mexicanos. Historically, the rates among Mexicanos have been among the lowest of any nationality group (along with Canadians) (Garcia, 1981). It has been suggested that factors such as a high degree of political chauvinism for Mexico, lack of cultural and political integration with the United States, and physical proximity to Mexico have served as major contributors. As a result, permanent resident aliens do not naturalize in significant numbers. In the early part of this decade, the National Association of Latino Elected and Appointed Officials (NALEO) began a major organizational effort to promote naturalization among foreign-born Hispanics. The organizational rationale was the size of this group, the potential for an immediate expanded political base, and continued migration from Mexico. Recent research has identified a different set of factors that explain the low rates of naturalization. These factors include apprehension among resident aliens to interact with the Immigration and Naturalization Service, lack of knowledge about the naturalization process, and the absence of known linkages between citizenship and concrete benefits. Current promotion drives and large-scale naturalization ceremonies are being utilized to promote further these efforts. Clearly, the political activation and concentrated attention on this segment of the Mexican-origin community remains as a major item on a Chicano agenda.

Chicano Leadership and Organizations

Our discussion of Chicano political involvement and activities within the Chicano community is also reflected in its leadership and organizations. One of the major thrusts of the leadership has been to enhance the presence and impact of Chicanos in national political arenas. The development of a national

Hispanic community (a topic to be discussed later) has been a major contributor to the directions and context of Chicano leadership and organizations. The content of a Chicano national agenda has included the economic betterment of the community (i.e. employment, economic development, and protection from discrimination in the workplace), educational equity and access at all levels of the educational pipeline, preservation of cultural pluralism in the United States, social service and social welfare policies that meet the needs of Chicano household configurations and geographic location, and protecting the interests and networks within the Chicano community with any immigration reform legislation (Polinard et al., 1984).

Part of the development of Chicano leadership has been affected by the increase in the number of Chicano elected officials. In 1985, over 3,000 Hispanics held elected office in all political jurisdictions (Garcia, 1986). This represents a 50 percent increase from the number of Hispanic officeholders in 1980. Again, the imperatives of redistricting played a major role in opening opportunities for contesting political offices; and Chicano leadership, particularly in voter registration and education efforts, served to "sensitize" the Chicano community about the opportunities for electoral victories.

One consequence of greater electoral activites in seeking political offices is the need to systematically examine the dynamics of Chicano electoral politics with a variety of structural, historical, and demographic conditions. Success at gaining political office has centered largely at the local level. In 1982, ten Hispanics served in the U.S. Congress, all in the House of Representatives (Welch and Hibbing, 1985). Although that number almost doubles Hispanic Congressmen since 1970, it only represents 0.3% of all elected officials. The gains have occurred at the local level—city councils, mayoralties, and school boards (McManus and Cassell, 1982). Previous research has suggested that a critical electoral mass and the presence of local organizations have facilitated successful electoral campaigns (Browning et al., 1984; Lovrich and Marenin, 1976). Yet the number of communities in which a substantial percentage of the local community is Chicano with long-standing electoral organizations is limited.

Thus research on electoral strategies, styles and bases of Chicano leaders, and communities' previous experiences with Chicano candidates and officeholders represents a gap in need of more enlightenment. One way in which to illustrate this point is a brief discussion of the two mayoral elections involving Frederico Pena and the City of Denver. Although Chicanos represent a growing community in this city, their overall percentage is still small (approximately 10–15 percent) (Lovrich and Marenin, 1976). The role of economic elites and the "probusiness" ethos insure that any candidate must incorporate support and pay attention to this segment. An examination of the Pena initial election and recent reelection would suggest a combination of strategies that addresses the interests of the minority community, as well as economic elites, other neighborhood groups, and other interest aggregations in the local community. Coalitional politics that bridges distinct interrelated subcommunities is a dynamic that becomes very applicable for Chicano aspirants, leaders, and organizational interests dealing with enhancing political representation.

The work by Browning, Tabb, and Marshall (1984) illustrates these historical links, organizational density and purposes, leadership cluster, and demographic base from which the strategies and consequences of Chicano political participation take shape. More work that incorporates not only the diversity of the Chicano community (i.e., among its leadership, class composition, etc.) but that includes the situational and structural factors that influence the parameters and responses to electoral goals among Chicanos is needed. Another example has been the unsuccessful efforts in McAllen, Texas, to place a Chicano in the mayor's office in a community that is over 90 percent Chicano. Our previous discussion of the increases in Chicano voter registration and voting would suggest the pivotal role in which leaders and organization can play to efficiently and effectively convert an expanding base into regular actors in the political arena.

It is within this area that linkage politics between Chicano leaders and the community suffers from systematic examination. If one follows the previous discussion about the need for effective leadership and more aggressive participation, then regular and clear communication between the leadership and the community is essential. One area that received some attention about this link is that of immigration reform legislation. With major components of the Simpson–Rodino bill, including employer sanctions, legalization of undocumented aliens, antidiscrimination provisions, and expanded border surveillance, there were some different positions taken by Chicano leaders and the Chicano public. Based on several polls, the public was more supportive of employer sanctions, although less than the general public. The Chicano public also supported a more liberal legalization program than their leadership. Previous work on elite-mass linkages has always demonstrated public opinion differences on policy areas. Yet we know virtually nothing of the extent of those potential differences for Chicano leaders and the community nor its implications for public policy debates.

The whole area of public opinion has only recently interested researchers and Chicano organizations to identify and relate the public opinion "map" among Chicanos. A conference held at the University of Texas–Austin in 1986 focused on the means and substantive issues involved with polling the Chicano community. Underlying the need for such efforts were the factors of major informational voids about this community, the possibility of a cluster of salient issue areas for most Chicanos, and the linkage need to identify and articulate Chicano public opinion before policymakers. Besides the immigration reform controversy, foreign policy issues related to Central America and policy initiatives by the United States have some interest for the Chicano community. On the one hand, migration patterns of Central American migrants have had direct impact on Chicanos as the residential areas of settlement are in already established barrios. On the other hand, informational levels about the political complexities of Central American countries and competing factions are not well understood by most of the American public. What initiatives that are taken by Chicano leaders in this foreign policy area may well be influenced by public opinion in their community.

Similar discussion can take place with a variety of domestic policy areas such as social welfare reform, a balanced budget, job training programs, educational vouchers, bilingual education, school prayer, abortion, and the like. Public opinion polls conducted by the Southwest Voter Registration and Education Project during the 1980s have consistently reported on the economy (in the form of unemployment and inflation), education (particularly bilingual education), and social welfare reform (i.e. food stamps, aid for dependent children, housing, job training, etc.). Similar polls among elites, although more purposefully selected, reveal the predominant concern for domestic issues, especially those related to the economy.

Although public opinion polls help to identify or reinforce the sentiments of the Chicano community, two other general concerns have also surfaced. The first deals with discrimination and the perception of its persistence among many Chicanos. For the most part, Chicanos—irrespective of class standing—feel that discriminatory practices against Chicanos still occur and that governmental intervention to halt it is necessary (Buzan and Phillips, 1980). The other area would fall under the rubric of *empowerment*. These polls would suggest that Chicanos feel that their power status and position in American society are insufficient and thus warrant significant efforts to attain greater political and economic influence. Empowerment also includes more political representation and access. Thus there is some consensus in the public opinion "map" about the primary concern for greater empowerment with special issues that have greater salience than others.

Although we have not discussed Chicano organizations very extensively in this essay, two areas of research are important to mention. The first deals with the continuation of historical accounts and analysis of previous or contemporary Chicano organizations such as LULAC, GI Forum, National Council of la Raza, and MANA (Allsup, 1981; M. Garcia, 1985). These studies document the development of these organizations, their prime objectives and goals, arenas of operation, ideology, and leadership base. Part of these efforts serves to provide historical continuity with organizational efforts on behalf of Chicanos and to illustrate the sophistication in dealing with major institutions and actors. Some of the works that have dealt with contemporary organizations focus on the adaptations (organizational and leadership) over time with different moods and sentiments expressed by the Chicano community as well as changes in the political climate. These provide valuable insights as to the evolution of Chicano organizations and strategies for social change.

The second research area lies with the focus of organizational impact on the broader Chicano community (Comer, 1980; Garcia and de la Garza, 1985). Such research examines identification and awareness of organizations, extent of contact and membership within organizations, and the influence that organizations have on the community. Organizational penetration and influence are still limited, and the question of how organizational strategies and objectives mobilize a wider sector of the community is left open for the remainder of the decade. Factors such as salient issues, levels of information about political institutions and processes, perceived utility of participation, and leadership articulation with the Chicano community serve as important considerations for more effective Chicano organizations.

Chicanos and Hispanic Politics

One cannot deal with the development of Chicano political behavior in the 1980s without some discussion of the nationalization of Hispanic/Latino politics. The rise of national attention to the growing presence of Chicanos in the United States has been couched in terms of the Spanish-speaking-origin community. Chicanos' regional concentration in the Southwest has contributed to the characterization of this group as primarily a regional minority. Despite the longtime and still-growing Chicano communities in the Midwest, the regional description still persisted. The formulation of a larger Spanish-speaking-origin grouping provided a greater national standing with the incorporation of Cubans, Puerto Ricans, and Central and South Americans, along with Chicanos.

The net result was a geographic expansion of political bases, augmenting the population base by over 40 percent. That is, Chicanos constitute over 60 percent of the Latino national community, with "other Spanish" being the next largest group at 20 percent (this segment is the more nebulous and diverse). With these gains in size and a national base, an aggregation that contained similarities of language, culture, and history was also produced yet one with real differences in relationships with the United States and geographic locations. Thus the benefits of nationalization for Chicanos include a larger base and visibility, with a potential for a greater resource base and leadership pool. At the same time, one can view Hispanics as a coalition of similarly situated groups in the polity that is still working out areas of communality and cooperative efforts.

The strength and/or fragility of such a coalition can be seen in the definition of important issues and policy preferences, as well as cooperative arrangements between essentially Chicano, Cuban, and Puerto Rican organizations. Such coalition experiences serve to realize the potential national force contained within a Latino/Hispanic community. In addition, cities like Chicago afford researchers a valuable urban "lab" in which to observe and analyze the dynamics of Latino coalition politics among various Latino nationality groups as well as black–Latino coalitions.

The other research issue contained in the nationalization of Hispanic politics deals with the development of a Latino/Hispanic identity. Much attention has been focused on ethnic identity and its relationship to political consciousness and mobilization (Garcia, 1981; Miller et al., 1981). Selection of ethnic labels serves as political maps of ideology, political involvement, and cultural affinity. Padilla's (1985) work on Latino consciousness focuses on the utilitarian purpose of Latino identification to enhance political capital. The argument deals with situational identity such that individuals identify as Latinos, realizing the effect and impact they can have when dealing with other political actors. In this manner, the depth of such an identity can coexist with other, more general social identities. Nevertheless, the activation of some degree of identity with being Hispanic/Latino becomes a key factor in the nationalization process among Chicanos.

In essence, an operating Latino community in the fullest sense of community (attachment, cohesiveness, identifiable boundaries, etc.) projects Chicanos and other Hispanics into a visible force in the national political arena. One can characterize the contemporary status of Chicanos as including the formation of a national coalition with other Latinos with the primary purpose of empowerment. Levels of sophistication of strategies, broader base organizations, and connected leaders with their communities serve as continual building blocks of political development. Specific issues will arise, but the ability of the Chicano and national Latino community to define, communicate, advocate, and shape the policymaking process remains as the crux of future political involvement.

References

Allsup, Carl. 1982. *American GI Forum: Origins and Evolution*. Austin: Center for Mexican American Studies.

Antunes, George, and C. Gaitz. 1975. "Ethnicity and Participation: A Study of Blacks, Mexican Americans, and Whites." *American Journal of Sociology* 80: 1192–1211.

Barrera, Mario. *Race and Class in the Southwest: A Theory of Racial Inequality*. Notre Dame: University of Notre Dame Press.

Browning, R., D. Rogers Marshall, and D. Tabb. 1984. *Protest Is Not Enough*. Berkeley: University of California Press.

Buzan, Bert, and D. Phillips. 1980. "Institutional Completeness and Chicano Militancy." *Atzlan*, pp. 33–64.

Cain, B. and D. Kiewert. 1984. "Ethnicity and Cultural Choice: Mexican American Voting Behavior in California 30th Congressional District." *Social Science Quarterly* 65: 315–327.

Comer, John. 1980. "Correlates of Recognition and Approval of Ethnic Organizations in a Non-Reinforcing Environment: Mexican in Omaha, Nebraska." *Journal of Political and Military Sociology* 8: 113-120.

Davis, James. 1983. "Does Authority Make a Difference? Locus of Control Perceptions of Anglo and Mexican American Adolescents." *Journal of Political Psychology* 4: 101–120.

de la Garza, Rodolfo, and R. Brioschetto. 1982. *Mexican American Electorate: Information Sources and Policy Orientations*. San Antonio: Southwest Voter Registration and Education Project.

_____. and Adela Flores. 1983. "The Impact of Mexican Immigrants on the Political Life of Chicanos: A Clarification of Issues and Some Hypothesis for Future Research." Paper presented at the Annual Meeting of the Southwest Political Science Association.

_____. and D. Vaughn. 1984. "The Political Socialization of Chicano Elites: A Generational Approach." *Social Science Quarterly* 65: 290–307.

Estrada, L., F. C. Garcia, R. Macias, and L. Maldonado. 1981. "Chicanos in the U.S.: A History of Exploitation and Resistance." *Daedalus* 110: 103–131.

Garcia, John A. 1981. "The Political Integration of Mexican Immigrants: Exploring the Naturalization Process." *International Migration Review* 15: 608–25.

_____. 1981. "Yo Soy Chicano . . . Self-Identity and Sociodemographic Correlates." *Social Science Quarterly* 62: 88–98.

_____. 1986. "VRA and Hispanic Political Representation." *Publius* 16: 49–66.

_____. 1987. "The Political Integration of Mexican Immigrants: Examining Some Political Orientations." *International Migration Review* 21: 377–89.

_____ and R. de la Garza. 1985. "Mobilizing Mexican Immigrants: The Role of Mexican American Organizations." *Western Political Quarterly* 38: 551-564.

Garcia, Mario T. 1984. "Americans All: The Mexican American Movement and the Politics of Wartime." *Social Science Quarterly* 65: 278–289.

Gutierrez, Armando, and H. Hirsch. 1973. "The Militant Challenge to the American Ethos: 'Chicano or Mexican American.'" *Social Science Quarterly* 53: 830–45.

Lovrich, N., and O. Marenin. 1976. "A Comparison of Black and Mexican American Voters in Denver: Assertive vs. Acquiescent Political Orientations and Voting Behavior." *Western Political Quarterly* (June), 284–294.

McManus, S., and C. Cassell. 1982. "Mexican Americans in City Politics: Participation, Representation and Policy Preferences." *The Urban Interest* 4: 57–59.

Miller, A., P. Gurin, G. Gurin, and O. Malanchuk. 1981. "Group Consciousness and Political Participation." *American Journal of Political Science* 25: 494–511.

Padilla, Felix. 1985. "On the Nature of Latino Ethnicity." *Social Science Quarterly* 66: 657–664.

Polinard, J., R. Wrinkle, and R. de la Garza. 1984. "Attitudes of Mexican Americans toward Irregular Mexican Immigration." *International Migration Review* 18: 782–799.

Portes, Alejandro. 1985. "The Political Adaptation Process of Cubans and Other Ethnic Minorities in the U.S.: A Preliminary Analysis." *International Migration Review* 19: 35–63.

Welch, Susan, and J. Hibbing. 1985. "Hispanic Representation in the U.S. Congress." *Social Science Quarterly* 65: 328–335.

Indians and the Social Contract

Joyotpaul Chaudhuri

Arizona State University

A lexis de Tocqueville's interest in America was partly sparked by his interest in prisons. De Tocqueville assumed that a comparative study of prisons was a good way of gauging how societies, particularly democratic societies, work. An equally fascinating scholarly challenge can be found in examining how societies treat their aboriginal populations. This is particularly true of democratic societies operating under the myths of comprehensive social contracts as the foundations of civil society.

The relationships between American Indians and the American governmental system touches on practically every operational point in democratic theory. To begin with, American Indians historically were outside of the social contract because Indians were in America before there was a contractual America. Consequently, beginning with the legitimacy of the social contract, every other democratic concept including consent, rights, obligations, taxation, voting, education, privileges, immunities, and property could be examined in the context of U.S.–Indian relations.

Unfortunately, despite the vast and quite uneven literature on American Indians, few students of politics have systematically examined American Indian affairs. This bibliographical essay is intended to be a brief guide to those who might wish to examine some aspect of politics or policy dealing with American Indians.

General Indian Policy Related Literature

The general boundaries of politics are marked by the study of power, authority, and the authoritative allocation of values. Looking at Indian politics from these boundaries, political scientists are part of the last group of scholars to enter into the vineyards of Indian affairs scholarship. Military historians, lawyers, anthropologists, and sociologists had earlier starts. Although students of politics and administration are latecomers, they have some potential advantages in starting late. Two of these advantages are particularly noteworthy. The literature on Indian affairs is truly vast, albeit uneven in quality. Second, much of the literature misses the politics of the subject. Consequently, there is much to be done for students of Indian politics.

A good starting point in doing bibliographical searches is to look at the series of bibliographical minivolumes published for the Newberry Library Center for the History of the American Indian by the Indiana University Press. There are over twenty volumes of bibliographical essays and references in the Newberry series. Many of the volumes deal with the literature on specific tribes, including the Pawnees, Indians of the Southwest, Cherokees, Creeks, Indians of the Northwest, California Indians, Indians of the Subarctic, Plains Indians, Sioux, Navajos, Choctaws, Apaches, Maryland and Delaware Indians, Cheyennes, Ojibwas, and others.

In addition to the specific tribal volumes, there are several general cross-tribal volumes including *Native American Prehistory* by Dean R. Snow and *Native American Historical Demography* by Henry Dobyns. Two volumes that are important starting points for political scientists or policy analysts are Francis Paul Prucha's *United States Indian Policy* and Russell Thornton and Mary Grasmick's *Sociology of American Indians*. Prucha's bibliographical essay divides the literature along historical lines or periods. The references are stronger in historical literature and less comprehensive in treating recent policy issues. Another weakness in Prucha's bibliography is that there are very few references to the views of Indians of their own history. Although a couple of the works by Vine Deloria are cited, the main Deloria book of protest, *Custer Died For Your Sins*,[1] is not highlighted. There are no references to works by Indians, the Indian newspapers and publications, including newspapers such as *Akwesasne Notes*, *Wassaja*, and books published by the Indian Historian Press.

The Thorton/Grasmick volume in the Newberry series concentrates on sociological and, to a lesser extent, anthropological literature. The bibliographical essay is divided along standard sociological topics, including demography, sociocultural change, religion, social stratification, social control, social psychology, urbanization, and a small section on "politics." Political scientists will not find the section on politics particularly helpful because the book represents a common sociological perspective that underestimates the role of structure, law, and power.

Although the Prucha and Thorton/Grasmick bibliographical essays are good historical and sociological beginnings, where does a political scientist really begin? A good introduction to the policy issues is found in Deloria's edited collection of essays by various authors entitled *American Indian Policy in the Twentieth Century*.[2] The lead article by Chaudhuri entitled "American Indian Policy: An Overview" outlines one version of the main policy and theoretical issues. Single-volume histories of Indian tribes and tribal issues have their methodological limitations. For general introductions, Debos's work or the abbreviated history by Spicer are good beginnings.[3]

For general histories of U.S. policy as opposed to tribal histories, Taylor's and Tyler's works[4] provide basic introductions. Both works are useful for providing the names and dates of relevant legislation. However, both works show almost no evidence of any Indian perspectives, nor are they useful for highlighting the policy issues involved in the legislation.

If we move away from general Indian history to the political and cultural history of specific tribes, the literature is vast and Prucha's work will provide a beginning. Thus even though the late Edward H. Spicer's work on Yaquis lacks a Yaqui perspective, it is the most definitive extant book on Yaqui political history to date.[5] If one is studying the politics of a specific tribe, a good history of the tribe is essential to understanding the nuances of behavior. It is important, however, to search for what Indian perspectives are available. The early Indian activists from the 1960s like the late Clyde Warrior and Hank Adams did not write systematic histories. Vine Deloria's writings[6] capture the common thrust of Indian critiques of non-Indian social science. Since the first wave of Deloria's writings, other Indians have begun entering the field of Indian history. These include Bea Medicine, Tom Holm, Roxanne Dunbar Ortiz, and Kirke Kickingbird.[7]

Indian perspectives on government and policies can be found in the oral history collections at several universities in Indian country including the Universities of South Dakota (Vermillion), Florida (Gainesville), and Oklahoma (Norman). Many of the studies were sponsored by the Doris Duke foundation. Also helpful will be the various Indian publications, many of which have had a chequered history. *The Native American Directory* is a good source of names and addresses of Indian tribes, organizations, and publications.[8] The publications of the Indian Historian Press are an additional source of Indian viewpoints.[9] Typical activist viewpoints can often be found in *Akwesasne Notes*.[10] Somewhat more conservative Indian viewpoints can be found in the work of the National Tribal Chairmen's Association.[11] American Indian legal advocacy is often best represented by the work of the Denver-based Native American Rights Fund.[12]

Besides background materials in Indian studies, students of politics can comb the literature for institutional and then behavioral materials.

Institutions: Structure, Law, and Policy

Until 1871, treaty making provided much of the basic structure of U.S.–tribal relationships. The treaty collections by Charles Kappler and the reissue by the Institute for the Development of Indian Law provide the basic source materials in the treaty stage.[13] Besides the treaties, the foundation of Indian Law till the 1940s is to be found in Felix Cohen's classic *Handbook of Federal Indian Law*.[14]

There are several good casebooks in Indian law, including one edited by Price[15] and the more recent one by Getcher, Rosenfelt and Wilkinson. There is also Title 25 of the *Code of Federal Regulations* that deals with Indians.

Besides the treaties and casebooks, there are several works dealing with the structure of Indian policy. One of the best is Deloria and Lytle's *American Indians, American Justice*.[16] The Deloria/Lytle book provides a good and current review of U.S. Indian policy and proceeds to outline the jurisdictional issues in law enforcement and the administration of justice. For basic knowledge about the tribes, the profile of the tribes provided by the U.S. Department of Commerce is helpful. There are also the sample sketches of the structure of tribal governments assembled by students of Indian law.[17] In the late 1970s, as a response to Indian activism, Congress created the American Indian Policy Review Commission that included Indians and non-Indians charged with making recommendations on needed changes in Indian policy. Much of the scattered and uncoordinated work of the commission has fallen by the wayside. The mood of reform was slowed by the Carter, Ford, and Reagan administrations' retreat to not-so-benign neglect as the governing theme in Indian policy. Gone was the considerable interest in Indian affairs shown in quite different ways during the Nixon and Johnson administrations. The documents, hearings, and reports of the Indian Policy Review Commission would be of some help to students of reform.[18]

In addition to legislative issues, students of Indian policy need to look at the politics of Indian resources, because all the resources of America were, at one time or another, associated with Indian tribes. The starting point of the law and the structure dealing with resources are to be found in the literature already cited. Additional reference points can be found in the works of Ortiz, Custo, and Mumme/Ingram.[19]

In addition to resource policy, there are separate routes for literature survey for tax policy, educational policy, welfare policy, and other policy contexts. Irrespective of the context of policy, the scholar can be lost and bewildered without perspective on Indian tribes and Indian rights.

A journey into theory is inescapable, given the complexity yet elusiveness of Indian studies. Chaudhuri's overview of the issues in Indian policy[20] might illuminate the contexts in which scholars need to have their own perspectives. Deloria's books and essays provide other sources. For a background on the evolution of policy, Deloria's essay entitled "The Evolution of Federal Indian Policy Making" will be particularly useful.[21]

Among political scientists, Chaudhuri's emphasis arises from theories of rights in democratic theory. Deloria brings an integrated blending of themes from theology, law, and political history, while Michael Edward Melody has done important work in examining the political theory implied in Indian legends.[22]

Instead of political theory, law, or voting behavior, some political scientists have preferred to depend on survey research. (For one example, see M. M. Murdock, *Ethnicity and Political Trust: Arapahoe and Shoshone Children*, Eric Documents No: ED 224 759.)

Urban Indians

In dealing with Indian policy, there needs to be care in distinguishing between issues that are common to the tribes and those that are region-specific or tribe-specific. Additionally, the distinction between reservation (rural or urban) or off-reservation urban Indians needs to be kept in mind. Although there are some reservations in urban areas, most urban Indians are off-reservation Indians. Of approximately 1.5 million Indians, over half live in urban areas.[23]

For a general introduction to urban Indian issues, see Chaudhuri's essay entitled "Native Americans and the Unheavenly City: A Study in Inequality."[24] There is extensive sociological and anthropological literature on urban Indian pathology, but very few are policy-oriented. In addition to general literature, there are studies of specific urban areas. Some of these include studies involving Los Angeles,[25] by Price, Denver,[26] by Graves, Phoenix/Tucson/Flagstaff, by Chaudhuri, and Phoenix, by Christy.[27]

In addition to institutional literature, students of policy may be interested in a profile of the work done on Indian political behavior.

Political Behavior: Native American Voting

General Elections

The literature on Indian voting in nontribal elections is fairly sparse. There are many reasons for this sparsity. The comparative lack of dramatic, visible, and sustained interest-group activity makes it easy for Indian electoral behavior to escape the attention of most political scientists. Also, as Daniel McCool points out in one of the very few articles on Indian voting,

> There are a number of reasons why so few data exists on Indian voting. For one, many Indians live in remote areas in the country. There are obvious language and cultural barriers. These factors make survey research difficult. There is also considerable difficulty in separating Indians and non-Indians in aggregate data. In many voting studies Indians have simply been classified as "other."[28]

McCool's work provides a good review of the literature on voting in addition to his own presentation of Indian voting data in Arizona elections. The literature on Indian voting behavior at a national level is even more meager than the state and local literature. Helen L. Peterson's 1957 essay in the *Annals*[29] is an example of one of the first post-World War II reviews of Indian participation. World War II had a major impact on Indian political participation. American Indians had a very high level of participation in the war effort. Even though Indians have had their difficulties with the federal government, there is a sophisticated and rational distinction between loyalty to their country when threatened and their feelings toward federal Indian policy. The return of the Indian G.I. from the war resulted in a rise in political participation. Helen Peterson barely captures this important phenomenon in her article where she notes a "modest increase" in registration and voting levels, including a 31% to 37% increase in voting in three Plains Indian tribes between 1952 to 1956.

Leonard C. Ritt's work[30] is an interesting and solitary efort in the 1970s in generalizing about national Indian behavior. Ritt's work depended on a national sample polled between 1972 and 1978 by the National Opinion Research Center. Given the size of the sample (around 100) and the heterogeneity of tribal membership, there needs to be considerable caution about any serious conclusions from the study. Ritt himself draws rather bland conclusions that Indians tend to be "moderate" and that there were more Democrats than Republicans in the sample.

Given the diversity of tribal identification and the scattered location of Indian populations, it is difficult to make generalizations about national Indian voting behavior. There are, of course, issues common to large groups of Indians, but what studies there are have not concentrated on them. What we do know about Indian electoral behavior corresponds to common sense and is almost tautological in that Indians tend to vote when they perceive a relevant interest. However, there are several contexts in which good studies of national Indian behavior could take place. Two such contexts come to mind. In the presidential nomination process of 1968, Robert F. Kennedy on the Democratic side appeared to have a widespread Indian following. Examining shifts and changes in Indian turnout, crossover voting, regional differences, party loyalties, and tribal differences may still be possible with electoral data from that election. Also, because concern about the loss of trust status for Indian lands and the termination of the status of recognized tribes is widespread, tracing Indian voting in areas of concentrated Indian residency could illuminate the extent and nature of Indian electoral behavior in key Senate and House elections in Indian country. Such studies are rare.

If we turn our attention to state and local electoral behavior, the literature is a little richer than is the case for national studies. Government research bureaus or their counterparts—universities in such states as Arizona, Oklahoma, and South Dakota—have occasional papers and special studies that lend support to some fairly simple generalizations. Indians tend to vote more heavily in contested tribal elections than they do in nontribal elections. Further, Indian voter turnout tends to be less than is the case for other major ethnic groups. This should not be surprising. Voting is not only a method of choosing officials, it is also an act of consent to, and reaffirmation of, the legitimacy of the contractual political system. Indians constitute the least involved group in the social contract.

One of the best sketches of state-level Indian electoral behavior is found in Daniel McCool's article about Indian voting in Arizona, 1952–1980. Marked tribal differences are self-evident. Papagos tend to register and vote Democratic. Navajos, the largest Indian group, used to register heavily Republican in the 1950s in national elections, but the picture has shifted in the 1970s and 1980s. As a result of the perception that Senator Goldwater was pro-Hopi in the Navajo/Hopi land dispute, the Navajos voted heavily Democratic in Senate and gubernatorial elections. They returned to their traditional behavior to some extent in presidential elections by slightly favoring Ronald Reagan in 1980.

The shift toward more democratic voting in the 1970s by the Navajo illustrated at least two things. The Navajos voted on the basis of Navajo interests and second, they can have an important and decisive impact in close elections. This impact was illustrated in the election of Governor Raul Castro in Arizona in 1974 and the election of Governor Jerry Apadaca in New Mexico. In both cases, Indian votes appeared to make a difference in close elections.

Indian votes can make a difference in general elections that are close and in areas with concentrations of Indian population. The study of Indian voting in general elections is still in a primitive state. However, for understanding basic Indian behavior in elections, there is no substitute for research. Analogies from the behavior of other minorities have their limits. As Daniel McCool points out: "No other minority group voting data is comparable to the Indian experience, however, nor can the same generalizations be made about Indian voting."[31] The literature on Indians and elections continues to be primarily dependent on journalists,[32] case law[33] and anthropologists.[34] There is still much work to be done by political scientists. The advantages of doing research include the fact that Indian voting did not occur in any scale till the 1950s with the possible exception of Oklahoma. Several states in Indian country, including Arizona, New Mexico, Washington, and Idaho, prevented Indian voting till the late 1940s or the early 1950s.

There are special caveats that are in order to students of Indian voting compared to most other voting groups. These include (1) differences in census definitions of who is an Indian; (2) differences in tribal definitions of who is an Indian; (3) varying self-definitions of Indianness; (4) identifying tribal membership; (5) identifying reservation/off-reservation and rural/urban distinctions; and (6) blood quantum. The latter does not involve a study of genetics. However, blood quantum roughly can correlate with positions that break along "traditional" and "modern" lines. An additional caveat is in order. Lockean values and Anglo-American democratic theory generally infer that nonvoting implies consent. Whether this is empirically true is a debatable matter. However, what is less debatable is that for many Indian groups at different times, nonvoting implied disassociation from the political system. Nonconfrontational dissent by abstention is a form of political behavior in many traditional groups. This was the case for many Hopis who opposed modern government and did not take part in the ratification of the Hopi constitution devised under the Indian Reorganization Act of 1934.

The effects of this kind of nonparticipation do not simply disappear. The effects of the silent dissent of the 1930s provided some of the seeds of factionalism in more recent times.

Tribal Elections

Tribal governments in some contexts have a legal status higher than that of states. Tribal governments initially had treaty-making powers under the U.S. Constitution. However, Congress unilaterally, in a rider to an appropriation bill in 1871, brought about an end to treaty making. Soon afterward, with the creation of reservations through executive orders and other nontreaty legislation and arrangements, Indian governments, with some exceptions in Indian territory (Eastern Oklahoma), lost most of their powers. Some of their powers were restored by the Indian Reorganization Act (IRA) in 1934 for many but not all tribes. Here again, there were exceptions in Oklahoma where the southeastern tribes had to wait till the 1960s to shift to elections deciding their principal chiefs rather than having the U.S. president appoint them.

With the coming of contractual governments in the IRA and the rise of various forms of Indian activism in the 1960s and 1970s, Indian elections have become hotly contested affairs. Indian participation in tribal elections is generally higher than that of Indian participation in nontribal elections. There are several good histories of the politics of the IRA that brought about elected governments, but few of them have been written by political scientists. However, political scientists can profit from the more historical works in order to understand the evolution of tribal elections. Although there is extensive literature on the IRA, one of the best places to begin is Kenneth R. Philp's book, *John Collier's Crusade for Indian Reform*.[35] A good beginning in reading the relevant documents can be found in Francis Prucha's *Documents of United States Indian Policy* and Vine Deloria's *Of Utmost Good Faith*.[36]

Although the historical literature on the foundations of tribes as political entities is extensive, the same is not true of good contemporary studies of Indian tribal elections. Navajo and Hopi elections have been intensely contested affairs since the 1970s. The Sekaquaptewa and Sidney campaigns in Hopi country and the Zah–MacDonald rivalries in Navaho country have all of the features of non-Indian elections: issues, registration drives, religion and rectitude, trust, interest group activity, platforms, ideology, and finances. A study of the Pine Ridge Sioux reservation elections after the 1973 siege of Wounded Knee would be a very interesting study. With the cleavages of blood quantum and ideology, the race between Richard Wilson, a mixed blood establishment figure, Russell Means of the American Indian movement, and Gerald Onefeather, a full-blood tribal administrator, was an interesting race. All over Indian country, there are interesting and hotly contested elections, but there is not a single empirically based comprehensive study of Indian elections.

Among the nonquantitative studies a good study is provided by Tom Holm's "The Crisis in Tribal Government."[37]

He captures an important common theme in many tribal elections:

> In many cases, tribal factionalism has been along "traditional" versus "modern" lines and is directly tied to different concepts of authority. (p. 136).

Holm proceeds to point out the inherent conflict between what Sir Henry Maine labeled as "status" versus "contract" being the source of authority. In a skillful way, he outlines these issues in the Pine Ridge and Creek elections. However, the next step needs to be taken—the study of the turnouts, the registration, the surveys of voter preferences, and all the other tools of empirical research. Careful observation, insight, and intuition are valuable tools of understanding, but election research remains in a primitive state in Indian country for general as well as tribal elections.

Concluding Remarks

The bibliographical references are not intended to be exhaustive. The essay primarily has highlighted studies and references that will be of service to students of politics and policy.

American Indians share with many other ethnic groups and most minorities common challenges in making the dominant political system responsive. However, American Indians, in addition to issues of civil rights, have very unique relationships to the American political system. The references in the essay have been selected with that distinction in mind—the highlighting of the unique aspects of Indian policy should not be taken to mean that Indians do not share many of the same problems faced by blacks, Hispanics, and other minorities. However, even if the basic issues of civil rights facing minorities were resolved, there still would be a host of unresolved issues that relate to the aboriginal nature of Indian people. In that sense, the clarification of a just Indian policy remains as an important part of America's unfinished business.

Notes

1. Vine Deloria, *Custer Died for Your Sins: An Indian Manifesto* (New York: Macmillan, 1969).
2. Vine Deloria, ed., *American Indian Policy in the Twentieth Century* (Norman: University of Oklahoma Press, 1985).
3. Angie Debo, *A History of the Indians of the United States* (Norman: University of Oklahoma Press, 1970). Edward H. Spicer, *A Short History of the Indians of the United States* (New York: Van Norstrand-Reinhold Company, 1969).
4. Theodore Taylor, *The States and Their Indian Citizens* (Washington: U.S. Bureau of Indian Affairs, 1972). Lyman Samuel Tyler, *A History of Indian Policy* (Washington D.C.: Department of the Interior, Bureau of Indian Affairs, 1973).
5. Edward H. Spicer, *The Yaquis: A Cultural History* (Tucson: University of Arizona Press, 1980).
6. For a brief expression of common Indian views on Indian policy, see Vine Deloria, *Behind the Trail of Broken Treaties: An Indian Declaration of Independence* (New York: Delacorte Press, 1974).
7. See Roxanne Dunbar Ortiz, *The Great Sioux Nation* (Berkeley: University of California Press, 1977); Kirke Kickingbird and Karen Duchenaux, *One Hundred Million Acres* (New York: Macmillan, 1973); Robert Burnette, *The Road to Wounded Knee* (New York: Bantam Books, 1974); and Thomas Holm, "Fighting a White Man's War: The Extent and Legacy of American Indian Participation in World War II," *Journal of Ethnic Studies* 9(2)(1981):69–81.
8. *Native American Directory*, National Native American Cooperative, P.O. Box 5000, San Carlos, Arizona, 85550–0301; for a listing of Indian reservations, see *Federal and State Indian Reservations* (Washington D.C.: U.S. Department of Commerce, 1976).
9. Rupert Costo and Jeanette Henry, *Indian Treaties: Two Centuries of Dishonor* (San Francisco: Indian Historian Press, 1977).
10. *Trail of Broken Treaties: B.I.A. "I'm Not Your Indian Anymore* (Rooseveltown, N.Y.): Akwesasne Notes, 1974.
11. *Congressional Testimony by the National Tribal Chairmen's Association* (1978), Eric Document Reproduction Service Nos. ED205-304 and 305.
12. *Annual Reports* (Boulder: Native American Rights Fund).
13. Charles J. Kappler, *Indian Affairs: Laws and Treaties* (Washington D.C.: U.S. Government Printing Office, 1902). *A Chronological List of Treaties and Agreements Made by Indian Tribes with the United States* (Washington D.C.: Institute for the Development of Indian Law, 1973).
14. Felix Cohen, *Handbook of Federal Indian Law. With Reference Tables and Index* (Washington D.C.: U.S. Government Printing Office, 1942); Reprinted, Albuquerque: University of New Mexico Press, 1972.
15. Monroe E. Price, *Law and the American Indian: Readings, Notes and Cases* (Indianapolis: Bobbs-Merrill Co., 1973); David Getcher, Daniel Rosenfelt, and Charles Wilkinson, *Federal Indian Law* (St. Paul: West Publishing Co., 1979); *Code of*

Federal Regulation. Title 25. Indians (25 CFR 1.2) (Washington, D.C.: U.S. Government Printing Office, 1972).

16. Vine Deloria and Clifford M. Lytle, *American Indians, American Justice* (Austin: University of Texas Press, 1983).
17. *Indian Tribes as Governments* (Washington D.C.: American Indian Lawyer Training Program, 1975).
18. Congress of the U.S. (1977). American Indian Policy Review Commission, *Final Report, Appendices, and Index Submitted to Congress*, May 17, 1977; see also the study entitled *New Directions in Federal Indian Policy: A Review of the American Indian Policy Review Commission* (Los Angeles: American Indian Studies Center, University of California, 1979).
19. R.D. Ortiz, ed., *American Indian Energy Resources and Development* (Albuquerque: University of New Mexico, Native American Studies Development Series, No. 2, 1980). R. Costo, "The American Indian and Environmental Issues, *Wassaja/Indian Historian* 13(2):51–55. Reprinting by Eric Document Reproduction Service. No. EJ 232786; Stephen Mumme and Helen Ingram, *Politics of Southwestern Water and American Indians*. Paper delivered at the 1985 Annual Meeting of the American Political Science Association, New Orleans, August 29–September 1, 1985.
20. Joyotpaul Chaudhuri, "American Indian Policy: An Overview." In Deloria, *America Indian Policy*, pp. 15–34.
21. Ibid., Deloria, pp. 239–56.
22. Vine Deloria and Clifford Lytle, *The Nations Within: The Past and Future of American Indian Sovereignty* (New York: Pantheon Books, 1984). See also Michael Edward Melody, *The Sacred Hoop: The Way of The Chiricahua, Apache and Teton Lakota*, doctoral dissertation, University of Notre Dame, 1976.
23. U.S. Department of Commerce, Bureau of the Census, *1980 Census of the Population; General Characteristics, Part I United States Summary* (Washington D.C.: U.S. Government Printing Office, 1983. See also, Theodore Taylor, *American Indian Policy* (Mt. Airy: Lomond, 1983).
24. Janet K. Boles, ed., *The Egalitarian City: Issues of Rights, Distribution, Access and Power* (New York: Praeger, 1987, pp. 61–75).
25. John A. Price, "The Migration and Adaptation of American Indians to Los Angeles, *Human Organization* 27 (1968):168–175.
26. Theodore Graves and Minor Van Arsdale. "Values, Expectations and Relocation: The Navaho Migrant to Denver." *Human Organization* 25 (1966):300–7.
27. Joyotpaul Chaudhuri, *Urban Indians of Arizona*, IGR Series (Tucson: University of Arizona Press, 1974); Mary Rose Christy, *American Urban Indians, A Political Enigma: A Case Study, The Relationship between Phoenix Urban Indians and Phoenix City Government*, M.A. thesis. Tempe: Arizona State University, 1979.
28. Daniel McCool, "Indian Voting," p. 118. In Vine Deloria, ed., *American Indian Policy in the Twentieth Century*, pp. 105–133. (Norman: University of Oklahoma Press, 1985).
29. Helen Peterson, "American Indian Political Participation," *Annals, American Academy of Political and Social Science* 311 (May 1957).
30. Leonard G. Ritt, "Empirical Approaches to the Study of American Indian Political Behavior," paper delivered at the meeting of the Southwestern Political Science Association, Houston, Texas, April 2–5, 1980; see also, another version of the same material by Ritt in "Some Social and Political Views of American Indians," *Ethnicity* 6(1) (March 1979): 45–72.
31. McCool, "Indian Voting," p. 130.
32. Tribal newspapers like the *Navajo Times* or general newspapers in Indian country like the *Arizona Republic* or the *Tulsa Tribune*.

33. *Harrison* v. *Laveen*, 67 Arizona 337 (1984) extended voting rights to Indians in Arizona.
34. See, for example, the brief article by Stephen J. Kunitz and Jerrold E. Levy, "Navajo Voting Patterns," *Plateau* 43(1) (Summer, 1970): 1–8.
35. Kenneth R. Philp, *John Collier's Crusade for Indian Reform, 1920–1954* (Tucson: University of Arizona Press, 1976).
36. Francis Paul Prucha, *Documents of United States Indian Policy* (Lincoln: University of Nebraska Press, 1975); Vine Deloria, ed., *Of Utmost Good Faith* (San Francisco: Straight Arrow Books, 1971).
37. Tom Holm, "The Crisis in Tribal Government." In *American Indian Policy in the Twentieth Century.* Vine Deloria, ed., pp. 135–54.

Book Reviews

Abigail Thernstrom, *Whose Votes Count? Affirmative Action and Minority Voting Rights* (Cambridge, Harvard University Press, 1987) x + 316 pp.; ISBN 0-674-95195-6 (cloth).

The enactment of the Voting Rights Act (VRA) in 1965 dramatically changed the political landscape of the South; millions of previously disenfranchised blacks were registered to vote in a rather short time. If you read Abigail Thernstrom's revisionist interpretation of the VRA, *Whose Votes Count? Affirmative Action and Minority Voting Rights*, you would conclude that all the federal government should have done was to register previously disenfranchised blacks and then allowed "covered" jurisdictions to police themselves. A cursory reading of Southern history shows that when federal troops were withdrawn from the old Confederacy after 1877, those jurisdictions systematically withdrew the right to vote from their black citizens. The events of Sunday March 6, 1965, made it clear to the nation that Southern jurisdictions were not going to willingly grant the vote to their black citizens. During the legislative debate in 1965, Southern members of Congress made it clear that they were not supportive of the VRA. Data presented during legislative hearings prior to the renewal of the VRA in 1970, 1975, and again in 1982 has shown that local jurisdictions have not complied with all of the provisions of the act. As a consequence, I find it very hard to understand how anyone could assume that Southern jurisdictions would willingly comply with the act.

The thesis of Thernstrom's book is that the federal government has gone too far in its enforcement of the VRA. The author is particularly disturbed that provisions of the act granted broad authority to both the Department of Justice and the federal judiciary to implement the act. The author has failed to come to grips with the fact that if Congress was disturbed by the power of both the Department of Justice and the federal judiciary, it has had three opportunities to revoke that authority, which it has failed to do. I think that the evidence is overwhelming, if the federal government had not taken a proactive role in minority voting rights, blacks and Hispanics would still be the victims of blatant discrimination as far as voting is concerned.

Besides considering the federal government as too proactive in its enforcement of minority voting rights, Thernstrom is of the opinion that the VRA has blurred the division of powers between the federal government and the states, even though the Supreme Court has affirmed the constitutionality of the act and concluded that the act does not violate the division of powers between the states and the federal government. It should also be noted that states' rights arguments were always used by Southern jurisdictions to justify their discrimination against blacks.

Thernstrom also has this very naive notion that white Southerners will willingly vote for black candidates. Numerous studies and the testimony of many expert witnesses in voting rights cases have shown that racial bloc voting is persistent. Nevertheless, Thernstrom still holds to the belief that biracial coalitions can work in the South.

In 1969, the focus of the debate on minority voting rights shifted from vote denial to vote dilution; as a consequence, the Department of Justice (DOJ) along with the U.S. District Court for the District of Columbia was granted greater responsibility to enforce minority voting rights. Vote dilution is much more subtle than vote denial. The Supreme Court in *Allen v. State Board of Elections* 393 U.S. 544 (1969) ruled that all electoral procedures from annexations to at-large elections were to be considered part of the voting process. If a "covered" jurisdiction under the VRA changed any electoral procedure, it had to seek "preclearance" either from the DOJ or from the U.S. District Court for the District of Columbia. Most "covered" jurisdictions found it easier to seek "preclearance" from the DOJ than to seek a declaratory judgment from the district court. A careful reading of the Congressional testimony during the legislative debates over renewal of the VRA in 1970, 1975, and again in 1982 indicates that the preclearance process was essential to minority voting rights. It is Thernstrom's contention that the use of Section 5 violated the separation of powers and gave the staff of the Civil Rights Division of the Department of Justice too much authority over the electoral process in "covered" jurisdictions. Again, if that were the case, Congress has had ample time to overturn the provisions of Section 5 during the subsequent renewals of the act, and it has chosen not to do so.

In 1980, the U.S. Supreme Court in *City of Mobile v. Bolden*, 446 U.S. 55, ruled that black plaintiffs had to prove discriminatory intent, not effect, under Section 2 of the VRA. During the legislative debate in 1982, Congress overturned the Supreme Court's decision and stated that all plaintiffs had to prove in Section 2 cases was discriminatory effect. It is Thernstrom's contention that, in overturning the *Bolden* decision, Congress created proportional representation for black and Hispanic voters, even though Congress has explicitly stated that it did not do so. One important fact seems to elude Mrs. Thernstrom when she rails against the *Allen* decision and Section 5, and that is, it had ample time to overturn the Court's decision as it did with *Bolden* in 1982.

Even though most of the arguments presented by Thernstrom were discredited during the debate over renewal of the act in 1982 there is still an audience for these views. William Bradford Reynolds, the assistant attorney general for civil rights, along with other judicial conservatives in the Reagan administration, would support the positions articulated by Thernstrom; as a consequence, no matter how spurious the arguments may appear to be, they will continue to be given legitimacy as long as conservatives and neoconservatives are making civil rights policy. *Whose Votes Count?* should be read by anyone interested in gaining a clear understanding of conservatives' intellectual approach to civil rights, and particularly voting rights.

Lorn S. Foster
Pomona College

David L. Kirp, Mark G. Yudof, and Marlene Strong Franks. 1986. *Gender Justice* (Chicago: University of Chicago Press) x + 246 pp.; ISBN 0 226-43762-0 (cloth)/0-226-43765-5 (paper).

In *Gender Justice*, David Kirp, Mark G. Yudof, and Marlene Strong Franks attempt to derive a comprehensive prescription for gender policy from the principle of equal liberty. The authors argue that the purpose of gender policy should be to protect and enhance the capacity of people to make choices about their lives without regard to gender. Inequities that arise from this exercise of choice do not concern them. Only those inequities that result from overt discrimination or other explicit barriers to free choice are deemed by the authors to require a public remedy. They distinguish their approach from those of the feminists on the Left and the naturalists on the Right in that theirs is a process-oriented rather than a result-oriented conception of equality. The first section of the book sets out the authors' theoretical framework, whereas the second provides specific recommendations for employment, family, and constitutional policy. Although their formulation may be attractive in the abstract, it falls short in the application.

Several of the authors' policy prescriptions can be readily perceived as enhancing equality of choice. For example, their support for nondiscrimination legislation and flexible working hours, their advocacy of family allowances rather than government-sponsored day care, and their proposal to allow nonworking spouses to accumulate social security benefits in their own names are clearly consistent with this principle. However, in other instances, the link between the principle of equality of choice and the policy prescription is less clear. It is difficult to understand how their suggestion that states continue to refuse to enforce private marriage contracts furthers the principle of equal choice. Moreover, the authors present a convincing argument that wages for housewives would be infeasible, but they fail to consider community property as an alternative. It is also difficult to comprehend how, as they propose, the Supreme Court could enhance equal choice by permitting the military to require that female officers prove their husbands' dependency in order to qualify for spousal benefits while allocating these benefits to male officers and their spouses automatically, or by permitting states to prefer males over females in appointing administrators of estates. In short, many of their policy recommendations are not

easily reconciled with the objective of enhancing equal opportunity for choice.

The authors' discussion of constitutional policy is flawed in other respects as well. They are understandably critical of the Supreme Court's inconsistencies in gender cases. However, like most traditionalists, they imply that the Court is a single-minded entity rather than a collegial body composed of nine individuals. Many of these doctrinal inconsistencies were not caused by sharp shifts in logic but rather by shifts in the votes of one or two justices whose personal philosophies were consistent.

Their recommendation that the Supreme Court look to religion rather than to race for a model for adjudicating gender-based classifications is puzzling. They argue that use of the religious model would provide a legal basis for accommodating a wider variety of personal choice in gender-related matters, the free exercise of gender. However, the protection of religious liberty rests on a different legal basis than the protection from invidious gender-based classifications. The First Amendment contains parallel clauses that are in tension with each other, one protecting free exercise of religion, the other prohibiting government establishment of religion. Because the Fourteenth Amendment's Equal Protection Clause does not include this tension, it is not as easily adapted to balance vigilance and accommodation. Furthermore, it is not clear that a more accomodationist approach would be desirable. Gender and religion are qualitatively different. Unlike religion, gender is apparent to most causal observers and cannot be changed easily. In these respects, it is more similar to race and ethnicity than to religion.

In their effort to distinguish sex discrimination from racial discrimination historically, the authors overstate their case. They portray nineteenth-century paternalism toward women as fundamentally benign and genuinely protective. They dismiss many of the harsher manifestations of this system, in some cases quite cavalierly. For example, in discussing the status of wives, in particular the inability of wives to deny their husbands sexual relations, the authors state that "although husbands theoretically had such power, reported instances of exercise were rare" (p. 32). Given the status of women, particularly married women at that time, absence of reported incidents should not be assumed indicative of an absence of incidents. They also fail to consider the plight of nineteenth-century women with alcoholic or spendthrift husbands or unmarried women unable to earn a living because of social and economic discrimination.

This tendency to trivialize opposing arguments is not unique to the discussion of paternalism. The authors' discussion of alternative conceptions of gender inequality is fraught with scarecrows to be knocked down. Both the leftist feminists who perceive gender inequality as emanating from oppression and the naturalists who perceive gender differences as reflecting a divinely ordained social order take on the dimensions of caricatures. Nuances of opinion and shades of gray do not enter into the authors' discussion. For example, consider their discussion of sex-segregated job markets. They conclude that arguments that find the source of this segregation in employer or client prejudice "strain credulity" because this is a "couple oriented, not a 'night out with the boys (or girls)' society, why should work and leisure preferences differ?" (p. 149).

In short, although Kirp, Yudof, and Franks criticize other theorists for oversimplifying the problem of gender inequalty, they appear to fall victim to the same temptation. They underestimate the interrelationship between the public and private spheres and the inherent tension between liberty and equality. Perhaps the greatest contribution of *Gender Justice* is that it illustrates the difficulty of devising a public policy remedy for gender inequality.

Jilda Aliotta
Miami University of Ohio

The *NATIONAL POLITICAL SCIENCE REVIEW* (NPSR), a publication of the National Conference of Black Political Scientists, invites authors to submit manuscripts for its next volume. The NPSR welcomes contributions on any important research problem in political science but is particularly interested in theoretical/empirical research that focuses on politics and policies that advantage or disadvantage groups by reasons of race, ethnicity, sex, or other such factors.

Contributions should be no longer than 30 typewritten pages double-spaced, and should follow guidelines of the *Chicago Manual of Style*. An abstract of no more than 150 words should appear just beneath the title and before text begins. Author's name should be placed on a separate cover sheet. Five copies of each manuscript should be sent to Lucius J. Barker, Editor, *NATIONAL POLITICAL SCIENCE REVIEW*, Department of Political Science, Washington University, St. Louis, MO. 63130.

Requests for book reviews should be sent to Paul D. McClain, Book Review Editor, School of Public Affairs, Arizona State University, Tempe, AZ. 85387. Inquiries about standing orders should be addressed to Transaction Publishers, Rutgers–The State University, New Brunswick, N.J. 08903.

For Product Safety Concerns and Information please contact our EU
representative GPSR@taylorandfrancis.com
Taylor & Francis Verlag GmbH, Kaufingerstraße 24, 80331 München, Germany

www.ingramcontent.com/pod-product-compliance
Lightning Source LLC
Chambersburg PA
CBHW081434270326
41932CB00019B/3203